CHICANOS, CATHOLICISM AND POLITICAL IDEOLOGY

Lawrence J. Mosqueda
University of Colorado at Denver

UNIVERSITY PRESS OF AMERICA

LANHAM • NEW YORK • LONDON

Copyright © 1986 by

University Press of America,® Inc.

4720 Boston Way
Lanham, MD 20706

3 Henrietta Street
London WC2E 8LU England

Library of Congress Cataloging in Publication Data

Mosqueda, Lawrence J., 1949-
  Chicanos, Catholicism, and political ideology.
  Bibliography: p.
  Includes index.
  1. Mexican American Catholics—Political activity.
2. Catholics—Mexico—Political activity.   3. Catholic
Church—United States—History—20th century.
4. Catholic Church—Mexico—History.   5. United States—
Church history—20th century.   6. Mexico—Church
history.   I. Title.
BX1407.M48M67   1986   306'.2'08822   86-5498
ISBN 0-8191-5318-4 (alk. paper)
ISBN 0-8191-5319-2 (pbk. : alk. paper)

All University Press of America books are produced on acid-free
paper which exceeds the minimum standards set by the National
Historical Publications and Records Commission.

To

PHIL MERANTO
1938–1985

Internacionalista, Brigadista

Profesor y Compañero

And To

PATTY

TABLE OF CONTENTS

PREFACE

The discussion of religion and politics is inherently one that becomes embroiled in controversy. This is especially true when the two are mixed in an attempt to give new insight into a people's reality. The author hopes that debate will ensue over many of the issues raised in this book.

The intent of the work was not simply an exercise in problem-solving, but an attempt to examine the religious-political development of the Chicano, the relationship between religion and politics and the changes which have occurred over time. In order to make the book more than a descriptive narrative, it was important to assess the process of these changes, and the consequences both now and in the future.

I wish to thank many people without whose help this project would have been much more difficult to complete. The original research was conducted for my doctoral dissertation under the late Phil Meranto. He was a true friend and compañero in graduate school and later. It is difficult to find the words that can give him his proper respect. David Olson gave generously of his time in his copious notes and comments which were always challenging and cogent. Others who deserve thanks for reading all or parts of the work include Dan Lev, Margaret Levi, Mario Barrera, Carlos Muñoz and several of the Southern California foco of NACS.

I would also like to thank Steve Thomas, who has demonstrated that it is possible to be an effective and prodding chairman and still remain entirely humane. Juanita Ramirez was both efficient and gracious in the typing and preparation of the manuscript. I owe her a special note of thanks.

Without Patty's strength, patience, and insights this work could not have been finished.

The usual disclaimer, of course, applies. Any errors in facts or analysis remain mine. I trust the reader will find more than enough to compensate for any which are found.

vii

CHAPTER I

INTRODUCTION: PERSPECTIVES ON STUDYING CHICANOS AND THE CHURCH

The Catholic Church is often assumed to be an important influence on the culture and values of the Chicano community. This study attempts to examine the strength of that influence. That the Church permeates the Chicano community is beyond dispute. Of the nearly ten million Chicanos in the United States, 90 percent are estimated to be Catholic. Chicanos constitute at least 20 percent of the total Catholic population in the United States and 67 percent of the Catholics in the five southwestern states.[1] The study does not emphasize, for the greater part, matters of Church and state. Rather the emphasis is on the Catholic belief system. Church teachings on matters of faith and morals, Church laws on behavior, and papal proclamations--and their dissemination to the Chicano community--will be examined for their impact on the ideology and behavior of Chicanos.

Religion attempts to give answers to the ultimate questions in life, i.e., those dealing with death, living, the "sacred." It provides a meaning for the major life events. Edward Cleary has observed:

> . . .the Church in Latin America does that and more; it also attempts to provide an ideology, a system of meaning to explain one's place in society. As a result such an ideology can become a facilitator or an obstacle to change in society.[2]

While Cleary was concerned with Latin America and this study is focused on Chicanos, the same issues can be raised. Does the Church provide an ideology for its members that explains one's place in society? If it does, what is the ideology, and what are the implications of the explanation? Of course, the Church is only one factor that can contribute to the formulation of ideology; but the numbers of Chicanos who are Catholic would tend to indicate that it is one whose influence may be highly significant within that community.

The literature on the Church and its social implications for the Chicano is limited and primarily impressionistic. This treatment gives rise to an image of the Chicano people as predominantly Catholic, very religious and therefore conservative and docile. Madsen ascribes a fatalism to the Chicano because of his religion, conservatism if he is part of the middle class and superstition if he is part of the lower class.[3] Broom and Shevky

1

see the Church as "the principal agency of cultural conservatism for Mexicans in the United States."[4] Warner and Srole assert that the Church is a powerful instrument for the conservation of the ethnic tradition, although less important than the discrimination endured by minorities in the United States.[5] Acuña states that historically the Church has been an instrument of social control in the United States. He maintains that it became a pacifying agent after the Mexican-American War, encouraging the conquered Mexicans to accept the occupation, and to be complacent in the face of discrimination and exploitation.[6] These authors' works suggest that the control the Catholic Church exerts in the Chicano community is broad and the impact of the Church tends to promote conservatism.

Other writers, such as McNamara, Grebler, D'Antonio and Samora, have indicated that the Church has had a history of reactionary politics and influence, but that there are signs that the Church can be useful in acculturation, assimilation, and other social concerns and therefore beneficial to Chicanos in facilitating their incorporation into the mainstream of American life.[7]

Much of the literature that addresses the Chicano and the Church is focused on the rural Chicano and the immigrant, rather than on the urban native-born population. These studies are largely anthropological and rely on stereotypes, use culture as traditional and static rather than historical, and look at development as linear rather than as dialectical.[8] This study attempts to avoid these perspectives by focusing on urban residents who constitute over 80 percent of the Chicano population, and Chicanos whose religious training came principally from the United States Church rather than from the Mexican Church.[9] The study blends a combination of research techniques which will be discussed below, and does not rely solely upon an anthropological analysis. Although a study that examines religion is inherently concerned with culture and needs an anthropological input, culture and religion are also profoundly sociological, psychological, political and economic.[10] What was looked for in this study was not a pattern of static tradition but the resolution of contradictions, the tensions of opposites that are internal to individuals and internal and external to the institution under observation (the Catholic Church) and the group under observation (Chicanos).

The goal of the research is not to make a final judgment of the Chicano community, but to search an understanding of a people's present realities rather than a stereotype. We wish to understand a vital, living, changing community and its relationship to an institution that is pervasive in that community with-

2

out denying the complexity or vitality of either the people of the institution.

Although the vast majority of Chicanos are Catholic, there are some who are not. Among those who are Catholic, not all are believing or practicing Catholics. Among those who believe, some believe more and differently than others. The purpose of the research is not to state that all Chicanos believe "X" and therefore the Church is the predominant factor in their individual and collective lives, but rather that it is important to study the Church as an institution which undoubtedly has some influence on the Chicano community, both for those who believe and those who do not. Whatever conclusions are reached must be tempered to avoid stereotyping, and must be noted in varying degrees among individuals; but must also be noted as having a cumulative effect on the community as a whole.

In summary, this research will analyze some commonly held assumptions about Chicanos:

1. The Catholic Church is a predominant factor in the lives of Chicanos.

2. The Catholic Church is a conservative factor in the formation of Chicanos' political ideology.

Terminology

Before proceeding to outline the methodology, it is first important to define the terminology that has been and will continue to be used in this study. Key concepts such as religion, culture, and ideology need a uniform definition, or more importantly, a conceptualization understood by both the reader and the author.

The Concept of Religion

Religion is a concept that needs to be defined in a study of this nature because the Catholicism that many Chicanos know and practice is not always the textbook-catechism religion that is taught to children in parochial schools. Religion is never merely metaphysical; it is bound to the social realities of the people who believe and practice it. It is much more than just another intellectual commitment or an ideal; it demands and receives both physical and emotional involvement. For some who believe, it is not just a part of their life--it can be their life.

Clifford Geertz has captured the essence of the effects of religion in his definition of religion:

(1) a system of symbols which acts to (2) establish powerful, pervasive, and long-lasting moods and motivations in men by (3) formulating conceptions of a general order of existence and (4) clothing these conceptions with such an aura of factuality that (5) the moods and motivations seem uniquely realistic.[11]

Annemarie de Waal Malefijt complements Geertz's definition with her understanding that religion is both social and cultural. She defines religion as "a system of actions and interactions based upon culturally shared beliefs in sacred supernatural powers."[12]

If one accepts these definitions, it is quite probable that as religion conditions and socializes one in patterns of believe and behavior with a God, to other persons, to oneself, and to the state--that the least important function that religion performs (at least to an observer studying religion) may be the training for interaction between man and a God. Even the most religiously indoctrinated person, with the possible exception of those members of a few dwindling religious orders, does not spend all of his or her time in continuous prayer and devotion. There is little religious activity that is not of a social nature, especially in Catholicism. Furthermore, an individual spends a considerable amount of time in personal interaction with other human beings, including political interaction and inaction.

Religion expresses the values of a people or a society, and "attempts to safeguard them by endowing them with divine sanctions."[13] The values which are expressed in one's personal behavior are much more important (again to the observer and society) in how one interacts with other people rather than with a God. At this point it should be emphasized that a judgment is not being made here on the values that a religion might impose on a person or society, but rather the suggestion is being made that other humans are the main benefactors and/or victims of those values--not the deity.

For many who believe, religion can be all-consuming. The inference should not be made, however, that those who are not totally consumed by religious beliefs and practices are not liable to accept the values of their previously learned religion. Unless one has made a conscious decision to reject ones previous religious training, and does not merely consider himself/herself

4

a sinner, one is more likely than not to accept the values of the religion being ignored--with the added condition of guilt.[14]

Part (2) of Geertz's definition illustrates the condition of the "sinner" who is nevertheless a believer: ". . . to establish powerful, pervasive, and long-lasting moods and motivations in men by . . . ." A disposition toward religious belief and activity does not necessarily mean that religious activity will be performed regularly, but that there is the probability of religious activity being performed under certain circumstances.[15] To be pious is not to be performing something we would call an act of piety, but to be liable to perform such acts.[16] Similarly, to be trained by religion to react in human interactions in a certain manner is not to say that one will act that way all the time, but to have a tendency to act in such a manner, and to have one's behavior, choices, and outlook influenced by such training.

The establishment of "powerful, pervasive, and long-lasting moods and motivations in men" has long been a field of inquiry for scholars. It is one that is fraught with a lack of consensus by the masters, and by those who use their studies. The variations in the sociology of religion are almost as diverse as the variations in religion itself. While Max Weber was not the first to write of the sociology of religion, his works are considered among the classics, and a starting point for much research on the effects of religion.[18] Yinger notes that Weber's thesis in The Protestant Ethic and the Spirit of Capitalism has unquestionably been examined--with various conclusions--more than any other issue in the sociology of religion. Weber's theses,

> . . . that Protestantism, particularly
> its Calvinist phase, was one important factor in
> the development of the spirit of capitalism,[19]

has been used by some to mistakenly attempt to prove that religion is the primary force in secular affairs.[20]

Weber is more careful than some of his adherents. He was not attempting to attribute a causal primacy to religion, but rather attempting to note the relationships between religious, political, economic and social forces.[21] Birnbaum and Lenzer note that Weber's analysis is not one that attributes a primacy to religion nor one that attempts a unified general sociology of religion:

> For Weber, religion was in the last analysis an
> expression of the fact that we lived or that
> historical men lived in a plurality of value
> universes . . . there could hardly be a general

5

sociology of religion, but rather a sociology of religious (and non-religious) structures.[22]

In this study we will not directly examine Weber's most famous thesis concerning the Protestant ethic and capitalism, but we will delved into the more general inquiry of the relationship between religion and politics within one population.

Marx saw religion as more than just its observable functions. It is also a perception where one's total reality can become cloaked in a non-realistic basis. For Marx, religion was a fantastic reflection of the real world in the minds of men. He saw religion as both an escape and a protest against the misery of the world.

> Religious distress is at the same time the expression of real distress and also the protest against real distress. Religion is the sigh of the oppressed creature, the heart of a heartless world, just as it is the spirit of spiritless conditions. It is the opium of the people.[23]

Marx's writings on theology and religion were scattered throughout his career, but are primarily concentrated in his earlier works. His main criticisms of religion are contained in his doctoral dissertation and in On the Jewish Question.[24] Among his other early works, the Economic and Philosophical Manuscripts also contains many theological references. Saul Padover notes that after Marx's early years, he wrote only intermittently of religion, and primarily as it affected politics and economics.[25]

It was not that Marx had lost interest in theology and religion (as intellectual subjects) as he grew older, or that his aversion for religion diminished, but rather he saw that to attack religion directly was to misdirect his analysis. As the quote above indicates, Marx realized that religion was an expression and a protest against distress; it was not a primary cause of distress. Thus Marx directed his efforts to attacking the social conditions which he felt gave rise to religion, rather than religious expression itself.[26]

This is perhaps best expressed by Marx in his Introduction to the Contribution to the Critique of Hegel's Philosophy of Law:

> The immediate task of Philosophy, which is at the service of history, once the holy form of human self-estrangement has been unmasked, is to unmask self-estrangement in its unholy forms. Thus the criticism of heaven turns into the

6

criticism of the earth, the <u>criticism of reli-</u>
<u>gion</u> into the <u>criticism of law</u> and the <u>criti-</u>
<u>cism of theology</u> into the <u>criticism of poli-</u>
<u>tics..</u>[27]

This study will inevitably examine Marx's theses: whether
criticism of religion does become criticism of politics, and
(since Chicanos as a socio-economic group certainly qualify as
part of the oppressed masses) whether religion can be the opium
of the people.[28]

While the impact of religion is subject to considerable
controversy and disagreement, one aspect of religion that is
widely accepted and highly relevant to this study is that of
religion as a form of social control.[29] It should be noted that
social control in itself need not be sinister activity, but a
natural process for the perpetuation of a society or group.
Value judgments enter into the evaluation of social control when
considering who is the instigator of the control, the methods
used, and (when it can be ascertained) the motivation of those in
control.[30]

All modern societies practice social control. Whether a
society is ruled by an economic, political, or military elite, a
bourgeois or social democracy, or a dictatorship of the proletariat, someone is in control and utilizes the resources available to them to maintain and strengthen that control. Some
institutions and social structures which function as instruments
of social control are armies, police, economic units, law, social
class, the family, education, science and technology, peer pressure, and of course, religion.[31] The forms of social control
thus range from overt physical coercion to the subtle--i.e.,
those that are a part of the consciousness of the subject being
controlled. The subtle controls are primarily self-administered
after much training and internalization.

In the evaluation of religion as an instrument of social
control, the primary task is not to ask whether religion <u>is</u> a
form of social control. The answer to that is obvious--it <u>is</u>.
Among the questions to be explored should be: How is religion a
form of social control? Who is being served by this control?
How strong is the control? What conditions strengthen the control and what conditions weaken it? What are the consequences of
the control for the society and the group under control?

Since the Catholic Church is the specific institution being
studied, a definition of the institutional Church is needed. In
this study the Church is a teacher of a specific body of formal

7

doctrine, and/or its officials acting precisely in their capacity as the Church's hierarchical representatives.[32]

The Concept of Culture

If one accepts Malefijt's contention that religion and culture are intrinsically linked, it is necessary to have a workable definition of culture. The concept of culture enjoys no uniform definition in the social sciences. One author has found over 160 different definitions of culture.[33] Another author lists 25 definitions of political culture.[34] Geertz has stated that it is important to choose a concept that is workable, not because there is only one correct direction in which to move, but simply because there are so many. Geertz conceives of culture as such:

> Believing, with Max Weber, that man is an animal suspended in webs of significance he himself has spun, I take culture to be those webs, and the analysis of it to be therefore not an experimental science in search of law but an interpretive one in search of meaning.[35]

In studying the culture of any group it is important to understand not only the benefit of using this concept, but just as importantly--if not more so--the limitations involved. Much damage has been done to Chicanos by social scientists using a mistaken interpretation of culture. Romano and Hernandez have effectively demonstrated that culture reported and interpreted in error, and imprecisely, can be used to show that Chicanos are basically "undisciplined," "content," "emotional," "passive," and "fatalistic."[36] Studies such as those reviewed by Romano and Hernandez use culture as static, quantifiable, and traditional. The studies assume that everyone in the group has the same attributes. They do not recognize that there is diversity within each culture and that there are few universals. These studies view culture as a snapshot of a group (an old out-of-focus one) instead of as a moving picture that is still in the process of being made and which has no end in sight. The authors receiving critical attention by Romano and Hernandez use a concept of culture that is basically traditional and ahistorical, and primarily as causative rather than reflective of society.

Romano has suggested that the concept of "traditional culture" as used by social scientists should be dropped. Instead the concept of Historical culture should be used.[37] The concept of "traditional culture" is non-dialectical--it denies change and conflict, both internal and external, and it denies progress. It denies that a culture and a people can be complex and thus

8

implies that they are "simple" and can be understood easily if just given enough time. Culture is, of course, complex and it is not simply understood.

The fact that cultural systems are complex does not imply that they do not have at least some minimal degree of coherence and cohesiveness, "else we would not call them systems; and, by observation, they normally have a great deal more."[38] It is extremely difficult to correctly quantify a people to fit a tight model and thus proclaim that one has captured their essence in a coherent pattern. Coherence itself cannot be the major test of validity for a cultural description. ". . . there is nothing so coherent as a paranoid's delusion or a swindler's story."[39]

Eugene Genovese has noted that culture is ever changing and thus historical. He also states that culture is profoundly political, especially to an oppressed people because it provides a way of surviving both materially and spiritually, and this in turn helps a people forge their politics.[40]

In a similar vein Raul Fernandez utilizes culture in such a manner (especially in regard to Chicanos) that the "webs of significance" which have been previously discussed can be seen to evolve from the social context of the people's reality. He notes that culture involves two aspects which are not separate but mutually interdependent, i.e., formal and material culture:

> The formal aspects of culture would include such things as ideas (art and science), values, rules of personal behavior, social institutions, and fundamentally, a given set of social relations in the process of production. The material aspects of culture, on the other hand, would be composed of all artifacts and material goods resulting from human activity in a given society.[41]

Culture so understood incorporates religion not only as an aspect of formal culture, but also subject to the influences of the material world of the population. This does not mean that religion is a mere by-product of the material world at a given point in time, but rather that the ethereal world of religion, the relations it engenders among the laity and between laity and clergy, operate in a temporal world.

The Concept of Ideology

The concept of ideology has meant various things to various people at different times. The term has come to mean for many people a false perception of reality per se. Many persons envision ideology as a nonscientific, dogmatic, and incorrect way of looking at reality.[42] Geertz has stated that few social scientists would claim to have an ideology but are willing to apply the term to those with whom they disagree.

> Almost universally now the familiar parodic paradigm applies: 'I have a social philosophy; you have political opinions; he has an ideology.'[43]

The confusion over the use of ideology has led Geertz to suggest that perhaps too much time is spent attacking or defending the term and it might be possible to drop the term "ideology" from scientific discourse, and let it die a natural death. But as Geertz also points out, there does not appear to be any other usable term at present to replace it.[44]

The immediate task here is not to expand on the theoretical debate on the concept of ideology, but to define it in such a manner that it is relevant and useful to the study. As utilized below, political ideology is the belief of:

> (1) how the present social, economic, and political order operates, (2) why this is so, and whether it is good or bad, and (3) what should be done about it, if anything.[45]

A more precise conceptualization is needed if ideology is to play a central part in this study. Dolbeare and Dolbeare's tripartite utilization of ideology is a useful concept here.[46] Political ideology consist of:

1. A World View. As used here, a world view consists of an "image of social reality" or "image of power and process." It entails one's understanding of what is happening in the world and why. The understanding may be correct or incorrect, but it is the individual's general perspective on how economic and political systems work today, for whom, and why.

2. Values and Goals. Every ideology has values that are central to its continuation. Some values tend to be more important and critical than others.

The crucial questions are the way in which values are understood or defined by the ideology, and how they are ranked in priority when they conflict with each other.[47]

The goals become specific guideposts, often interim, that attempt to bridge the gap between the values of the society and the present conditions as defined by the world view. A combination of world view, values, and goals provides a sense of scope and direction of social change to achieve the goals and values that emerge.

3. Tactics for Social Change. Based then upon the world view, the goals and values and the scope and direction perceived as needed, certain tactics become acceptable and certain tactics do not. The controlling factor in the process by which change is sought is not the scope of change sought, but "the ideology's world view definition of present circumstances and power distribution within the society.[48] Is violence necessary? Does the desired change require or forbid certain activities? Even if some tactics could work, would the cost be too high?

With this conceptualization of ideology, we see that it encompasses both theory and practice. Ideology is more than what people say they believe, it is also what they do. It is also more than what they do now but also envisions what they can potentially do and not do--based on the self-limitations of their ideology. It is possible (as we shall see in subsequent chapters) that individuals may have very similar goals and values, but because their world views have fundamental differences, they will have different tactics for social change. From a political standpoint, this creates a situation where the convergences may be more apparent than real.

Perspectives on the Study of Chicanos

As previously discussed, the study of Chicanos has often been based on erroneous conceptions of culture and its applicability to Chicanos. The narrowness of the studies discussed by Romano and Hernandez resulted from the limited perspectives that were emphasized by the researchers. Raymond A. Rocco has effectively demonstrated that social scientists who study a people as a whole (in this case Chicanos) but who use limited perspectives obtain narrow and often distorted views of the group.[49] The study of a people and their culture requires that the researcher transcend those limited concepts that are normally restricted to his discipline and entertain other perspectives.

The questions that are raised will greatly influence the results of the research, and the assumptions of the researchers will influence what questions are deemed worth raising. As Robert Lynd has stated, "the controlling factor in any science is the way it views and states its problems."[50] A major problem with the political study of Chicanos is that many political scientists in the past have not made any assumptions at all and those who have, have often based their assumptions on impressionistic stereotypes.[51] This is not because the Chicano was not important enough to study or was "invisible," "sleeping," or "silent," but rather because the social sciences refused to learn. As Hernandez has stated:

> Ralph Ellison, a Negro, has insightfully noted in Invisible Man, that he knew he was invisible because no one saw him. The Mexican American has been labeled often as the 'silent minority'--we know we are silent only because no one hears us. This writer is of the belief that no one, particularly social scientists, has heard us because they have not listened.[52]

Recently, of course, some political scientists have listened to and studied Chicanos, but as with any "new" subject, a tradition in theory is lacking, and many studies are largely descriptive.[53]

It is relatively easy to write about what institutions do for a people externally. For example: What does the Church do-- the amount of charity given, the number of schools built, the number of hospitals built, etc.? It is much more difficult to determine what institutions do to a people internally--to formulate methods for determining why a people behave the way they do without falling into the social science dilemma of stereotyping groups.[54] This writer wishes to state that there should be no inference that whatever conclusions are reached can be applicable to every Chicano, or, in fact, that the Chicano can be successfully stereotyped at all.

The Catholic Church as an institution to be studied does not present as great a problem of diversity as do the Chicano people. There are, of course, "deviants" and these will be duly noted in the body of the study, but the Church as defined in this study as a system of definitive teachings and its officials acting in their capacity as the representatives of the Church's hierarchy, presents a reasonably unified (although not monolithic) body to study.[55] The Catholic Church is not a loose confederation of autonomous congregations as is much of Protestantism or other major religions. It has a leader--the Pope. It has a body of notables (princes) which chooses a new leader when the old one dies--the College of Cardinals. It has governors who oversee and regulate their flocks and who enjoy regional discretion in administration--bishops. And it has lieutenants who perform the daily functions of the institution--priests. Therefore, it is acceptable to study the Church as an institutional body (while noting variations in its membership) and to try to determine what it does to and for a people, who, like all people, defy definitive stereotyping but who nevertheless do constitute a group.

Methodology

In this study it was thought best not to borrow or use a model that someone else has developed since many sociological and anthropological cultural studies of Chicanos in the past have been found to be inaccurate, and the few political studies of Chicanos in the past have not dealt extensively with religion. It was therefore necessary to combine research techniques which were interdisciplinary to develop a paradigm that attempted to encompass the vast and complex subject of the study.

Theory

Clifford Geertz, an anthropologist, has already been mentioned for his concise definitional concepts of religion and culture. He proposes that culture be viewed as a field of inquiry, but not in the tradition of those who merely look at events and describe what they have seen with little or no analysis. Geertz calls this type of study "thin description." What is needed is "thick description," i.e., "thinking and reflecting"--the ability not only to record and report but also to decipher and sort out what is felt and implied.[56] Cultural analysis requires much more than just the tabulation of observable activity; it requires an understanding that comes through experience.[57]

The "experience" that is mentioned here is not meant to imply that one need by a member of a group in order to study that group or their behavior, but that one should not necessarily apply "used" concepts and models from other studies of other cultures and try to impose them on a new subject that may or may not be able to fit into preconceived ideas. What is also not needed is a metaphysical or spiritual linkage with the subjects involved. Culture is not found merely in the "hearts and minds of men," but is public because the human behavior that acts out culture can be observed and analyzed.[58]

If all this seems somehow incomplete--it is.

> Cultural analysis is intrinsically incomplete.
> And, worse than that, the more deeply it goes
> the less complete it is.[59]

Geertz has asserted that the closer one comes to a definitive
explanation using only culture, the more one suspects himself and
is suspect by others that one is not quite getting it right. He
explains that one can escape this dilemma by

> . . . turning culture into folklore and collect-
> ing it, turning it into institutions and class-
> ifying it, turning it into structures and toying
> with it. But they _are_ escapes.[60]

The point of cultural analysis--good cultural analysis, i.e.,
thick interpretation--is to try to understand people, not just to
learn about and classify them.

The concept of culture has value, especially in the study of
religious impact, because it helps us to understand activities
that otherwise could not be explained, but it is not the answer
to the political universe. Geertz is well aware that culture,
even by those who use thick description, can become essentially
single factor analysis which can only lead to incomplete analysis
masquerading as complete analysis. Geertz argues that to guard
against this, it is necessary to observe the "hard surfaces of
life."[61]

Marx is one who studied the "hard surfaces of life," and as
such is important to this and every study that wishes to add to
the body of knowledge about the human condition. A major theoretical foundation of this work is the utilization of Marx's
dialectical and historical materialist tradition.

The richness of Marx's materialist conception of history is
demonstrated in the following famous passage from the preface to
A Contribution to the Critique of Political Economy:

> In the social production of their life, men
> enter into definite relations that are indis-
> pensable and independent of their will, rela-
> tions of production which correspond to a de-
> finite stage of development of their material
> productive forces. The sum total of these rela-
> tions of production constitutes the economic
> structure of society, the real foundation, on
> which rises a legal and political superstructure

and to which correspond definite forms of social consciousness. The mode of production of material life conditions the social, political and intellectual life process in general. It is not the consciousness of men that determines their being, but, on the contrary, their social being that determines their consciousness.[62]

Marx continues with a passage that is especially relevant to this study:

> With the change of the economic foundation the entire immense superstructure is more or less rapidly transformed. In considering such transformations a distinction should always be made between the material transformation of the economic conditions of production, which can be determined with the precision of natural science, and the legal, political, religious, aesthetic or philosophic-in short, ideological forms in which men become conscious of this conflict and fight it out.[63]

In these comments Marx states that the elements of the superstructure, including religion, are shaped (but not mechanically determined) by the material forces of production, and that the changes in the economic foundations alter the superstructure "more or less rapidly."[64] As we shall see throughout this work, the Catholic Church does change with changes in the economic foundations. The changes are, however, less rapid than the economic changes but not imperceptible. The analysis of changes in the ideological forms, including religion, is also not as precise as the more apparent economic conditions.

The focus of this study is complex with such key concepts as ideology, religion and culture. A fusion between Geertz and Marx is desirable because the unique problem under scrutiny does not lend itself to borrowing one preconceived paradigm and applying it here.[65]

Research

For part of the contemporary period of this study interviews were conducted with various members of the Chicano community. A detailed questionnaire evolved, one not meant to be coded and computerized but one that became in effect, a modified oral history-directed interview, with attitudinal responses, specific to the religious and political development of the respondents.

15

It is important to note that this type of interview is limited to and dependent upon persons who have the time to give to someone who is usually a stranger, and who can be persuaded to answer questions that are somewhat personal, and (as was an observed) at times painful, and (speaking as an individual, not as a researcher) are in reality none of the stranger's business. In a very real sense the interviewee's privacy is being invaded. One of the results of this type of interview is that often questions are raised in the minds of the interviewees that they had not previously given much consideration. Some beliefs that they may have taken for granted seem challenged by the necessity to explain them. This produces a situation where answers seem remarkably candid, especially considering the subject matter.

To explore the complexities and subtleties of the connections between religious and political ideologies, it was important to ask people what they feel, perceive and understand; and taking them at their word is a useful and valuable way to obtain information. Moreover this method provides information which other methods cannot. The modified oral history aspect of the interview fills in the gaps which are missing from written documentation. As Willa K. Baum notes, oral history

> . . . can flesh out the bare bones of official documents and minutes of meetings, much as the private letters and diaries of notables did in bygone ages when personal writing was in vogue.[66]

A total of thirty-five people in the Los Angeles area were interviewed. At least ten persons were sought in each group described below, with as much diversification as possible. A total of twelve leaders were interviewed, thirteen persons in the general population, and ten members of the present or past clergy. In order to obtain candid answers, anonymity was promised to all participants except those whose identity would have a particular and unique bearing on the study.[67]

The study is a qualitative analysis and is not a mass survey of only present attitudes, but a process to try to understand the ideological development of each respondent and to observe trends within the Chicano community. The individual interviews were to be taken as a whole to indicate how the respondent perceived reality and for what reasons, not dissected into each question to try to lay a certain secular act to a specific religious teaching.

The study explored how Chicanos perceive their political and religious roles and subsequently act out those roles in relation

16

to a God, to themselves, to other people, and to the state. Also sought was the degree of devoutness and/or active church participation of each respondent. A practicing Catholic was defined as one who attends mass regularly, receives the sacraments, and who observes the fundamental laws of the Church. However, it should not be assumed that practicing Catholics are the only persons who can be influenced by the Church. The study also attempted to assess the extent to which nominal Catholics and "fallen-away" Catholics are influenced by the religion which they appear to ignore.

The subjects interviewed were divided into three groups:

1. Chicano notables--those who are perceived by Chicanos and/or Chicano literature, media or Anglo media as "leaders" or as having some influence with or on Chicanos. There were two ways that a person was classified as a leader: A) One can be imposed on the Chicano community by governmental appointment, by virtue of one's occupational status and/or attention by the media from which one emerges as a spokesperson; B) One can arise indigenously from community organizations and earn the respect and trust of the people one works with.

Although the former tends to be, by definition, more of an outsider than the latter, he is not necessarily less of a real leader in the sense that he has a following within the Chicano community. The degree of that following, both quantitatively and qualitatively, is determined by the actions of the person during his tenure in the position that gives him a leadership role.

The indigenous leader is not the spokesperson for the universal population (Chicanos) but is a spokesperson for a fraction of it. In practice, his position is made more secure than that of the non-indigenous leader by the power base from which he emerges, but is also made more tenuous by the number of adversaries he has developed both within his power base and outside of it. The line separating these two types of leaders is often obscure, but what is intended here is not a discourse on the concept of leadership, but a statement of how the Chicano notables were perceived by this study.

Obvious leaders, those who were in fact the most notable and were known to this author, were interviewed first. New names emerged, i.e., those who were perceived by others as community leaders. These leaders were then interviewed. Especially sought were persons having some connection with the Church (other than as a private member), either as a friend or adversary.

17

2. <u>Chicano population in general</u>. As described above, this study is a qualitative, not a quantitative effort, whose focus is on observing changes and trends within the Chicano population. However as much variation as possible was sought in regard to sex, age, occupation, income, and educational background of those interviewed. While numbers and percentages are rarely used (for the <u>original</u> information generated) in this study to avoid the appearance of quantitative analysis, the people interviewed approximate the diversity in the urban Chicano population.

It is important to document the lives of non-elites, not only with survey research (which certainly has an important place in scholarship), but also with their own words and actions. Due to the sensitivity of the subject matter, referrals from other individuals were often sought to obtain interviews.[68] However, unlike the leaders, no effort was made to find those who had known connections with the Church (as friend or adversary) other than as a private member.

3. <u>Clergy</u>. These may or may not be Chicano but are somehow responsible to a Chicano constituency in their particular assignments. I sought out Chicano priests who were active within the Chicano community, ecclesiastically and/or secularly. I also sought referrals to other Chicano and Spanish-surnamed priests in the Los Angeles area (whether they were active or not).

Also desired and subsequently interviewed were individuals whose contributions may have been particularly relevant to this study, such as the two Spanish-surnamed bishops of Los Angeles; and the Reverend Chris Hartmire, a Protestant minister who heads the National Farm Worker Ministry; and the Reverend Mark Day, former Catholic chaplain to the United Farm Workers.

Ideology, as previously defined, involves tactics, as well as world view, and goals and values. Therefore it was important to examine not just the history, perceptions, attitudes, and beliefs of Chicanos and the clergy, but also their actions and behavior, their actual practice. The method chosen for this task was to examine organizations that attempt, or have attempted, to have a socio-political impact on Chicanos and/or the Church. It was important to see if persons who work within these Chicano organizations felt that the Church helped or hindered their active involvement (and how they then conceptualized helping and hindering). The investigation of Chicano organizations was an important effort to go <u>beyond</u> the individual interviews (although there was some overlap) in observing Chicano political ideology and behavior.

Three types of organizations were desirable:[69]

1. An in-house Church group that worked largely within the confines of the Church, one whose members are very knowledgeable about the structure, teachings and internal politics of the Church. PADRES, an Hispanic clergy organization headquartered in San Antonio, Texas, but active where there are a number of Hispanic clergy (such as in Los Angeles), best fit this description.

2. A group that was primarily an outside pressure group whose members were still practicing Catholics in varying degrees and whose primary thrust was directed at the Church itself. Catolicos por La Raza (CPLR) was the group chosen. Although CPLR is no longer active, it is important to study since it was a group that reflected the frustrations, goals and tactics of a significant segment of the Movimiento of the late 1960's and early 1970's.

3. A group that is outside the Church and whose main thrust is in a non-Church direction, but whose leadership and membership show a strong affinity toward religious symbolism, and desire the Church's support. While this study is primarily concerned with the Chicano urban population, and the United Farm Workers (UFW) is, of course, composed principally of rural persons in its formal membership, it is important to observe the relationship between the Church and the UFW. The UFW is obviously more than just another farm union organization. It has significant ties with the urban population both for symbolic and concrete support. Its influence is felt well beyond the fields and areas of its principal focus, and it is thus important to this study.

Subsequent Chapters

Chapter Two reviews the historical literature pertaining to the development of the Chicano and his relationship to the Church to 1960. Obviously this encompasses a large time period that cannot adequately be covered in one chapter or perhaps in an entire book. But it is necessary to provide an historical base, however brief, in order to have an understanding of the present.[70]

Chapter Three analyzes the contemporary Chicano and the Church. Examined are the cumulative effects of the past, current literature, the result of the Chicano interviews, and the lay Chicano organizations previously described.

19

Chapter Four is an examination of the clergy and the official Church teachings on morality and social issues. Current Church literature is examined as well as papal encyclicals that have social and political implications. The results of clergy interviews are also examined. Chapter Four continues with dissident views in the Church from liberal pressure groups to radical clergy. The "revolutionary" Church in Latin America is also briefly examined since the progression of the left spectrum of politics eventually leads to some taking a revolutionary road, such as the late Father Camilo Torres.

Chapter Five is the conclusions.

NOTES

[1]Hermanas-PADRES National Encuentro News Release, August 15, 1978, San Antonio, Texas. Also see Y. Arturo Cabrera, Emerging Faces the Mexican-American (San Jose, California: William C. Brown Co., 1971), pp. 48-57 and Luis Valdez and Stan Steiner, Aztlan, An Anthology of Mexican American Literature (New York: Vintage Books, 1972), pg. 389.

[2]Edward Cleary, "The Church and Change in Latin America," Pitt Magazine, May 1975, pg. 10.

[3]William Madsen, Mexican-Americans of South Texas (New York: Holt, Rinehart and Winston, 1964), see particularly Chapters 3 and 7.

[4]Leonard Broom and Eshref Shevky, "Mexicans in the United States: A Problem in Social Differentiation," Sociology and Social Research 36 (January 1952): 157.

[5]W.L. Warner and Leo Srole, "Differential Assimilation of American Ethnic Groups," in American Minorities, ed. by Milton L. Barron (New York: A.A. Knopf, 1957), pg. 436.

[6]See Rodolfo Acuña, Occupied America: The Chicano's Struggle Toward Liberation (New York: Canfield Press, 1972), pp. 5, 65, 144, 147.

[7]See Patrick H. McNamara, "Catholicism, Assimilation, and the Chicano Movement: Los Angeles as a Case Study," in Chicanos and Native Americans, The Territorial Minorities, ed. Rudolph O. de la Garza, Z. Anthony Kruszewski, and Tomas A. Arciniega (Englewood Cliffs, New Jersey: Prentice-Hall, 1973), pp. 124-130; Patrick Hayes McNamara, "Bishops, Priests and Prophecy" (Ph.D. dissertation, University of California, Los Angeles, 1968); Leo Grebler, Joan W. Moore, Ralph C. Guzman, The Mexican-American People (New York: The Free Press, 1970), Chapter 19; and William V. D'Antonio and Julian Samora, "Occupational Stratifications in Four Southwestern Communities," in Mexican Americans in the United States, ed. John H. Burma (Cambridge, Mass.: Harper and Row, 1970), pp. 363-375.

[8]For reviews of such literature see Octavio Ignacio Romano-V., "Social Science, Objectivity, and the Chicanos," and "The Anthropology and Sociology of the Mexican-Americans," in Voices, Readings from El Grito (Berkeley: Quinto Sol Publications, 1973), pp. 31-56; and Deluvina Hernandez, Mexican American Challenge to a Sacred Cow (Los Angeles: Chicano Studies Center, University of California, 1970). Some of the works

reviewed by Romano and Hernandez are Madsen, Mexican-Americans; Ruth Tuck, Not With the Fist (New York: Harcourt, Brace, and Company, 1946); Munro S. Edmonson, Los Manitos: A Study of Institutional Values (New Orleans: Middle America Research Institute, Tulane University, 1957); Florence Rockwood Kluckhohn and Fred L. Strodbeck, Variations in Value Orientation (New York: Row, Peterson and Company, 1961); and Celia S. Heller, Mexican-American Youth: Forgotten Youth at the Crossroads (New York: Random House, 1968).

[9]While the historical relationship between Mexicans and their Church is duly noted in the following Chapter, the prime focus of the study is concerned with the current period and there are substantial differences for Mexicans north of the border vis-a-vis Mexicans south of the border in their relationship to their Church: 1. The Mexican National Church is composed primarily of Mexican leadership. 2. The United States Church is composed primarily of Anglo leadership. Of some three-hundred United States bishops, there are currently only seventeen Spanish-surnamed bishops, most of whom are auxilary bishops. All of these Spanish-surnamed bishops have been appointed since 1970. 3. Mexican Nationals, of course, comprise the vast majority of the membership of the Church in a country where the Catholic Church is the predominant religious institution. 4. Chicanos are a minority in the United States Catholic Church, and the Catholic Church is a minority Church in the United States. Chicanos therefore constitute a minority group in a minority Church.

Unless otherwise noted, the term "Chicano" is used throughout this study to designate all long-term permanent residents and citizens of the United States who are of Mexican descent. Mexican nationals are designated as "Mexican." Occasionally the term "Hispanic" is used; this entails all Spanish-surnamed individuals.

[10]See Eugene Genovese, "Class, Culture, and Historical Process," Dialectical Anthropology 1 (November 1975): 71-79; Clifford Geertz, The Interpretation of Cultures (New York: Basic Books, Inc., 1973.) Chapter 4; and Annamarie de Waal Malefijt, Religion and Culture (New York: The Macmillan Company, 1968).

[11]Geertz, Interpretation of Cultures, pg. 90.

[12]Malefijt, Religion and Culture, pg 12. Elsewhere Malefijt notes that:

> "Religion, like culture itself, consists of systematic patterns of beliefs, values, and behavior, acquired by man as a member of his

22

society. These patterns are systematic because their manifestations are regular in occurrence and expression: they are shared by members of a group: (pg. 6).

[13]Ibid., pg. 9.

[14]Most religions, of course, consider man to be imperfect, and a "sinner." What is meant in the text is that one may consider oneself an extraordinary "sinner" and perhaps unworthy of forgiveness.

[15]Geertz, Interpretation of Cultures, cites Gilbert Ryle's The Concept of Mind to illustrate this point (pg. 95).

[16]Ibid.

[17]There are many works which review the sociology of religious literature. Among some of the more complete anthologies and interpretations are Norman Birnbaum and Gertrud Lenzer, Sociology and Religion (Englewood Cliffs, New Jersey: Prentice-Hall, 1969); Roland Robertson, The Sociological Interpretations of Religion (New York: Schochen Books, 1970); and Robert N. Bellah, Beyond Belief: Essays on Religion in a Post-Traditional World (New York: Harper and Row, 1970). In Bellah, see especially Chapter 1, "The Sociology of Religion."

[18]Max Weber's classic works are The Sociology of Religion (Boston: Beacon Press, 1963); and The Protestant Ethic and the Spirit of Capitalism (New York: Charles Scribner's Sons, 1958). Both works are available in numerous editions.

[19]J. Milton Yinger, Religion, Society, and the Individual (New York: The Macmillan Company, 1957), pp. 214-215.

[20]Ibid., pg. 215.

[21]As Yinger notes, Weber's study of Protestantism and the spirit of capitalism was one part of a series of monographs in which he explored the significance of religion for economic matters. Weber also wrote Ancient Judaism, The Hindu Social System, and The Religion of China. "In each case, he took account of the political economic, and other social forces at work, thus sketching a broader picture than in his essay of Protestantism, in which he described only one side of the causal chain." Ibid., pg. 216.

[22]Birnbaum and Lenzer, Sociology and Religion, pg. 13

[23]Karl Marx, Introduction to Contribution to the Critique of Hegel's Philosophy of Law in Karl Marx, Frederick Engels, Collected Works, Vol. 3 (New York: International Publishers, 1975), pg. 175 (emphasis in original).

[24]Saul K. Padover, ed., Karl Marx, On Religion (New York: McGraw Hill Book Company, 1974), pg. ix, Marx's dissertation was Difference Between the Democritean and Epicurean Philosophy of Nature.

[25]Ibid.

[26]Birnbaum and Lenzer, Sociology and Religion, note that

"When Marx declared that for Germany religious criticism had ended and that political criticism had begun, he meant in effect that head-on attacks on religion were useless so long as the social condition which gave rise to religion persisted. This was part of the shift in emphasis in Marxist theory which led Marx and Engels to move from a statement of the theoretical presuppositions of human liberation to a consideration of its actual pre-conditions: from critical philosophy to revolutionary praxis" (pg. 5).

[27]Marx, Critique of Hegel's, in Collected Works, pg. 176 (emphasis in original). The Critique was written in 1843.

[28]It appears to this author unnecessary to fully document the Chicanos' historical and contemporary position as a predominantly poor, working class, minority population. For those, however, who wish more factual information on the conditions of Chicanos, I refer them to the information presented in the following chapters, especially II, III and IV.

[29]Gary Marx in his Protest and Prejudice (New York: Harper and Row, 1967, 1969) notes several writers to illustrate and social control aspects of religion for Blacks. More importantly he notes;

"In a more general context, the social control consequences of religion have been noted throughout history from Plato to Montesquieu to Marx to Nietzsche to Freud to contemporary social theorists" (pg. 95).

Also see Gary Marx's Chapter on "Religion: Opiate or Inspiration of Civil Rights Militancy?" pp. 94-105.

[30]Joseph S. Roucek's broad definition of social control is used in this study:

> "Social control is a collective term for those processes, planned or unplanned, by which individuals are taught, persuaded, or compelled to conform to the usages and life-values of groups."

Social Control (New York: D. Van Nostrand Company, Inc., 1947), pg. 3.

The motivations of those practicing social control are often obscure and may be of secondary importance in observing social control. The primary research effort should be the search for impact. Whether the controller has a "benevolent" rationale for his actions is relatively unimportant if the objective impact is detrimental to the subjects under control. While Roucek recognizes that motivation is often too complex or too obscure for easy analysis, he offers three general purposes for the agents of social control:

> "(1) exploitative, motivated by some form of self-interest, direct or indirect; (2) regulatory, based upon habit and the desire for behavior of the customary types; and (3) creative or constructive, directed toward social change believed to be beneficial" (pg. 8).

[31]For a more complete classification of types of social control see Roucek, Ibid., and Paul H. Landis, Social Control (Chicago: J.B. Lippincott Company, 1956), especially Chapter 19, "Means of Social Control Classified."

[32]This is the definition used by McNamara, "Bishops, Priests, and Prophecy," pg. 32n.

[33]See A.L. Kroeber and Clyde Kluckhohn, Culture (New York: Vintage Books, 1952).

[34]Walter Rosenbaum, Political Culture (New York: Praeger Publishers, 1975), pg. 5.

[35]Geertz, Interpretation of Cultures, pp. 5, 14.

[36]See Octavio Ignacio Romano-V., "Social Science," and "The Anthropology" in El Grito; and Deluvina Hernandez, Mexican American Challenge.

[37]Romano, pg. 55.

[38]Geertz, Interpretation of Cultures, pg. 17.

[39]Ibid., pg. 18.

[40]Eugene Genovese, "Class, Culture," pg. 72.

[41]Raul A. Fernandez, The United States-Mexico Border: A Politico-Economic Profile (Notre Dame: Notre Dame Press, 1977), pg. 152. Also see pp. 1-35; 149-157. A very good essay on Chicano culture which takes a materialist approach is Juan Gomez-Quinones, On Culture (Los Angeles: Popular Series No. 1, UCLA, Chicano Studies Center, 1977).

[42]Raymond K. Dehainaut, Faith and Ideology in Latin-American Perspective (Cuernavaca, Mexico: CIDOC Sondeos Series No. 85, 1972), notes that

> "Today, the term can be used to signify any set
> of doctrines or beliefs, visionary theorizing,
> false consciousness, dogmatic politico-social
> programs, revolutionary ideas, the doctrine of
> the social origin of ideas, etc." (pg. 1/3).

[43]Geertz, Interpretation of Cultures, pg. 194.

[44]Ibid., pg. 200. Geertz lists other terms that denote a similar concept of ideology--Plato's "noble lies," Sorel's "myths," Pareto's "derivations;" but as Geertz states, "none of them has managed to reach any greater level of technical neutrality than has 'ideology.'"

[45]Kenneth M. Dolbeare and Patricia Dolbeare, American Ideologies: The Competing Political Beliefs of the 1970's, 3rd ed. Chicago; Rand McNally College Publishing Company, 1976), pp. 2-3.

[46]The following is extracted from Ibid., pp. 5-11.

[47]Ibid., pg. 7.

[48]Ibid.

[49]Raymond A. Rocco, "The Chicano in the Social Sciences: Traditional Concepts, Myths, and Images," Aztlan 1 (Fall 1970): 78. Rocco notes that

"conclusions that are made utilizing only one perspective should neither be put forth nor accepted as anything more than simply parts of a much larger multidimensional mosaic: the Mexican American."

[50]Quoted in Ira Katznelson, Black Men, White Cities (Chicago: University of Chicago Press, 1973, 1976), pg. xi. Katznelson in noting that the "systematic study of race politics is in its infancy" (pg. xi) reviews the previous directions in the research and develops his own research approach. As part of his approach he utilizes a concept that is attractive to this author. In discussing "objectivity," Katznelson does not pretend disinterest or noninvolvement, but rather uses Erik H. Erikson's "disciplined subjectivity, " i.e., one is

". . . involved with the subject of inquiry, yet disciplined by the canons of scholarship. This approach recognizes the essential links between scholar, subject, the audience; the social scientist is both in and of his world. This is a persuasive approach, for why study society unless you care about society? Moreover, since social science scholarship has political and moral consequences, social scientists must face up to their political and moral responsibilities" (pg. 11).

[51]In addition to the critiques of Romano, El Grito, and Hernandez, Mexican American Challenge, also see Carlos Muñoz, "Toward a Chicano Perspective of Political Analysis," Aztlan 1 (Fall 1970): 18. As recently as the Fall of 1970 Muñoz was able to write correctly: "Of all the social sciences, however, political science is perhaps the only discipline that has almost totally ignored the Chicano . . . ."

The "discovery" of Chicanos by political scientists has been relatively recent and to a large extent by young Chicano political scientists themselves. Muñoz quoted an ad hoc committee on the Mexican American in the profession to note that in 1970 there were only two political scientist Ph.D.'s of Mexican descent in the United States.

[52]Hernandez, Mexican American Challenge, pg. 22.

27

[53]For a brief but very good summary of the development of the research conducted on (and primarily by) Chicanos in the last decade see Tomas Almaguer, "Interpreting Chicano History: The 'World System Approach to 19th Century California'" (Berkeley: Institute for the Study of Social Change, Working Papers Series #101, University of California, 1977), pp. 1-3.

[54]Not all social scientists consider stereotyping to be a dilemma, but rather that stereotyping is what social scientists do. Bronislaw Malinowski is quite correct and candid when he states that stereotyping is what sociology is all about. The same can largely be stated to apply to the other social sciences:

> "First of all, it has to be laid down that we have to study here are stereotyped manners of thinking and feeling. As sociologists, we are not interested in what A or B may feel qua individuals, in the accidental course of their own personal experiences--we are interested only in what they feel and think qua members of a given community."

Argonaut of the Western Pacific, quoted in Buford H. Junker, Field Work, An Introduction to the Social Sciences (Chicago: The University of Chicago Press, 1960), pg. 57.

[55]Malefijt, Religion and Culture, notes that religions consist of systematic patterns of beliefs, values, and behaviors that are regular in occurrence. However, she also states:

> "But regularity is not to be confused with homogeneity. In all religions there are differences of interpretation of principles and meanings. There will be found dissenters and believers, innovators, and traditionalists. Dissenters and innovators do not, however, deny regularity: they merely protest against it." (pg. 6).

[56]"Felt and implied" are the terms of Buford H. Junker, Field Work, pg. 1.

The possibility of different people accurately recording an event while arriving at different conclusions is related in the following anecdote by Allen Spitzer:

> "We once overheard two American Catholic clergy-men express their reactions to the Basilica and Shrine of Our Lady of Guadalupe in Mexico City. Impressed by the huge edifice and the throngs of

28

pilgrims crowded into it, one turned to the other and said, 'This is the Faith!' and his companion countered rhetorically, 'This is the Faith?'"

"Religious Structure in Mexico," Alpha Kappa Deltan 30 (1960) 54-58.

[57]For a complete explanation of "thick description" see Geertz's "Thick Description: Toward an Interpretive Theory of Culture," in Interpretation of Cultures, pp. 3-30.

[58]Ibid., pp. 10-12.

[59]Ibid., pg. 29.

[60]Ibid., (emphasis in original).

[61]Ibid., pg. 30.

[62]Passage from Robert C. Tucker, ed., The Marx-Engels Reader, 2nd ed. (New York: W.W. Norton and Company, Inc., 1972, 1978), pg. 44.

[63]Ibid., pg. 5.

[64]It is important to note that there is no dichotomy between using Marx and the concepts of culture and religion in the formation of ideology. It should be clear to those who have read Marx that Marx was not an economic determinist or that materialism precludes any mental activity from having an influence on the course of history.

Erich Fromm, among others, has noted that historical materialism has been interpreted to be essentially a psychological theory indicating that man's main motive is to gain money and to have more material comfort. As Fromm states, this is an incorrect interpretation:

" . . . [H]istorical materialism is not at all a Psychological theory; it claims that the way man produces determines his thinking and his de- sires, and not that his main desired are those for maximal material gain. Economy in this con- text refers not to a psychic drive, but to the mode of production; not to a subjective, psycho- logical, but to an objective economic-sociologi- cal factor."

29

Erich Fromm, Marx's Concept of Man (New York: Frederick Ungar Publishing Company, 1961, 1966), pp. 11.12. (Emphasis in original)

[65]The fusion of Geertz and Marx does not assume to be the definitive answer or approach to studying religion or the specific topic under investigation: Chicanos and Catholicism. As will be noted again in the concluding chapters, the topic of the Church and Chicano has rarely been investigated (although sometimes discussed), and then primarily by clerics. I have attempted to devise an approach (the theory described above and the research described below) that does not merely add to the preexisting information but may diverge from it. It is not (and as Marx explains above, and cannot be) as precise as studying economic conditions or natural science. As some of the leading members of the Society for the Scientific Study of Religion note in a work that examined the classics on religion:

> "If social science generally does not yet measure up fully as a science in the sense that its compelled, accumulated record is meager, then it is not surprising that the social scientific study of religion would also lag behind. Indeed, religion, having in some degree regarded science and the scientific perspective with suspicion, may have been especially resistant to scientific scrutiny . . . . " (pg. 413).

> "Our thesis here is only that, beginning with a spectacular set of classics by Marx, and by those that followed him, the scientific study of religion has still not consolidated the traditions of problem finding and methodology which would indicate how these contemporary phenomena should be approached. As we said before, present-day researchers may be inspired but hardly compelled by the classics as they take up these questions. It is our hope, as well as one of the purposes of this book, that in the future this situation will no longer exist. After all, if the social scientific study of religion is worth doing at all, it both deserves sustained effort and promises accumulated knowledge. As of now, it is probably accurate to say that we are not very far beyond the classics" (pg. 417).

Charles Y. Glock and Phillip E. Hammond, eds., Beyond the Classic? Essays in the Scientific Study of Religion (New York: Harper and Row, 1973), pp. 413,417.

[66]Quoted in Rolando A. Juarez, "What the Tape Recorder Has Created: A Broadly-Based Exploration Into Contemporary Oral History Practice," Aztlan 7 (Spring 1976): 104. See the whole of the article for an oral history critique. For other related works see James W. Wilkie, Elitelore (Los Angeles: Latin American Center, Univeristy of California, 1973); and Oscar Lewis, The Children of Sanchez (New York: Vintage Books, 1963).

[67]Physical limitations imposed by time, resources and manpower restrict any study to its practical confinements. In this study, the primary research is limited to the Los Angeles area, although the literature reviews the Southwest and historic Mexico. The Los Angeles area has more persons of Mexican descent than any other area outside of Mexico City.

[68]Aside from the theoretical methodological problems in studying religion, there can also be problems in a practical sense because religion is often considered to be a "personal" affair. For problems others have encountered in studying Chicanos and the Church, see Chapter V, footnote four.

[69]All of these groups are further defined and elaborated upon at appropriate times in the body of the text.

[70]The historical review of the literature is an integral aspect of the study. As will be shown in the subsequent chapters, the present relationship of the Chicano and the Church should not be attempted without this foundation. Katznelson, Black Men White Cities, quotes Charles Beard to illustrate a similar point in his own race politics study:

> "' . . . many of our neglects, overstresses, and simplifications are due to the divorce of political science from history.'" (pg. 23)

CHAPTER II

A HISTORY OF MEXICANS/CHICANOS AND THE CATHOLIC CHURCH:
THE EVOLUTION OF CHICANO-CHURCH LINKAGES AND INTERACTIONS

The heritage of Chicano is, of course, Mexican, and the
history of the Mexican people is inseparable from the Catholic
Church. The Church's influence over the Mexican people has gone
through phases that generated and are reflected in the major
historical events that have shaped the present realities of the
Chicano people. In order to have a clear perception of how the
present day Chicano views his Church and is viewed by the Church,
we must have an historical perspective that presents a background
of these significant events--the foundations for the present.
Some of these events are the Conquest and "conversion," the War
for Independence, the War of 1848 and its aftermath, the Revolution of 1910, and the "Americanization" of the Chicano. It is
only with such a background that one should attempt to interpret
the religious nature of the contemporary Chicano.[1]

Spanish Conquest to the War for Independence

When Cortes landed in what is today Mexico, he encountered a
civilization that in many respects rivaled those of Europe. The
inhabitants had sophisticated architecture, economies, arts, and
urban centers, the greatest of which was Tenochtitlan. Cortes
also found a society that was highly theocratic. As has been
recounted by many historians of the conquest, Cortes was able to
use the beliefs of the Aztecs that he might be a god to his
advantage in the military defeat of Tenochtitlan.[2]

The Spanish had--in addition to the economic and military
ambitions of the Spanish kingdom as an inducement--a profound
sense of mission to civilize and Christianize the newly discovered people. Religion was not only a justification for exploration, colonization and any resultant excesses that would
follow, but also a motivation. During the conquest, the Spanish
Church and the Spanish State acted essentially as one force. Due
to the patronato real (royal patronage) granted by Pope Julius II
to King Charles V in 1484, the head of the Church in Spain was
the King, and the Church's hierarchy served with his approval.
The Church-State relationship was more than one of cooperation;
it was one of unification. In the conquest and formation of
Mexico, the Church assumed an important role in the establishment
and administration of the colonial government. Cumberland has
noted that the relationship between the Church and State was so
intimate as to be virtually indistinguishable. "The Church acted
for the State, the State for the Church, and both for Spain."[3]

Military victory by Cortes was only the first stage of the conquest. Equally important and perhaps more so was the attempted transformation of the defeated native population into willing subjects of the new regime. (The Church was to become the legitimating arm of State power.) The foundations of this transformation were laid in the theocratic nature of the pre-Colombian society and in the similarities between the Aztec and Catholic religions. The natives were already deeply religious and mystical. Significant portions of their lives were spent in religious ritual, prayer and sacrifice. Their interpretations of existence were defined by the priesthood, as was the responsibility for the discipline of the people.

The specific similarities between the religion of the natives and Catholicism were such that they caused some debate among the missionaries as to whether the native rituals might be the work of Satan duplicating the sacred rites of the Church in a pagan environment, or whether the new world had been visited by a Christian evangelist--some thought by the apostle Thomas. The native religion included the rituals of baptism, confession, and communion. Similarities in belief included an Eve-like figure (Cihuacoatl), belief in hell, limbo, and paradise; atonement for transgression by fasting and penance; and belief in a virgin birth (Huitzilopochli by Teteoinan). Similarities in form were evidenced in incense in Churches, pilgrimages, houses of virgins, and the cross.[4]

While Catholicism is monotheistic, the Spanish Catholicism of the 16th century gave the appearance of being polytheistic with its compartmentalized veneration of the Virgin, the Saints, and the use of relics, statues, and medallions. This eclectic blend of monotheism/polytheism, symbolism and ritual made the transition from native religion to the outward acceptance of Catholicism a relatively easy task for the native. With the military defeat of their nation and the apparent failure of their own gods to protect them, the new religion of the conquerors provided a metaphysical continuation that eased the confusion and pain of the defeat. As Eric Wolf has observed:

> Whatever their doubts, the formal similarities
> between the two religious traditions permitted
> an easy transition for the worshiper and gave
> him continuity precisely in the realm in which
> continuity was vital: The realm of religion
> behavior.[5]

However, to state that the natives underwent rapid mass conversion is imprecise since it was not an actual conversion but rather the submission to superior forces that followed military

defeat and the initiation of a new political and economic order.[6]
Tannenbaum notes that the rapid conversion seemed miraculous to
both the missionaries and the conquerors and helped to ease their
conscience by giving moral justification for the conquest.[7]

The utilization of native religious symbolism by the friars
was an unavoidable aspect of the conversion process. Of perhaps
greatest impact was the incorporation of the native Aztec goddess
Tonantzin into a native Catholic "goddess," the Virgin of
Guadalupe. In brief, the legend of the Virgin of Guadalupe is as
follows:[8]

On December 9, 1531, an Indian maiden appeared to a newly
converted native, Juan Diego, as he was passing the hill of
Tepeyac, northeast of Mexico City. She declared herself the
Mother of God and told Diego to ask the Bishop that a shrine be
built on the spot. According to the legend, the Bishop, Juan de
Zumarraga, was naturally dubious of the Indian's account and
demanded proof. On the third and final visit to Diego on December 12, 1531, the Virgin presented him with roses grown on the
barren Tepeyac. Diego gathered the roses in his robe and took
them to the Bishop. When the Bishop unfolded Diego's robe there
appeared upon it the image of the Virgin. Presumably, this
convinced the Bishop that a miracle had indeed occurred. More
importantly, it convinced a large part of the Indian converts
that their new religion was legitimate, that the religion now had
a native flavor because the Mother of God had appeared to them in
Indian form. While objectively the institutional Church was
still a Spanish Church,[9] subjectively for the Indian there was
now a native and national symbol. While their theological awareness had not changed, their symbolic commitment to the Church had
been strengthened.

While symbolism was important in the conversion and legitimization attempt, the Church also acted in a nonsymbolic and very
practical manner when it felt that it was necessary. The Church
and State were often rebelled against by the native population.
In the frontier the Church was often the only visible sign of
Spanish authority and as such was the target of the rebellions.
Revolts occurred in such areas as Oaxaca, New Galacia, Zacatecas,
and what is today New Mexico. The Church and State combined to
suppress these revolts.[10] This demonstrated that the Church was
less than successful in its mass conversions and that many of the
Christian Indians were Christian by virtue of obligatory baptism
rather than by intent or desire.

In its formation the Spanish Church in Mexico wantonly
destroyed native Mexican artifacts and documents including the
library at Texcoco. Much of the history of the native population

literally went up in smoke on the orders of the first Bishop of Mexico, Zumarraga. Since the State and Church were essentially one, the destruction of the legacy of the native population can be seen as more than just an overzealous act of a true believer attempting to save the Indians from their hedonistic past. It was also a political act to destroy a conquered people's past civilization. As such it attempted to counter not only a possible relapse of the native population into past religious practices, but also to stop the gestation of national revolutionary awareness among the natives. It was a political consolidation of power.

This consolidation of power was also implemented through other Church related institutions. The Holy Office of the Inquisition was brought to America in 1569, and the Index of forbidden books was used by the hierarchy to suppress undersirable thoughts from Europe. This list was continually updated for centuries in an attempt to keep out the ideals of such authors as Boyle, Montesquieu, Rousseau, Voltaire, and Locke.[11]

It should also be noted that while the institutional Church was a full partner in the Spanish State's conquest of Mexico, there was individual priests who assailed and crusaded--unsuccessfully--against the subjugation and exploitation of the Indian population. Priests such as Sahagun, Gante, Motolinia, Montesinos, Torquemada, and de la Casas labored for the native population.[12]

The case of Antonio de Montesinos, a Dominican, demonstrated that the Spaniards were not amenable to hearing about their exploitation of Indian labor; and in the final analysis, the institutional Church was not willing to support those who exposed the exploitation. In 1511, Montesinos denounced the treatment of the Indian population from the pulpit. His well-heeled congregation was not disposed to relinquishing their privileged lives because one priest interpreted their existence as sinful. They attempted to have Montesinos remove at the local level but were refused when his immediate superior, Fray Pedro de Cordoba, refused to deport him. After another verbal attack on his congregation, he was recalled to Spain for an audience with the King--the head of the Spanish Church. Montesinos was not returned to the Americas.[13]

The power that the Church possessed was also evident in the number of clerics in relation to the general population. In 1570, there were 63,000 Europeans in Mexico of which one in twenty-five was a cleric. By 1646, the number of Europeans had doubled and the number of priests had increased relative to the population with one of nineteen then members of the clergy. By

1770, the proportion of priests had dropped considerably with the influx of new immigrants—only one of seventy-eight were then men of the cloth out of a total European population of 750,000.[14]

During the formation of New Spain the Church was able to accumulate great amounts of wealth due to its continuity as an institution, its judicious use of acquired property, and through exorbitant fees charged for its services. By the end of the sixteenth century, the Church was estimated to own at least half of Mexico.[15] The Church and its orders generally used the land that it possessed rather than let it lie idle as did many large private landowners. This use of land (largely through Indian labor and Black slave labor) enabled the Church to accumulate capital and become the prime banking institution in the country.

Certain orders such as the Jesuits were not only landowners and gentlemen farmers, but also engaged in commerce on a considerable scale. Besides the standard commodities such as cattle, the Jesuit "College of St. Peter and St. Paul alone bought or sold more than 500 Negro slaves (carried on their books as 'items') in the course of the seventeenth century."[16] Chevalier, in an accounting of the Church's accumulation and use of its resources, notes that "Transactions such as these (slave and cattle transactions) were the logical, inevitable outcome of exploiting haciendas, droves, waving mills, and sugar plantations."[17] The accumulation of wealth among the Church members was the natural outcome of participation and leadership of a politico-economic order that saw no incongruities in vast differentials in wealth, status and prestige. The Church cannot be separated from the colonization. The Church as an institution reflected the society to which it gave moral guidance.

The wealth of certain segments of the Church was not a universal phenomenon among the clergy, however. There was a great deal of inequality of resources among the clergy itself.[18] The objective foundations for intraclerical disputes were established at an early stage of Mexican development, and these inequalities between the institutional Church and the masses, and among the clergy itself, continued into the nineteenth century. At the time of the revolution (1810) many parish priests earned barely one hundred pesos a year while the archbishop of Mexico City received a salary of one-hundred-thirty thousand pesos, with the bishops of Puebla, Valladolid, and Guadalajara receiving almost as much. These salaries put the hierarchy among the richest and most privileged men in Mexico.[19]

The War for Independence

On the morning of September 16, 1810, Padre Miguel Hidalgo y Costilla issued the Grito de Dolores and launched a revolution against the Spanish leaders of Mexico. His immediate goal was to rid Mexico of the Gachupin (native-born Spaniards) who were exploiting the masses of citizens. More a sincere humanist and humanitarian than a contemporary revolutionary leader, his ideas for the future were based more on nebulous concepts of love and liberty rather than on a well-thought-out plan of action.[20] Believing in the righteousness of his cause, Hidalgo and his co-conspirators (such as Ignacio Allende) had envisioned a movement more on the line of a Putsch or rebellion that would be readily joined by the other creoles (Spanish descendants) and the dominant Indian-Mestizo population. What Hidalgo received was a disorganized uncontrolled revolution that also assumed class distinctions rather than one based merely on race and nationalism.

The rebels early in the campaign took up the banner of the Virgin of Guadalupe. The use of the Virgin in banner and slogans should not be interpreted as giving the revolution a "holy war" rationale. To do so would be to mistake form for content and cause. The fact that Hidalgo transformed a religious symbol into a political one was based on the reality that the Virgin of Guadalupe was a native symbol rather than solely a religious one. The important use of religious symbolism in this instance does not translate into a religious primacy for the causes of the revolution. While the Church was beginning to be attacked by those influenced by the liberal philosophies of Europe, the religion of the people was not subject to widespread suppression. The cases of the revolution and the impetus for its duration and intensity were based on the concrete economic and political realities of the masses that had little to do with sprituality (although the Church was certainly involved as a politico-economic temporal unit).

The leadership of Hidalgo and the involvement of other parish priests gave little ecclesiastical legitimacy to the revolution. The hierarchy of the Church excommunicated Hidalgo and preached allegiance to Spain and to the King. The loyalists took up the banner of the Virgin of Los Remedios (a Spanish virgin)--who was declared General of the Spanish army. The competing forces of Catholic Mexico had thus pitted the Virgin against herself.[21]

Cumberland asks the appropriate question for the revolutionary period: Who spoke for the Church? The parish priest who helped lead the insurrection, or the bishops who excommunicated him? The priests captured and executed by loyalists, or the hierarchy that permitted the executions? Or even more paradoxically,

Vicente Guerrero who fought for independence but who signed a manifesto guaranteeing Catholicism as the sole religion, or Calleja who also guaranteed the status enjoyed by Catholicism even while he butchered Guerrero's followers?"[22]

Regardless of the specific answer to the above questions, notes Cumberland, "The hierarchy as a body condemned the revolution, and the hierarchy had the power of position--and of money."[23]

As consecrated bishops of the Church (apostolics), the hierarchy also had the power to speak for the Church--especially since the hierarchy acted as a body. The deviants from the Church were those who fought for the revolution. By all standards, the judgment should be that the church as an institution was against the revolution. The official Church was acting for the State, while many members and lower ranking priests fought against the Spanish State.

The revolution was never victorious although "independence" was achieved. The turmoils of the new world (South American was also in rebellion) were also felt in Spain. In 1820, a rebellion, initiated by soldiers back from South America, seized control of Spain. Influenced by the liberal philosophies of Europe and somewhat by the ideas of the French Revolution, the new Spanish government initiated reforms and acted to counter the influence of the Spanish Church. The hierarchy in Mexico, who had pontificated against and fought the independence movement, now decided that it was in their interest to separate themselves from Spain, fearing the new-found liberalism of Europe would spread to Mexico.

In conjunction with the bourgeois secular elements of Mexican society, the hierarchy chose Agustin de Iturbide to lead an independent Mexico. Iturbide met with the remaining leadership of the revolutionary movement, Vicente Guerrero (Hidalgo had been captured and executed in 1811), and pronounced for independence on February 24, 1821, in his Plan de Iguala.[24]

For the masses the change meant little in their daily lives, except the lack of allegiance to Spain. The leaders of the army, the Church, and even the bureaucracy were virtually indistinguishable from the past. The "independence" that Mexico had achieved was independence for the Mexican ruling class to rule without interference from the Spanish government, but for the general population the change was virtually non-existent. For the first time in the history of Mexico the Church was a "Mexican" Church (although its leaders were still essentially Spanish). The birth of the "Mexican" Church was not an attempt to institute reforms but rather to prevent them. The Church's chameleon loyalties and readily apparent hypocrisy added fuel to the growing liberal, anti-clerical movement in Mexico even as it achieved a temporary respite from the liberalism of Europe.

As liberalism is a nebulous concept, especially when applied out of one's domestic context, it is useful to discuss liberalism here. The liberalism that was the ideological influence on Mexican reformers was not based on perceptions of social or economic justice for the masses. Rather it was a bourgeois attempt to rid Mexico of the vestiges of feudalism which the Church helped to maintain. As Lloyd Mecham has noted:

> . . .early anticlerical were not reformers in
> the proper sense of the term. Their opposition
> was not based on spiritual, social or economic
> causes. The 'reformers,' recruited almost ex-
> clusively from the Creoles, had no complaint to
> find with Catholic dogma and tenets; representa-
> tives of a privileged social class, they mani-
> fested little interest in the welfare of the
> lower classes, and if they regarded clerical
> wealth as an evil, it was because this wealth
> made the Church powerful politically.[25]

While the liberals no longer had to deal with a Spanish Church, they were confronted with a Mexican Church which became politically more active because it could no longer count on the Spanish government to support its previous privileged position.[26]

The Church of Northern Mexico

While most of the political and ecclesiastical formation of Mexico was occurring on the central plateau of Mexico (Mexico City in particular), events were also shaping the future of the native population in the frontiers, particularly in what is today the United States Southwest. Isolated from the capital of Mexico by thousands of miles of deserts and mountains, areas such as New Mexico and California developed patterns of existence that were somewhat different and independent in their daily functions and formation. It was the Church rather than the civil authorities that often had the primary task of colonization in these regions. There were outposts of troops and governmental officials, but the cultural and, especially in California, economic life of the people was Church oriented.

The missions of California have been largely romanticized in
their popular recording. Junipero Serra has been described as a
"saintly genius" for his planning and developing of the mission
system.[27] John Tracy Ellis, Catholic Church historian, describes
the missionaries and their efforts in glowing and enthusiastic
terms.[28] Bolton writes that the missions and their Franciscan
overseers were ". . .a force which made for the preservation of
the Indians, as opposed to their destruction, so characteristic
of the Anglo-American frontier."[29]

Carey McWilliams, however, challenges the popularly held
notion that the missions were beneficial to the California
Indian. In a seemingly harsh indictment, McWilliams states that
". . .with the best theological intentions in the world, the
Franciscan padres eliminated Indians with the effectiveness of
Nazis operating concentration camps."[30]

The indictment is harsh only in the sense that the impact of
the Nazi actions were absolutely intentional, and the padres were
not; however, the distinction is unimportant to the victims.
During the missionization period of 1769 to 1834, the "wild" or
gentile Indians did not decline in number, but in the missions of
California 29,100 Indians were born while 62,600 died. Half of
the deaths were attributed directly to conditions within the
missions. Diseases introduced by the Spaniards took their toll,
as did crowded, unsanitary conditions of the missions themselves.
The major abuse was the forced-labor system that built the missions and their plantations—and intensified when the Franciscans
"began to assign neophytes to the presidios and to farm them out
as servant to the worthless Spanish soldiers."[31]

Regarding the issue of Indian acceptance of Catholicism, one
recent Catholic source strains credibility in its accounting of
the missions' theological impact on the native population; ". . .
the Eucharistic Lord, was as true known and loved by the Indians
in their rough, crude clothing as by Spanish lords and ladies in
their lace and finery."[32]

McWilliams seriously challenges the concept that the Indian
population earnestly undertook Catholicism as a belief or as an
intentional (i.e., willing) way of life.[33] An important indication that the Christianizing aspect of the missions was less than
successful in eliciting a commitment from the converts was that
most of the recorded offenses for which the Indians were punished
by the friars were political crimes—attempts to rebel or to
escape from the mission system.

The missions were not intended to be permanent institutions.
The life span of the mission was supposed to average ten years at

41

which time the Indians were to be sufficiently trained to be able to become productive citizens and owners of their land. The missions, however, showed little sign of relinquishing their holdings until 1830 when the rancheros (large-land owners) perceived the missions as economic competition, especially since the missions controlled much of the land and principal labor force available.[34]

By 1834 the missions had assets valued at $78 million. With so much at stake the rancheros began to undermine, with the active assistance of the friars, the plan to assign these holdings to the native population. The padres, angered with secularization, encouraged the Indians to take the assets that were non-valuable and portable, and the rancheros acquired through extra-legal and illegal means the capital property. By 1845, the mission property had been either leased or sold and had become large ranches, with Indian workers. Those Indians who knew their "rights" and refused to move were evicted. With the defeat of Mexico in 1848 and the takeover of northern Mexico by the United States, the Indians had no legal recourse for any action taken against them.[35]

In New Mexico the mission system was not developed on the same scale as it had been in California. Each village had its own church, often without a pastor; but there was no Serra to develop the chain of missions that had evolved in California. The relative isolation of the village made the dominant institutions interdependent upon each other. The patrons (feudal-type landowners) assumed a co-dominant relationship with the Church in terms of respect received from the populous. However, the patron often dominated the local Church since he was the one who financed religious activities and fiestas. When the priest was absent from the isolated areas, the patron actually became the religious leader, albeit on a layman status.[36] The institutional Church and the patron supplemented each other--at times, in an uneasy alliance. The uneasiness evolved not from the aspect of who would necessarily be the champion of the masses (although here again there were motivated priests who were truly concerned with the temporal welfare of the people), but who would be the dominant force.[37]

Pre-War Independent Mexico
And the War and Its Aftermath in the United States

The causes of the War between Mexico and the United States (1846-1848) have been discussed by various authors. The delineated reasons vary from Mexican aggression to United States imperialism (Manifest Destiny). This author is of the opinion

42

that the preponderance of evidence demonstrates United States' aggression and imperialism.[38] However, the immediate task of the current work is to examine the role of the Church before and during this time period.

As in many former colonies, a sudden plunge into nationhood provided the competing forces of society an arena for immediate conflict of both ideas and actions. As previously stated, the Church became even more politically active after separation from Spain. The influence of the Church as an institution cannot be overemphasized. The Church was the largest single entity in Mexican society, and its influence was more than that of one institution among many attempting to retain or improve its position in society.

In the past the Church had been a virtual arm of the State. However, with the succession of different political regimes in independent Mexico, the Church was often a power to content with, rather than the extension of the government as in the past.

The Church as owner of half of Mexico translated into a disproportionate impact on Mexican life. Much of the Church-owned land, of course, could not be considered liquid, but the Church's income demonstrated great ability to finance its immediate concerns. At the time of independence, the Church's income "was estimated to be well over one-hundred million pesos annually-five times that of the government."[39]

Parkes has stated that the two institutions that perpetuated a virtual state of anarchy and made democracy or even cohesion impossible after independence were the Church and the army. The corrupt generals' command of the armed forces gave them an independent position in society. The Church was by law not only free of taxation (a situation not peculiar to Mexico), but also had the independence of the fueros, the right to have the clergy answerable only to clerical courts for any transgressions, ecclesiastical or civil, that they might commit.[40]

As mentioned previously, there was a growing liberal movement in Mexico. The liberals who sought to counter the Church's influence did so from an anti-clerical perspective that primarily attempted to curb abuses. (There were, nevertheless, those who were overtly anti-religious and demonstrated an almost evangelical atheism.) It was not that the liberals chose the Church as a scape-goat for the condition of Mexico, but that anyone concerned with Mexican development could not escape the Church. As Cumberland has noted:

It impinged on every aspect of Mexican life. .
The definition of the proper role of the Church
became the critical issue; the history of Mexico
from 1821 to 1872 could be written in terms of
the search for that definition.[41]

With the outbreak of hostilities between the United States
and Mexico, the Mexican government turned to the prime banking
institutions in an effort to finance the War. In 1847, the then
current president, Valentin Gomez Farias, demanded a loan of
fifteen million pesos from the archbishop of Mexico. Pleading
poverty, the archbishop refused the loan.[42] In regard to the
eventual outcome, United States victory, the refusal probably had
little impact. However, the anti-clericals had another opportunity to propagandize against the Church as unpatriotic and not
contributing to the war effort. They did not consider the
Church's offers of prayers for victory a sufficient substitute
for material contributions.[43]

While the Church in Mexico did not support the Mexican war
effort, the Church in the United States supported the American
war effort and viewed it as an opportunity to prove their pa-
triotism and counter the growing nativist activities. However,
some Catholics serving in the American army in Mexico were dis-
turbed by Mexican press reports that United States troops were
desecrating the churches and were intent on destroying the
Catholic religion. Such actions caused a contingency of Americans, largely Irish Catholic, to desert and form the San Patricio
battalion, and fight with the Mexican army. The battalion was
captured by the United States army, and several of its members
were hung as deserters.[44]

The ultimate defeat of Mexico was total. The resultant
settlement, the Treaty of Guadalupe Hidalgo, ceded half of Mexico
to the United States. However, the Mexican negotiators insisted
on protecting the rights of the people in the region. Incor-
porated in the Treaty were guarantees that Mexicans in the conquered lands be granted equal treatment and protection under the
Constitution and the law, recognition of land titles, protection
of the culture including the language, exception from taxation
for property sold in order to move back to Mexico, and freedom of
religion.[45]

It is generally agreed that the guarantee of the right of
the Mexican to practice his religion was honored. However, there
is abundant documentation that the other political rights and
land title guarantees were pervasively if not systematically
violated.[46]

Land rights have been trampled upon; the language has been suppressed by legal, extra-legal, and illegal methods; basic civil rights have been at best ignored, at worst totally violated (lynchings, etc.). But the Mexican was allowed to keep his religion. There are at least two possible reasons for this:

1. The Catholic religion was not an exclusive institution of the Mexican, but also had a substantial and growing influence in the United States. Whatever feelings of racial or ethnic superiority that the Anglo-American perceived over the conquered Mexican could not be attributed solely or primarily to religion. There was, undeniably, a strong current of nativist anti-Catholic bigotry (Know-Nothings) among the Anglo population that contributed, especially among the Protestants of the Southwest, to the distrust of the Mexicans.[47] Distrust of Catholics was no doubt a contributing but not sufficient factor explaining distrust of the Mexican. These nativist feelings could not be fully utilized as a basis of systematic oppression when there were significant and growing segments of the population who were not Mexicans, the only logical step would have been to do this among the Irish and other Catholics also. Once a form of bigotry has been unleashed, it becomes extremely difficult, if not impossible, for the perpetrator to control either its direction or intensity. The previously mentioned defection of some Catholic Americans during the War would have served notice to those in power that such a policy of official nativism would not only be politically unwise, but possibly militarily dangerous.

2. Whether by conscious intent or not, it was probable that the reason the religious freedom proviso of the Treaty was honored, was that it was the only one that actually served a useful purpose for the expansion of the American empire. Even if there were those in the government of the time who harbored anti-Catholic views, it would be apparent to them, or it soon became apparent, that the Church would not be a threat to expansion, but would in all probability be quite useful. Unlike the other provisos of the Treaty (land rights, civil rights, etc.) which, if enforced, would have solidified the Mexicans' political position as a cohesive vested group in the United States, the religious right proviso helped to undermine their position.[48]

Catholicism in the "new nation," the United States, turned out to be a stronger agent of social control than it had been when the Southwest was part of Mexico. The transfer of political power for the region also brought a transfer of religious hierarchy. Although the lines of communication from the Southwest were equidistant or further to the new center of the national Catholic power (Baltimore) as they had been in the former nation (Mexico City), the linkages and discipline were much tighter. Rather than act as a champion of the people in an assertion of their political rights, the Church limited itself to spiritual guidance. The United States Church acted to counter any indigenous religions leadership among the Mexican population that could challenge either it or its country's legitimacy.[49] This aspect of Church collaboration with the "Americanization" of the Southwest was to be expected. Just as the Church in Mexico reflected Mexican society, the Church in the United States reflected United States society. Despite the perceptions of the nativist, the Catholic Church in the United States has traditionally been a strong defender of the fundamental policies of the United States.[50]

The clearest example of the linkages to the East and the "Americanization" aspect occurred in New Mexico. At the time of the War, New Mexico was part of the diocese of Durango. After the occupation, a new diocese was created north of the new border and French-born Bishop Bautiste Lamy was appointed the new vicar. Lamy, knowing little of the land or the people he was to serve, was decidedly an outsider whose lack of understanding of the local population was to cause a virtual schism in the New Mexican Church.

When Lamy arrived in New Mexico, his attempts to set up "a little Auvergne" were met with resistance by the native clergy, especially by Padre Antonio Jose Martinez. Padre Martinez was a very respected cleric, who possessed progressive religious and political views. He refused to collect the tithes from the poor, he set up a co-educational school (at a time when such a concept was virtually unknown), and he opposed large estates, advocating that the land be distributed among the poor.

Lamy's mission was to "Christianize" a region that had been served by the Catholic Church for over three centuries. The manner in which the American Church and Rome viewed New Mexico Catholicism was indicated in the title of his appointment, i.e., in "partibus infidelium, 'in the region of the infidels.'"[51] He immediately set out to replace the native clergy with those who had his confidence. He excommunicated five native priests and replaced them, and others who were lost through natural attrition, with French priests.[52] He made little attempt to incorporate the native population into the priesthood.

Padre Martinez protested the Bishop's actions. His methods of protest were entirely legal under Canon Law and he went through the proper channels to call to the attention of Lamy the results of his actions.[53] Lamy could not easily dismiss Martinez because he had more than a religious following; he also had a political base. Martinez had served as territorial representa-

46

tive of his region six times before northern Mexico was taken by the United States. He had also served as a member of the terri-torial Council of Legislative Assembly between 1852 and 1861.[54] When Lamy reinstituted the tithes, however, Martinez's strong protest eventually led first to his suspension, and then to his excommunication. Martinez, well versed in Canon Law, did not recognize the excommunication as valid. He continued to minister to the people until his death in 1867, although he was offcially out of the Church. The schism diminished with the passing of Martinez, but the influence of the Martinez era is still felt today in New Mexico. He remains a folk hero to many of the New Mexican Catholics, even though he is still officially excommuni-cated.[55]

In the literature it is not documented that Bishop Lamy's actions were intentionally racist, or based on personal malice. Like the Franciscan frairs of the California missions, he pro-bably had the best of theological intentions. However, as with the missions, the test of theological and temporal worth lies with the impact on the population, not with the intentions of the clergy.

The vigor with which the Catholic Church undertook Ameri-canization can well be explained as a reaction to nativism. The Church itself was under attack as foreign, even though it was composed principally of United States citizens--Irish Americans, Italian Americans, etc., and permanent immigrants. The Church wanted to prove to United States society that it was just as Anmerican and loyal as was Protestantism. The Catholic Church's desire to Americanize its flock can be seen as a defensive move against the nativist and the Know-Nothings--a move that was not necessarily vicious in its intent, but nevertheless destructive in its result.

The Catholic European immigrants wanted to be Americanized, and were willing immigrants to the United States.[56] The Mexicans were a conquered indigenous people who did not necessarily con-ceive of themselves as immigrants. Furthermore, the Mexicans did not recognize the border as a significant barrier because, in fact, it was not a barrier. The Mexicans had a tradition already established in the Southwest and perceived little need to change to suit the occupying forces.

That the Church reflected the mores and values of nineteenth century America is further exemplified in the Church's position on slavery. At the time of the conquest of the Southwest, it would have been unreasonable to expect the Church to be overly concerned with the civil rights of the Mexican, since it had demonstrated an insensitivity to the issue of slavery in Mexico and the United States.[57] The Church no doubt considered the Mexicans to be free men, with their fate in their own hands; and according to the Treaty of Guadalupe Hidalgo, they had the choice of returning to Mexico within a year of the conquest. Thus, according to the Treaty, those who stayed had exercised their option to "willingly" join the United States. The condition of the Mexican during this period (post-Mexican War) could not appear seriously repressive to a hierarchy and Church that considered the enslavement of another racial minority to be morally acceptable.

The circumstances of the Church and the Mexican in California after the War varied somewhat from that of New Mexico. The objective conditions of the people were different. In New Mexico the Mexican population was a majority and the population had a certain degree of homogeneity.[58] In California, due largely to the discovery of gold, the native Californio bacame a minority with the influx of Anglo-Americans. The territory, while retaining much of its Mexican flavor, eventually became a predominantly Anglo and Protestant state. By 1880, Mexicans would constitute only 21 percent of the total population in the Los Angeles area.[59]

The combination of events of secularization of the missions, the War, and the death in 1846 of California's first bishop, Garcia Diego, put the state of Catholicism in California in a weak position. One author has suggested that Catholicism in the new American territory was "near extinction."[60] The task of reconstructing the Church was given to Bishop Joseph S. Alemany in 1850. Alemany, like Lamy in New Mexico, was responsible ultimately to the center of Church power in the United States, Baltimore. The Church leadership directed Alemany to (1) obtain control of the Pious Fund, the former Mexican Church's fiscal source for California; (2) introduce the tithe; and (3) solidify the control over the mission property.[61] While all of these actions would affect the Mexicans, and to a degree the newly arrived Catholic Anglo resident, the provision that earned the most controversy was the institution of tithing. Since the native Californios had largely not previously supported the clergy by the method of the tithe, they balked at this imposition. The Indians had, of course, supported (i.e., physically) the friars through their labor in the missions and through the surplus wealth that they had generated. However, the demand for the tithe was a direct and undisguised substantial subsidy. With the large scale refusal to pay the tithe, and the Eastern priests' conception of how Mexicans should behave, the Church threatened to, and in some cases actually did, disrupt services to the population.

On at least one occasion the result of this disruption of
services led to clashes between the Anglo Catholics and the
native Californios. In 1856, a Los Angeles priest refused to
bury a woman in the church cemetery, ostensibly because the woman
had died in "sin." Angered, a group of Mexicans buried her in
the cemetery. The priest was outraged and had the group arrested
on charges of desecrating the holy grounds. The Anglo Catholics
were also enraged and charged that the "entire Mexican race was a
'mutinous rabble.'"[62] Significantly, the _ricos_ (rich native
Californios) while denouncing the racist attack, also denounced
the Mexicans who took the actions. The Church in this explicit
instance demonstrated: (1) the ability to divide its congregation on arbitrary grounds that provoked Mexican protest and Anglo
reaction, and (2) that the Mexican reaction to the Church cannot
be predicted purely on racial grounds, but that class differentiation _among_ the Mexican subgroups is equally as important if one
is to understand the reaction of Mexicans to institutional
action.

Post-War Mexico

While the division of Mexico naturally created a new era for
the Mexican people in the new Southwest, events in the old
country continued to play a major role in the development of the
new Mexican-American or Chicano. Opinions of Chicanos, especially the immigrants, about the Church would be greatly influenced
by the Church's activities in Mexico. The proximity of the old
country meant that as events occurred in Mexico that would cause
people to emigrate, the population of the Southwest would be in a
constant flux with the arrival and departure (often forced) of
their fellow countrymen.

In 1854, the liberals revolted against President Santa
Anna's corrupt rule, and by 1856 they were in control of Mexico
and issued an important measure regarding the holdings of the
Church. The _Ley Lerdo_ required the Church to sell all land not
directly related to religious functions. A heavy sales tax was
to be paid to the central government. The law, however, was not
confiscatory; the Church was not stripped of its land by uncom-
pensated expropriation. While the Church protested this law, it
was not in a strategic position to immediately and physically
oppose the law. It was, however, in the position to threaten
spiritual reprisal against those who would take advantage of the
law by "denouncing" the land--the procedure for buying the
Church's surplus property.

The law was essentially a liberal reform that was not intended to communize the vast holdings of the Church for the

peasants. The leaders of the reform believed in the concept of individual private property. As such, and in an attempt to make it appear that the law was not aimed solely at the Church, the reform directed that all collective or institutional holdings be dispersed. Therefore, the law applied not only to the Church, but also to corporations, and communal land that was still owned by the Indian villages. Many of the non-Indians, unable to afford the holdings of the Church (and unwilling to confront the Church), denounced the Indian lands and obtained them for small amounts. Meanwhile, the Church was losing portions of its land to those individuals who could afford the going rate and were undaunted by the Church's ecclesiastical threats--often these were foreigners. The consequence was that the peasants did not benefit; instead of serving clerical masters, they now served secular bosses. Those Indians who owned land in common lost major portions of their remaining independence. And the Church, while losing some of its land, obtained a large cash surplus, therefore allowing it to continue as an important political and banking unit.[63]

The constitution of 1857 reaffirmed the Ley Lerdo and anti-clerical temper of the time. Among the liberties given to the people was the right of nuns and monks to renounce their vows. It also instituted (on paper) other reforms such as the subordi-nation of the military to civilian government, the abolishment of debtor prisions, the abolishment of hereditary titles; and it instituted civil liberties concerning freedom of expression.

> It was a faithful statement of French bourgeois reform, but utterly failed to reckon with the imperative Mexican problem of the landless Indian and his incorporation into national life.[64]

The government declared that all public officials must swear allegiance to the new constitution. While the Church's wealth was altered but not destroyed, the hierarchy considered the action as more than a major inconvenience as it converted its assets. The Constitution was a direct and precedent-setting threat to its continuation as an institution of privilege and prestige. The hierarchy, in one of its more open attempts to influence the political direction of Mexico, retaliated by excom-municating all who swore allegiance. Many officials refused to take the oath and resigned their positions. Many others, while largely anti-clerical but not necessarily anti-Catholic, took the oath but with deep regrets.

Furthermore, the Church was concerned with more than the tenor of the anti-clericalism. For example, the bishop of

Michoacan declared that the newly granted freedoms of speech, the press, assembly, and free elections were contrary to the laws of God and the Church.[65]

The Church in Rome gave its support to the Mexican hierarchy. Pope Pius IX declared that the new government and its constitution were illegitimate.

> We raise our Pontifical voice with apostolic freedom . . . to condemn, reprove, and declare null and void, and without any value, the said decrees.[66]

Incited by the national clergy and having been given the legitimacy of papal support, the reactionary elements of Mexican society launched the three year War of the Reform. Unable to secure victory by themselves, they invited the French to invade Mexico and establish a Catholic empire. Maximilian was chosen to be the new emperor of Mexico. Before coming to Mexico, he visited the Pope and received his blessing.[67] Maximilian's fate is well known. After the French withdrew in 1867, having no real political base he was captured and executed.

Thereafter (until the revolution of 1910) the relationship between the Church and the Church and the State was one of mutual hypocrisy with the Church refusing to publicly accept its subordination to the State and the State only selectively enforcing the "reforms." The hypocrisy of both institutions was especially evident during the dictatorship of Porfirio Diaz (1876-1910). Diaz and the Church agreed that in exchange for Diaz's approval of clerical appointments, the Laws of Reform would not be enforced. Diaz, however, realized that anti-clericalism was good politics regardless of one's "liberalness" or reaction, and he therefore periodically suppressed that Church for public consumption while he allowed it to increase its holdings and grow in numbers. The Church began to teach for the benefit of the dictator the gospel of law and order, even though the anti-clerical laws were still on the books. Though the Church and State were now antagonists in collusion rather than united as in Mexico's formation, the impact on the people was the same.[68]

The Twentieth Century

For the early part of the twentieth century the most significant event for the Mexican on both sides of the border was the revolution of 1910, and the two decades of upheaval that would follow. During the reign of Porfirio Diaz (the Porfiriato) the economy of Mexico expanded and developed. The people who bene-

fited from the despot's regime were primarily large landowners
and foreigners. For the masses of society, the landless peasants, the conditions of life degenerated from an already subsis-
tence level to one of degradation. The reasons for the poverty
were not lost on the peasant. As Brandenburg has noted:

> The contrast between mansion and hut--between
> the life of the hacendado and administrator on
> the one had and the peon on the other--bore
> heavily on the peasant as he daily entered the
> fields before sunrise and returned at sunset.
> To the peon, justice meant the unquestioned word
> of hacendado, administrator, jailor, and priest.
> And if the overlord needed assistance in keeping
> his peons in line, he simply called upon Diaz's
> rural shocktroopers. The poverty stricken pea-
> sant had no hope of a better tomorrow, no pro-
> mise of somehow raising himself from his deplor-
> able status.[69]

When Diaz stated that he did not intend to succeed himself
in 1910, the prospects for change became a viable possibility for
the population. Although Diaz retracted his statement, the national fervor for a new order could not be stopped.

For over thirty years the Porfiriato had suppressed opposition; therefore the opposition was not unified in a country as
vast as Mexico. The resultant upheaval was to last off and on
for nearly two decades with such figures as Madero, Huerta,
Carranza, Villa, and Zapata vying for power at various times
against each other. The telling of the Mexican Revolution has
been related from scholarship to folklore.[70] The immediate task
of the present study is to examine the Church's role in the
events during the Revolution and the impact on Mexicans and
Chicanos.

In the decade preceding the revolution, the Church, with the
surreptitious but evident collusion of Diaz, had come to live
with anti-clericals--not necessarily in a harmonious relationship
but one that generally avoided bloodshed. The Church was not the
most visible landowner, and therefore not the sole target of the
various revolutionaries. Nevertheless, the Church was still a
powerful landowner through its use of "front" charitable organizations,[71] and therefore had an interest in the outcome of the
Revolution.

The institutional Church, adhering to its pattern of political affiliations in the conflicts of the past, chose the side of
reaction in the upheaval. What the Church could not defeat

militarily owing to its weakened position in society, it tried to alter through proclamations and "reforms" of its own. In 1913, the Dieta de los Circulos, in accordance with the teachings of Rerum Novarum urged that the "Honorable and hard-working rural worker" should have sufficient land to support his family but only with due respect to the rights of the large landowners.[72] The Church opposed, however, those who were actually fighting (often among themselves) for the redistribution of power and land in Mexico. Zapata and others who advocated "socialism," however ill-defined were opposed by the Church as a matter of course.

The Catholic Social Action was the primary progressive arm of the Church. Started by Jose Luis Cuevas in order to promote the ideas of Rerum Novarum, it was dominated by members of the hierarchy since the intelligentsia of Mexico had long ago abandoned the Church.[73] The lay workers were not expected to be able to interpret the words of the pope. However, once the revolution had started, and the issues became more than academic or theological debate, but a concrete situation of armed struggle among the competing forces, this progressive arm of the Church became increasingly less important. As Quirk has noted:

> Catholic Social Action ultimately disappeared in the maelstrom of the revolution against Huerta and the subsequent wars among the revolutionary chiefs, all that was left of the program was the intransigence of the Church against radicalism . . . .Increasingly in the 1910's the fulminations of the Church were directed aginst radicals--to defeat socialism became the aim of the priest, not to aid the oppressed.[74]

The Constitution of 1917 seriously curtailed the Church's ability to function in Mexican society. The Church was, on paper, stripped of its ability to operate schools on the primary level and its property was nationalized. Priests were not to appear publicly in clerical clothing, nor were they to offer public services outside of the churches. The delegates who wrote the Constitution came close to adopting a provision that would have demanded that priests be married and another that would have banned oral confessions. One article provided that social reform measures (for the protection of workers) should be the province of the civil authorities and not the Church.

The Church was not in a position to challenge directly the Constitution since many of its leaders and priests were then in exile. However, from the hierarchy's vantage points in the United States and Rome came denunciations which attempted to invalidate the Constitution.[75] President Carranza, however, did

53

not enforce all of the provisions of the Constitution, and the clergy who did remain acted, when feasible, as if the Constitution did not exist.

The tenor of the Church's activity to help the Mexican worker was indicated in its unionization efforts. In 1921, the clergy formed Catholic unions to counter the growing influence of the Confederacion Regional Obrera Mexicana, C.R.O.M., a craft-union organization that closely resembled the American Federation of Labor. The clergy declared that to belong to C.R.O.M. was a mortal sin. However, the Church-controlled unions did nothing to implement their demands on employers. No Catholic union ever called a strike; the programs of the union were to be adopted by the owners through their "voluntary good will," and "the workers were told that obedience to their masters and resignation to their poverty were religious duties."[76]

Though no strike was called by a Catholic union, the priests of Mexico went on strike themselves. On July 31, 1926, the priests began a three-year strike by refraining from offering mass or other services to the population. The purpose was to bring pressure to bear upon the government through an expected outcry of the people being denied services. The strike was a grievous tactical error. In one of the most telling examples of the lack of dependency, and lack of commitment by the Mexican to actual Church dogma and institutional ritual, the clergy discovered, much to their dismay, that the people of Mexico were able to fulfill their spiritual needs without priests. The church buildings themselves were open and persons who wished to avail themselves of their use could do so. Many continued to go to church and pray sporadically, but the loss of priests was not an immediate concern to the lives of most people. Gruening observed that many persons actually preferred the absence of priests since they could then worship without having to pay for the privilege. There were, of course, those who missed their priests, but according to Gruening,

> There seems to be a definite relation between the peasant's concerns in the clerical contro-versy and the benefit they have derived from agrarian reform. Where they have received land they apparently care little, or less, about the absence of a priest, and his services. Land fills their lives.[77]

The active resistance to the government's anti-clericalism and the resulting clergy strike came not from the peasants but rather from the creoles and individual priests who, while not acting officially for the Church, did not incur the Church's disfavor. An armed insurrection of militant Catholics, the Cristeros, fought government troops between 1926 and 1927 in an attempt to reverse the Revolution. As with previous revolutionary situations in Mexico, both sides committed atrocities. The outrage that brought a specific governmental response against the Church was the dynamiting and burning of a civilian train between Guadalajara and Mexico City. The Cristeros had been actively assisted by priests who were fighting with them. The Church claimed that the clergy involved were only acting as chaplains to the insurgents. The government, under Calles, ordered that the remaining bishops of Mexico be deported to the United States. By May of 1927, Mexico had no viable institutional Church other than buildings where people could worship individually.[78]

The situation was one of a Catholic nation having no functional religion. Neither antagonist was in a position of moral strength although the government had the upper hand in the situation. The Church was obviously weakened because the expected mass outcry had not materialized and the limited armed insurrection it had helped to create,proved to be embarrasingly inept but brutal. The government, while attempting to implement anticlerical laws and limit the power of the Church, had helped to create a situation where it was not a tower of liberal secular enlightenment, but rather one of actual suppression of religious freedom. The situation was not conducive to the legitmization as institutions of either Church or State.

In this quandary, the mediation of an outsider was utilized. The then United States Ambassador, Dwight Morrow, arranged a compromise between then President Portes Gil and the Church. The compromise essentially put the Church and State in the same position they had been in before the strike and Criestero uprising. The Church was required to register its priests, the strike was called off, and the Church was allowed to teach its religion within the confines of the churches. On June 20, 1929, with Vatican approval, the Church began again to function as a religious institution.[79]

While the settlement was a stalemate, the Church lost more in the long run: (1) The Church recognized the right of the State to regulate its activities; (2) to the anti-clericals the Church had been exposed as weak; (3) to the militant Catholics, the Church appeared not only weak but also appeared to betray them with an agreement that had not only not restored the luster of the Church, but had given de facto recognition to the Revolution.[80] The decline of the institutional Church was evident in the phenomenal drop in the number of clergy in Mexico. Before the Revolution there were 4,493 registered priests in Mexico and by 1935 there were only 230.[81]

Throughout the early and middle 1930's, the Church was subjected to many anti-clerical laws that were more anti-Catholic than purely attempts to negate Church abuses. Some restrictions put upon the Church were petty and intended to harass the Church rather than establish a revolutionary program.[82] It was not until the beginning of the 1940's that Mexico evolved a Church-State relationship that was conducive to minimal friction. This was primarily due to the Church refraining from overtly public political stances rather than a return to purely ecclesiastical concerns. Also as Mexico entered the middle of the twentieth century, it could well be argued that the Revolution—while still primarily being given rhetoric—was essentially liberal capitalism.[83] At the same time the Church was losing its overt vestiges of medieval feudalism and becoming part of the capitalist society under which it operated. In short, the objective realities of both the State and the Church were becoming less dysfunctional and the subjective teachings of the Church were progressing from a reactionary adherence to the principle of feudalism to the tenets of modern capitalism. At the formation of the Mexican colony, the Church and State were the same and had the trappings of feudalism. By the nineteenth century, the State was developing a capitalist liberalism while the Church languished in the past. It was not until the twentieth century that the State was able to wrench the Church into the world of capitalism. Quirk has described the situation between the Church and State as a modus vivendi, a tactical agreement to disagree peacefully.[84] There should be little doubt that the personalities involved in the Church and State still viewed each other with a mutual distrust, and at times, jealously. However, they did not want to return to the conflicts that had plagued both institutions. But also it should be observed that the two institutions were/are, as the Church becomes less fuedal, having fundamentally less and less about which to disagree.

The Church in the United States

The United States Church, especially the Church in the Southwest, was faced with the problem of how to cope with the massive immigration from Mexico caused by the Revolution. The Church saw the Mexican immigrants and residents as a clientele population, in a crisis situation, who needed to be Americanized.[85] In addition, the Church considered the Mexican brand of Catholicism different from and inferior to the Catholicism practiced on the East Coast. In some respects the Catholicism of the Mexican—plus his reason for immigration to the United States—did differ from the eastern Catholics. As previously mentioned, the European immigrants, such as the Irish, voluntarily immigrated to the United States. When they came, they also brought

56

their own clergy with them. While often retaining their ethnic heritage, they strived to become Americans. Americanization, therefore, became a primary goal of the European immigrants, and not an unwanted imposition. The Catholicism of the Mexican immigrant, however, could well be interpreted as being different from his European counterpart. Moore notes that the immigrants who arrived during the great migration were often the ones who had the least training in a Mexican Church--a Church that was historically weak in eliciting overall commitment. As she notes:

> The immigrants appear, indeed, to have come from precisely that population group in Mexico among whom Catholic influence was weakest. They were unaccustomed to parochial schools, financial support of the Church, religious instruction, and regular attendance at mass, all of which are important to American Catholics.[86]

While many Mexican priests also fled to the United States, the relationship they had with their countrymen was not the same as the Irish with their priests. Many of the immigrants brought their anti-clerical views, and the number of priests who did immigrate from Mexico was insufficient to tend to the religious needs of those people who desired their services. The Church has viewed this as a "pastoral emergency" which continues in places to the present.[87]

The Church's efforts toward Americanization did not include an overt effort toward integration. Joseph H. Fichter, S.J., has noted that Catholics followed/follow "area practice" in regard to race and labor relations. This included Catholic participation in the enslavement and later discrimination against Blacks in the South, anti-Semitism in the Northeast, and discrimination against Mexicans in the Southwest.[88] Churches in the Southwest were often segregated either by, at best, neglect to include the Mexican population or, at worst, by actual intent of the congregation and pastor.[89]

Thus the Mexican Catholic in the United States faced a situation that was at once similar and different to that which he had grown accustomed to in Mexico. This added to the confusion of the immigrant in the new country. The Church, rather than being a source of comfort and continuity, was often a source of discomfort and confusion, even--if not especially--to those who wished to practice their religion. In Mexico, the people had been faced with a highly feudal Church which dominated much (if not most) of the wealth, charged excessive fees for services, and more often than not taught acceptance of the status quo. The Church was also relatively secure in its position as the Mexican religion. At the same time, it practiced race and class discrimination in the allocation of its resources. In the United States, the Mexican immigrant found a Church (especially in the Southwest) that was itself a minority (Protestantism was the dominant religion), pleaded inadequate resources, and was trying to prove that it also was American. In a direct impact on the immigrant, the Church attempted to change him by attempting to alter this heritage while at the same time treating him as an inferior because of his heritage. Similar to the Church in Mexico, however, it still taught general acceptance of the status quo. Thus those who were anti-clericals in Mexico had little reason to alter their position. Those who considered themselves devout Catholics (many of whom had not felt the discrimination in Mexico) had reason to feel either totally confused by their new racially inferior status, or to become an anti-cleric themselves because of the treatment received in the United States. The commitment of the immigrant to the Church was given little to nurture it.

In such a situation it would have been unreasonable for large numbers of Mexicans to become active Church members, even if they had desired to be devout. In the predominantly secularized urban areas of Southern California, the Mexican had the viable option of ignoring the Church. While the Church could be the focus of existence, this was not absolutely necessary in the city. The situation in the Mexican populated rural areas of the United States (as in Mexico also) was somewhat different. In addition to religion per se, the Church was the center of social life. Not to participate in Church-sponsored activities often meant not to participate in community life at all. This did not signify that Catholicism (as a body of dogma) had a tight rein on the rural Mexican, but that the institutional Church was integrated into village life.[90] However, overall religious influence, as a belief system, became less prevalent in the United States than in Mexico. The Mexican-American population did not become atheistic or non-religious, but the impact of Catholic beliefs became less than it had been in Mexico (though cultural forms such as baptism and and compadrazgo remained).

Thus it is not surprising that the observers of Mexican religious practices perceived the Mexican in the United States as being somewhat irreligious.[91] Protestant churches saw Chicanos as a people open to proselytizing, but for the most part these efforts were not successful. Estimates in the post-Revolution era of the proportion of Mexicans who were Protestant vary considerably from a very high 30 to 50 percent suggested by Oxnam, to a more reasonable estimate of 5 percent by Holland.[92] The 5 percent figure is the estimate that has held and is made by Grebler, et al., for the Chicanos in the 1960's.[93]

58

Mexicans/Chicanos did not convert to Protestantism in great numbers for several reasons. Blair has noted that being a Catholic is taken for granted in Mexico (and subsequently in the United States), and that in the past little knowledge of other forms of religious worship existed (i.e., Western religions in the post-Columbian era).[94] Historically to be Mexican is to be Catholic--not necessarily in belief but at least culturally, i.e., baptism, fiestas, etc. Although it was not considered unusual (especially for the men) to ignore religious practices, one would still define oneself as a Catholic, if only on one's deathbed. By the nineteenth century many liberals and radicals not only refrained from religious practices, but often <u>denounced</u> the Church and its clergy. However, to actually convert to another religion was extremely uncommon. To become a Protestant was in many respects a negation of one's past. Much more than the anti-cleric who denounced the clergy and attributed to priests the Mexican's lack of political development, the Protestant convert was often denying his heritage, culture, and often, family.[95] Refugees (and others) accepted Protestant charity, along with sermons, but there were few real conversions.

Protestantism is a myriad of denominations separated not only by different beliefs, but also by the class composition of membership.[96] Proselytizing among the Mexicans was not practiced by all denominations, nor in all localities. Some Protestant churches discriminated against Mexicans and discouraged their entrance into their congregations, either overtly or by making them feel unwanted.[97] Proselytizing was emphasized by those churches who socio-economic status was more conducive to reaching out to the new Mexican immigrant. These congregations were often fundamentalist and of a conservative nature in dogma and in form. These churches were usually austere and strict, and different from Mexican Catholicism which "placed high evaluation on ritual, fiestas, visual religious symbols, and tradition."[98] The demands of Catholicism were normally not as confining as the demands of Protestantism. Therefore while the immigrant could not be categorized as a "catechism" Catholic, Protestant proselytizing met little lasting success.[99]

Hence, many Mexicans were essentially a religious-Catholic people without a tangible Church. Conversion to Protestantism, for the majority, was not a viable alternative. However, the Catholic Church felt the necessity, if it was to retain its influence, to extend itself to the Mexican population. As a study notes:

> Contrary to the notion that the immigrant would seek the Church for support and comfort--a notion valid for most Catholic immigrants to the

59

East--the Church had to reach out for the
newcomer if it was to perform its function.[100]

However, this "reaching out" was slow in developing and did not
concern itself generally with the secular needs of the people.
In a 1937 editorial in the official Los Angeles diocesan paper,
The Tidings, Catholics who insisted that the Church address the
social welfare of the people were emphatically rebuffed. The
editorial stated that the Church was not concerned with

> . . . merely human worldly objects. . . . Christ
> did not found the Church to be a mere
> humanitarian institution. . . . She has, in
> fact, plenty to do to attend to her own
> business.[101]

While the Church did not lead the struggles of the Chicanos,
it did intercede at times, especially if a radical influence on
the Chicano community was seen. An example is the pecan shellers
strike of 1938 in San Antonio, Texas. During the strike the
fledgling, predominantly Chicano union was brutally suppressed by
San Antonio police chief, Owen Kilday, supposedly because of its
communist leadership. The sheriff's activities were not universally applauded by other government agencies. The Texas State
Industrial Commission and the National Labor Relations Board, and
even the governor of Texas criticized Kilday's behavior. However, he was able to weather the censorship because he had the
support of San Antonio's respectable community, including middle
class Mexicans and the local Catholic Church. Citing the communist leadership, the strikers did not get the support of the
Mexican Chamber of Commerce, the League of United Latin-American
Citizens (LULAC), nor of Archbishop Dorssearts. Drossearts
approved of the police actions against "communist influences."[102]
As in previous situations where the poorer Mexicans asserted
their rights, the Mexican bourgeoisie and the Church effectively
united against them.

An exception to the norm of hierarchy non-involvement with
secular matters was Archbishop Robert E. Lucey. At the time of
the pecan strike, Lucey was bishop of Amarillo, Texas. Despite
his later liberal credentials as Archbishop of San Antonio
(appointed in 1941), Lucey did not criticize Drossearts' actions.
However, it would have been a highly unusual action for a bishop
to publicly criticize another bishop. With Lucey's appointment
to San Antonio, he endeavored to initiate some social reforms.
Shortly after his installation in San Antonio, he outlined part
of his program. Lucey's program involved the right to collective
bargaining, sufficient wages to allow for investment and plan for
retirement, and that business regulate itself to cease illegal

practices.[103] Essentially this plan of action involved curbing a few excesses of the market economy, not the redistribution of wealth on any significant scale. While his concern for the plight of the Mexican worker appears genuine in his writings, they can be described as patronizing.[104] They also display a certain naivete about the influences on the incentives of public officials.[105]

It was, however, largely through Lucey's efforts that the Church in the Southwest recognized that a "Mexican problem" even existed. He helped to formulate the Bishop's Committee for the Spanish-Speaking in 1945. The Committee spoke out against the more blatant discriminatory practices, such as in the bracero program.[106] Since the Committee respected the prerogative of each diocese to handle its own affairs, it did not make mandatory any of its pronouncements on individual dioceses (or parishes) but left their implementation up to the individual bishops. Therefore its ultimate effectiveness for improving the overall condition of the Chicano was limited.[107]

What is significant about Lucey is not that he was radical-- he clearly was not--but that his New-Deal liberalism was considered very progressive for a member of the Church hierarchy. He was singled out for his social reform efforts by Church historians.[108] Lucey was the execption-not the norm. He was/is considered, by those who desire more Church involvement in the secular aspects of the poor peoples' lives, a model to emulate.

While Lucey's actions and those of the Bishops' Committee were of marginal effectiveness in their direct impact on the Chicano community, they did have important tangential effects with long-range implications for the Chicano. Two priests who attended a regional meeting in 1948 of the Bishops' Committee endeavored to begin pastoral work among the Mexican farm workers. Fathers Thomas McCullough and Donald McDonnell persuaded their Archbishop, John J. Mitty of San Francisco, to free them and two other priests from the usual parish assignments to minister to the migrants. A primary concern was that Protestants might make inroads among the unchurched Mexicans. The four priests formed the Spanish Mission Band whose primary purpose was to offer mass, hear confessions, and extend other services to the migrants.

Frs. McDonnell and McCullough, however, realized that it was difficult to minister to a people's spiritual needs when their material conditions were greatly inadequate. Based on the teachings of the social encyclicals, Rerum Novarum (Pope Leo XIII, 1891) and Quadragessimo Anno (Pope Pius XI, 1931), which call for the right of "workingmen's associations" to band together ith employers to establish "just wages," the priests sought to offer support for the organization of workers into an effective body to negotiate for better working conditions.[109] Obtaining permission from their bishop "to explain the teachings of the Church on management-labor cooperation,"[110] they began to help organize the workers, especially against the abuses of the bracero program.

"Cooperation" is the key concept here. The unions that the fathers helped to support were not militant or radical, but based upon the teachings of the Church. These teachings do not endorse class struggle or labor strife, but the working out of differences with mutual respect for the rights of labor and the rights of capital. Though seemingly moderate, the growers took the priests' actions as a threat. They began a campaign to bring pressure upon the diocese to stop the fathers' efforts.

Letters from various people suggested that teaching the social encyclicals would cause a rift between the growers (many of whom were Catholic) and the Church. One letter from a member of the San Joaquin County Farm Bureau Federation stated that relations between the Church, the workers, and the growers was "becoming of serious concern to the farmers of the entire county." Another letter from a Stockton priest suggested that the growers might retaliate by supporting Proposition No. 16 on the November, 1958, ballot. (Proposition No. 16 would have eliminated the Church is tax-exempt status.) A letter from a rural priest asserted that Fr. McCullough was not authorized to discuss the issue of employee-employer relations.[111]

Pressure to halt the fathers' efforts increased, including eventually pressure from another bishop. In December of 1960, the fathers, in an attempt to help the Agricultural Workers Organizing Committee (AWOC) went to El Centro, California. This proved to be a tactical error since El Centro was in the San Diego diocese and Bishop Charles F. Buddy complained to Archbishop Mitty. At that time Archbishop Mitty was ill, but auxiliary bishop Hugh Donohoe recalled the priests. Shortly thereafter the Mission Band was dissolved. Fr. McDonnell went to Brazil to work among the poor and Fr. McCullough was sent to a parish in Oakland, California. He was ordered to sever his affiliation with the unionization efforts and not to issue public statements regarding farm workers. "He had taken a solemn vow of obedience; he obeyed."[112]

While none of the participants have stated for attribution why the Mission Band was dissolved, the comments of Bishop Donohoe, are illuminating:

Well, the kind of opposition that developed to
the Mission Band is the opposition that develops
whenever the movement gets to the point of
identifying with particular problems, and in so
doing invariably they find themselves espeusing
(sic) the cause of the field worker . . . the
growers . . . took for granted that the priests
were not merely in favor of 'social justice' but
rather that they were union organizers . . .[113]

The implications of Donohoe's statement are evident.   In
theory the social teachings of the Church are valid.   If, however, they are applied to a concrete situation then it will
become clear that there is no neutral position in the search for
social justice.   Rather, the reasonable man will find himself
"invariably espousing" the cause of the farm worker because that
is where social justice is to be found.   The growers will, however, be in opposition to the unionizing effort, and will see
that the priests are not merely neutral, but in this situation in
favor of the farm workers.   The growers will then assume that
this is Church policy (when, in fact, it was the action of individual priests).   The Church could therefore be hurt because for
the Church the power lies with the growers, not with the farm
workers.

In this specific situation when the institutional Church had
the opportunity to legitimize the activity of two of its priests
involved in social action, it chose not to do so.   As in Mexico
during the 1910 Revolution, when the issues became concrete
rather than merely theoretical debate, the Church chose not to
enforce its own (and moderate) proposals.   Frs. McCullough's and
McDonnell's actions as individual priests were not sufficient
(despite the grower's beliefs) to qualify them as indicative of
the institutional Church (as is intimated in Bishop Donohoe's
statement).

The fathers' actions were not typical, as they were carried
out in a special situation.   They were not in a regular assignment and were acting on their own initiative.   Ultimately, of
course, they were answerable to the Bishop who, in the beginning,
allowed them to teach the social gospel.   The Bishop, however,
did not authorize union activity as such, and they found themselves on the periphery of the Church.   When the periphery became
a losing situation, the Church cut its losses.   The Church acted
on the basis of its own vested interests, rather than its stated
teachings.   If we are to take seriously the axiom that theory can
only be tested in practice, then it becomes clear that the theories of the Church involving labor justice have failed in specific
instances in regard to the Mexican people.   In Mexico and the

United States, when the rights of workers were attempted to be balanced with the rights of the owners, the Church eventually capitulated to the owners. It should be noted that while the fathers failed in the short term to instigate the social reforms they desired, they left an important legacy. That had preached to the farm workers that they had the right to organize as workers; that it was not a privilege given by the employers or the state. For the religious, there was the opportunity to hear that it was a part of morality to demand a just wage. For the religious and nonreligious alike, there was the chance to gain experience in unionizing, that is, before the fathers were stripped of their own right to work among those who needed their help. Equally important, the fathers, in a nonelitist manner, shared their knowledge and experience with other potential leaders who could and would continue the struggle. Two of these were Cesar Chavez and Dolores Huerta.

Chavez first met Fr. McDonnell in 1950 when he came to the Sal Si Puedes barrio of San Jose. McDonnell shared with Chavez his knowledge of farm labor problems. Chavez had the experience of a farm worker but little theory on how to change conditions. McDonnell provided an initial blend of theory and practice. The early influence of McDonnell on Chavez should not be minimized. As Chavez has stated:

> Actually my education started when I met Father Donald McDonnell, who came to Sal Si Puedes because there was no Catholic church there, no priest, and hundreds of Mexican-Americans . . . .
>
> . . . We had long talks about farm workers. I knew a lot about the work, but I didn't know anything about the economics, and I learned quite a bit from him . . . .
>
> . . . Everything he said was aimed at ways to solve the injustice. Later I went with him a couple of times to some strikes near Tracy and Stockton.[114]

During the beginning of the grape strike Chavez noted the early influence of McDonnell:

> (Fr. McDonnell) . . . sat with me past midnight telling me about social justice and the Church's stand on farm labor and reading from the encyclicals of Pope Leo XIII in which he upheld labor unions. I would do anything to get the Father to tell me more about labor history. I began going to the bracero camps with him to help with Mass, to the city jail with him to

talk to prisoners, anything to be with him so he could tell me more about the farm labor movement.[115]

It was also McDonnell who introduced Chavez in 1952 to Fred Ross of the Community Service Organization (CSO). Here he received practical experience on organization, which he was later to use so effectively with the United Farm Workers.[116]

Dolores Huerta, who along with Chavez was one of the driving forces behind the United Farm Workers, also was influenced early by one of the two fathers. Fr. McCullough introduced Huerta, one of his parishioners, to the CSO. Mrs. Huerta worked with Fr. McCullough in the early formation of the Agricultural Workers Association (AWA), a predecessor of the United Farm Workers.[117]

During the period of Frs. McDonnell's and McCullough's activity among the farm workers of California, the Church in Los Angeles, under the direction of Archbishop McIntyre (later Cardinal), was revitalizing a program of Americanization. The goals were not only to Americanize but in a real sense to Catholicize the Mexicans who were not yet perceived as real practitioners of the faith. There was evidence from a variety of sources by the midcentury that Mexicans, indeed, did not attend services at regular intervals, and these indications increased throughout the 1950's. Different localities from around the nation indicated Chicanos had various levels of Church participation, but in no cases did their regular mass attendance exceed 40 percent of the population. Humphrey reported that in Detroit, a 1944 study showed that church attendance was irregular and that children went basically to please their parents, and therefore might cease to attend when they became adults. Thurston reported that in 1949, of one hundred families in a Los Angeles colonia, only about fifteen went to church regularly, and those attendees were largely women and children. In a 1954 San Antonio study, Murray found that of 118 housing project families, 90 percent considered themselves Catholic; however, only 38 percent were regular Sunday mass worshippers. Less than that number received the sacraments regularly, and very few attended parish functions or sent their children to Catholic schools. In a telling, if somewhat exaggerated statement, Bishop Candeleria asserted that the Catholic Church was effectively ministering to only 10 percent of the Mexicans in California and the Southwest.[118] Clark in a study of the Mayfield district near San Jose, estimated that in 1955, about 35 to 40 percent attended church "fairly regularly," and only 20 to 25 percent participated in Church activities. Similar to the Murray study, however, most would identify themselves as Catholic and would seek out the Church at the major life events such as birth (baptism) and death (last rites). Clark also noted that most kept an image of the Virgin of Guadalupe somewhere in their homes.[119]

Faced with an apparent decline in religious practice among a prime Church constituency in the Southwest, the Los Angeles diocese began a program that aimed at the future--the youth. At the beginning of McIntyre's reign (1948), only 30 percent of the Chicano area parishes had schools as opposed to 58 percent of the other parishes.[120] The Church therefore started a school building program that would attempt to insulate the young Chicano from the secular values of public schools and stave off the prospects of protestant proselytizing. The Church assumed that the seeming lack of Catholic commitment among the Chicano population, at least in Los Angeles, was that public schools inculcated a secular outlook which made the Mexican have feelings of superiority over his parents, and their values, including those toward the Church.[121]

Through the Catholic schools, the Los Angeles Archidiocese hoped to inculcate their own values of a Catholic Americanism. Archbishop McIntyre was regarded as one of the bulwarks of Catholic conservatism, both politically and ecclesiastically. As such, he endeavored to guard against not only secularism but especially liberal secularism. In a speech in 1948, he recognized the growth potential (numberically) of the Chicanos and the desire to guide them (ideologically):

> The obvious to us is that the future citizens of this fair city and state will come in large numbers from the children of this eastern area of the city today. That they be safeguarded in their traditions and be preserved from an American brand of liberalism is our hope and prayer.[122]

McIntyre considered the school construction to be a priority item in his administration. With funds allocated by his predecessor, John J. Cantwell, for the construction of a new cathedral, he began the program of building schools in the Chicano areas. By 1960, nearly every parish in East Los Angeles had a parochial school. It should be noted that the use of general (i.e., diocesan) funds to create parish schools is not a usual practice. Each parish normally has the responsibility to build its own school; and during this period parishes were expected to contribute to the effort. Building Catholic schools in Chicano areas, of course, does not necessarily mean that Chicanos will automatically attend them. By the 1966-67 academic year in the high-density Chicano areas, only 15 percent of the eligible population were enrolled in grades one to six in Catholic schools; and 23 percent in grades seven to twelve.[123]

The school building program was not without its critics. A memorandum, presumably written by a Mexican/Chicano priest in 1947, was addressed, in a highly unusual procedure, directly to Pope Pius XII. The writer was concerned, as was the diocese, that Chicanos "today live for the most part far from the practice of their religion." He challenged, however, the concept of Americanizing the Chicano as the solution to this situation. Rather the writer suggested the Spanish-speaking (i.e., native Spanish speakers) priests be put in charge of churches in order that the customs of Mexican Catholicism be preserved and to increase Chicano participation--which would not occur in the American churches. The memorandum asserted that there was too large an area to be bridged between the Mexican and Anglos in "psychological race difference" and language; that Mexicans had a strong attachment to their traditions, and also objected to the tendency of "North Americans" to Americanize immigrants in general. The letter was submitted by the Apostolic Delegate in an unsigned version to the bishops of the Southwest for their comments. Only Archbishop Lucey of San Antonio acknowledged that "educational and social care does not suffice in the case of the Mexican" (i.e., to help him retain the practice of Catholicism).[124] The school-building program, however, continued on schedule. As late as the mid-twentieth century, the Chicano was still being seen as a virtual mission problem to which the hierarchy of the Church could not agree on a solution.

Conclusions

While general conclusions will be reserved for the final Chapter in order to present a unified view of Chicano-Catholic development and practices, some general observations need to be made before proceeding to examine the contemporary Chicano. After 450 years of virtual monopoly power over the religious development of the Mexican, the Church appeared to have failed to incorporate a deep commitment into the population. It had certainly engendered a pervasive attachment to things Catholic, but by most indications, especially in the United States, the obligations that the Church imposes on its members did not seem to be obligations that Chicanos felt needed to be practiced in their lives.

As this Chapter attempted to show, the foundations for the relationship between Chicanos and the Church was not found only in the United States but also throughout the history of Mexico.

The contradictory signals that the Mexican/Chicano received from his Church are not the basis on which intense commitments are built. Contradictions between the Church's theory and practices, between the commitment it expected from the people and the commitment it returned are evident in this Chapter.

The conquest and conversion made the natives subjects of a new power, but it did not necessarily make them believers in a new body of dogma. The institutional Church prospered during its unification with the Spanish State, but the religion of Catholicism appears to have faltered. The masses were not instructed sufficiently to internalize the obligations of the Church, but enough to be attached to the symbols, especially native symbols such as the Virgin of Guadalupe. The intellectuals increasingly became attracted to the liberal philosophies of Europe and perceived the institutional Church as an impediment to the implementation of their views in Mexico. When the liberals eventually assumed State power, they needed to consolidate their control and suppress the side of reaction.

While the institutional Church in Mexico was historically clearly on the side of reaction, there was also a long tradition of individual clerics becoming politically active and assuming leadership roles in reformist and revolutionary activities. The Mexican population thus received increasingly contradictory stimuli from the Church at the local and institutional level.

In the United States, the Mexican and Chicano also received contradictory stimuli that, while often lacking the historical drama of revolutionary situations in Mexico, were of no less importance in their impact on Chicano religious development. Historical events such as the Bishop Lamy versus Padre Martinez disupute, discriminatory practices, plus some well intentioned policies such as Americanization, all served to weaken Chicano commitment to the institutional Church, and thus make Chicanos appear "unchurched." As in Mexico, however, activist priests in the United States, such as Fathers McDonnell and McCullough, attempted to blend secular and pastoral work and reached out to the unchurched. When this effort was made, it was observed that the unchurched were still attracted and attached to the Church. However, when the fathers were pulled from their assignments (or in other historical examples, Padres Hidalgo and Martinez, both excommunicated) the commitment of Mexicans to the Church was necessarily weakened.

While the Mexican/Chicano has received contradictory signals from his Church, he also gives contradictory signals of his reaction to the Church. His continuous identification and attraction to the Virgin of Guadalupe, and resistance to Protestantism, suggest a strong attachment to the Church; his apparent lack of attention to the obligations of the Church suggests a weak commitment. Throughout the rest of this work, we will examine aspects of this complex dichotomized relationship. As we study the present manifestations of the relationship between the Chicano and the Church, we will also explore the prospects for the future.

[1]For an essay delineating the importance of outlining an historical perspective in order to understand the present conditions of the Chicano, see Juan Gomez-Quinones, "Toward a Perspective on Chicano History," Aztlan 2 (Fall, 1971): 1-49.

Since we are concerned with the ideological consequences of a dominant historical institution we would do well to remember Marx's observation:

> "Men make their own history, but they do not make it just as they please; they do not make it under circumstances chosen by themselves, but under circumstances directly encountered, given and transmitted from the past. The tradition of all dead generations weighs like a nightmare on the brain of the living." Karl Marx, The 18th Brumaire of Louis Bonaparte (New York: International Publishers, 1963), pg. 15.

[2]Cortes was thought to fit the description of the god Quetzalcoatl who was to return to Mexico the very time Cortes arrived. Quetzalcoatl was said to be white, bearded, long-haired--a description that fit Cortes. Although Cortes eventually had to conquer Tenochtitlan militarily, he was able to use the belief that he might be Quetzalcoatl to his strategic advantage. See Charles S. Braden, Religious Aspects of the Conquest of Mexico (Durham, North Carolina: Duke University Press, 1930), pp. 20-48.

[3]Charles C. Cumberland, Mexico: The Struggle for Modernity (London: Oxford University Press, 1968), pg. 59.

[4]For details of the Aztec religion see Eric Wolf, Sons of the Shaking Earth (Chicago: University of Chicago Press, 1959), pp. 168-175; Braden, Religious Aspects, pp. 21-75; G. C. Vaillant, The Aztecs of Mexico (London: Penguin, 1950), pp. 168-181.

[5]Wolf, Sons of the Shaking Earth, pg. 172. For a commentary on the blending of the native and Catholic religions, see B. C. Hedrick, Religious Syncretism in Spanish America, Miscellaneous Series (Greeley, Colorado: Museum of Anthropology, 1967).

[6]The Spaniards eventually recognized that the lack of actual conversions-despite mass baptisms-did not create the environment for a stable political or religious order. For example, the lessons of Mexico were utilized in the colonization of the Phil-

ippines where Christianization was also used as an instrument of political control, but with more of an attempt to actually instruct the conquered population in the rudimentary basics of Catholicism. For expansion of these comments see John Leddy Phelan, The Hispanization of the Philippines (Madison: University of Wisconsin Press, 1959), pp. viii; 31-89, especially 55-56.

Missionary work by its very nature presents itself a formidable task that is prone to failure rather than success. Rather than the subjugation of a people by primarily the force of arms and military conquest, missionaries attempt to transform the consciousness of a people. They attempt to change the world-view from that arising from the objective reality of the native population to that of the conquering (or missionary) force. This attempt to transform the native society in subjective terms, without the transformation of their objective reality, will quite naturally be met with resistance or subterfuge by the native population.

The success of missionary work should not be measured by the apparent acceptance or submission to the new religion while the missionaries or the agents are still present and are in a dominant position to enforce their new code of conduct; rather it should be judged as to its effectiveness after the departure of the missionaries and their agents (a rare and often non-occurrent situation). This presents a clearer view of how effectively the new religion has implanted itself into the consciousness of the population--i.e., whether the teachings have become ingrained in the minds of the colonized, or are only superficial. Vittorio Lanternari's The Religions of the Oppressed, A Study of Modern Messianic Cults (New York: Alfred A. Knopf, 1963) repeatedly demonstrates the ability of native populations to incorporate Christian ritual and symbolism into native cults. Perhaps more importantly, he shows how tenuous the religious change in native populations is when the missionary forces are abruptly removed from their outpost. As a striking example he uses the missions of certain New Guinea tribes, whose missionaries (German Lutheran) were interned as possible Nazis by the Australians during World War II. "No sooner had this occurred than pagan life sprang into the open, revealing a tremendous vitality clandestinely nurtured for many a long year" (pp. 318-319).

[7]Frank Tannenbaum, Mexico: The Struggle for Peace and Bread quoted in Bertha Blair, Anne O. Lively, and Glen W. Trimble, Spanish-Speaking Americans (New York: National Council of Christ, 1959), pg. 133, in an anthology of books edited by Carlos E. Cortes, et al., Church Views of the Mexican American (New York: Arno Press, 1974).

[8]The legend of the Virgin of Guadalupe has never been officially declared to be an absolute article of faith by the Vatican--as such it does not enjoy the status of "truth" or dogma in the Catholic Church. Catholics are free to believe or not to believe in the story. To argue the validity or non-validity of this or any other "miracle" is unimportant here. What is important for this study was/is the general acceptance of the legend by the native populaion and its consequences for the people involved. Richard M. Dorson has noted, "even if the event is historically false, it is psychologically true." Quoted in James W. Wilkie, Elitelore (Los Angeles: Latin American Center, University of California, 1973), pg. 21n.

[9]Robert Ricard emphasizes in his The Spiritual Conquest of Mexico (Berkeley: University of California Press, 1966), originally published as CONQUETE SPIRITUELLE DU MEXIQUE (University of Paris, 1933, translated by Lesley Byrd Simpson) that

> "a Mexican Church was not founded, and a Creole Church was barely founded. What was founded, before and above all, was a Spanish Church, organized along Spanish lines, governed by Spaniards, in which the native Christians played the minor part of second class Christians."

[10]For accounts of some of these revolts see Ricard, The Spiritual Conquest of Mexico, pp. 264-282; and John Upton Terrell, Pueblos, Gods and Spaniards (New York: Dial Press, 1973), pp. 291-315.

[11]See Raymond K. Dehainaut, Faith and Ideology in Latin American Perspectives, (Cuernavaca, Mexico: CIDOC, 1972), pp. 4/6-4/7. The Church's attempt to keep the liberal ideas of Europe out were less than successful due to smuggling. See Irving A. Leonard, "Visitas and Books," in ed. Frederick B. Pike, The Conflict Between Church and State in Latin America (New York: Alfred A. Knopf, 1964), pp. 65-77.

[12]See Cumberland, Mexico: The Struggle, pg. 60.

[13]Herbert Herring, A History of Latin America, 3rd ed. (New York: Alfred A. Knopf, 1968), pg. 171.

[14]Cumberland, Mexico: The Struggle, pg. 48.

[15]The exact amount of the Church's wealth is, of course, quite different if not impossible to determine. Church finances have been historically a well-kept secret. In addition to the confidentiality of the financial structure, there was also a

great diversity and guarded jealousy among the various religious orders and dioceses. It is quite possible that the Church itself did not have an exact accounting of its resources at a given point in time. However, the estimate of the Church owning half of Mexico by the end of the sixteenth century to at least the War with the United States (1846-1848) is the generally accepted figure by various scholars. See Francois Chevalier, Land and Society in Colonial Mexico, The Great Hacienda (Berkeley: University of California Press, 1963), pg. 234; Herring, A History of Latin America, pg. 331; Dehainaut, Faith and Ideology, pg. 4/59; and Cumberland, Mexico: The Struggle, pg. 177.

[16]Chevalier, Land and Society, pg. 249. Ironically, the slave trade in Spanish America was given a degree of "humanitarian" legitimacy when Father Bartolome de las Cases, who had been given the title of "Protector of the Indians" because of his work on behalf of the native--he urged that Negro slaves be imported to do the back-breading work the Indians were doing. See Herring, History of Latin America, pp. 109, 171-172.

Marvin Harris suggests a more practical reason for the importation of African slaves--i.e., the Indians were poor slaves and tended to die due to raids, disease, and excessive toil. See Marvin Harris, "Race, Culture and Manpower in Peoples and Cultures of Native South America," ed. Daniel R. Gross (Garden City, New York: Doubleday, 1973), pp. 395-408.

[17]Chevalier, Land and Society, pg. 249.

[18]See Herring, History of Latin America, pg. 182.

[19]Henry Bamford Parkes, A History of Mexico, 3rd ed. (Boston: Houghton Mifflin Company, 1969), pg. 111.

[20]See Cumberland, Mexico: The Struggle, pp. 113-123.

[21]See Parkes, History of Mexico, pp. 150-151.

[22]Cumberland, Mexico: The Struggle, pg. 175. While the Church is, of course, hierarchically structured, the Church that was visible and best known to the people was basically their local parish and local priest. Individual Catholic perceptions of the Church would primarily rest on that local priest. However, while the average Catholic knew little of the hierarchy, the overwhelming public opposition of the hierarchy to the War would cause confusion among the population.

[23]Ibid.

[24]For an account of this period, see Ibid., pp. 126-129.

[25]Lloyd Mecham, Church and State in Latin America (Chapel Hill: The University of North Carolina Press, 1934), pg. 64, quoted in Dehainaut, Faith and Ideology, pg. 4/23.

[26]Pike, Conflict Between Church and State, pg. 13.

[27]Transcript of "Mexican......and American" produced by NBC Religious Programs Unit in association with the Office for Film and Broadcasting, U. S. Catholic Conference. Airdate: February 15, 1976., pg. 3.

[28]John Tracy Ellis, American Catholicism, 2nd ed. (Chicago: The University of Chicago Press, 1969), pp. 7-8.

[29]Hubert E. Bolton, "The Mission as a Frontier Institution in the Spanish American Colonies," quoted in Ellis, Ibid., pg. 6. Ellis and Bolton portray the mission as important "civilizing" aspects that benefited not only the Indian but was also useful to the nation state. The benefits to the state were often indirect, which would be natural considering the distance involved from the centers of power. As such, the mission at times suffered from a benign neglect of the state. See John L. Kessell, "Friars versus Bureaucrats: The Missions as a Threatened Institution on the Arizona-Sonora Frontier, 1767-1842," The Western Historical Quarterly 5 (April 1974): 151-162.

[30]Carey McWilliams, Southern California: An Island on the Land (Santa Barbara: Peregrine Smith, Inc., 1973), pg. 29.

[31]Ibid., pg. 34.

[32]"Mexican......and American," pg. 3.

[33]McWilliams, Southern California, pg. 36.

[34]See Matt S. Meier and Feliciano Rivera, The Chicanos, A History of Mexican Americans (New York: Hill and Wang, 1972), pp. 40-41.

[35]See McWilliams, Southern California, pp. 37-41. For a padre's reasons for opposing the abolishment of the missions, see Zephyrin Engelhardt, "The Mission and Missionaries of California," in A Documentary History of the Mexican Americans ed. Wayne Moquin (New York: Praeger Publishers, Inc., 1971), pp. 203-210.

[36]See Clark S. Knowlton, "Patron-Peon Patterns Among the Spanish Americans of New Mexico," Social Forces 41 (October 1962): 12-17. While New Mexico is, of course, today a modern Southwest state, the relative isolation of certain mountain villages is still evident, as demonstrated by one priest who flies to his different congregations. See "'Flying Padre' Comes Out of the Blue, To New Mexico Mountain Parishes," Los Angeles Times, 9 July 1977, pg. 28.

[37]See Carey McWilliams, North from Mexico: The Spanish-Speaking People of the United States (New York: Greenwood Press, 1948, 1968), pp. 63-67.

[38]For several versions of the War see Ramon Eduardo Ruiz, ed., The Mexican War, Was It Manifest Destiny? (New York: Holt, Rinehart and Winston, 1963); for a view of Mexican culpability see Justin H. Smith, The War With Mexico, two volumes, (New York: The MacMillan Co., 1919); for a more recent work demonstrating United States aggression see Glenn W. Price, Orgins of the War with Mexico, The Polk-Stockton Intrigue (Austin: University of Texas Press, 1967).

[39]Cumberland, Mexico: The Struggle, pg. 177, (emphasis added).

[40]Parkes, History of Mexico, pg. 176. Up to this period the only time the Church had partially surrendered its authority over priests who committed civil offenses was during the Revolution between 1810-1820.

[41]Cumberland, Mexico: The Struggle, pp. 173-174.

[42]Ibid., pg. 183.

[43]When the government of Mexico attempted to confiscate five millin pesos from the Church to pay for the War effort, a civil war temporarily erupted. See Ibid., pg. 217.

[44]See McWilliams, North from Mexico, pp. 102-103; and Parkes, History of Mexico, pg. 220. Ellis, American Catholicism, challenges the belief that the American deserters were primarily a Catholic Irish battaion (pg. 262n).

[45]For a copy of the Treaty of Guadalupe see Moquin, Documentary History, pp. 241-249.

[46]See, for example, Rodolfo Acuna, Occupied America: The Chicano's Struggle Toward Liberation (San Francisco: Canfield Press, 1974); Gilberto Lopez y Rivas, The Chicanos (New York:

Month Review, 1973); Sam Kushner, Long Road to Delano (New York: International Publishers, 1975); David F. Gomez, Somos Chicanos, Strangers in Our Own Land (Boston: Beacon Press, 1973); and Moquin, Documentary History.

[47]For a review of the causes and rise of nativism, see Juan Hurtado, An Attitudinal Study of Social Distance Between the Mexican American and the Church (San Antonio, Texas: Mexican American Cultural Center, 1975), pp. 36-42; and Ellis, American Catholicism, pp. 41-83.

[48]That the Mexican was allowed to keep his religious rights (by the government) for benign reasons is possible but highly improbable. The Mexicans were a conquered people of the (new) Southwest United States. When one considers the historical treatment of Native Americans and Mexicans in the area, as well as violations of other civil rights (see sources in footnote no. 46), the benign rationale becomes less likely.

[49]See Acuna, Occupied America, pg. 64.

[50]While the Church in the United States has never held the position of power or leadership that it has held in Mexico, it did reflect and support the American system under which it operated. In no manner could the Church rationally be considered un-American. See for example Hurtado, Attitudinal Study, pp. 43-50; Andrew M. Greeley, The Catholic Experience (Garden City, New York: Doubleday and Company, 1967); and Ellis, American Catholicism.

[51]Juan Romero, Reluctant Dawn, Historia del Padre A.J. Martinez, Cura de Taos (San Antonio, Texas: Mexican American Cultural Center, 1976), pg. 14.

[52]Since there were only ten Spanish priests in the area at the time, Lamy's action effectively decimated the native clergy. The number of priests brought in and loyal to Lamy was indicated in the growth of his diocese from ten to thirty-seven priests. See Acuna, Occupied America, pg. 66.

The feelings between the surviving native clergy and French missionaries was one of mutual distrust.

The effects of Lamy's action are still resented by the native clery in New Mexico. Time has little tempered the anger or the judgment as indicated by these recent statements by some members of the clergy:

" . . . the people he [Lamy] brought here were worse than no priest at all, in some ways. They didn't come to serve the people, they came to dominate."

"Actually, a lot of them [French clergy] were flunkies--rejects who couldn't make it in France so they sent them over here. What was worse was the racism that was practiced. If a young Chicano wanted to become a priest they sent him to the brotherhood where he wound up sweeping floors and serving meals for the French priests."

Phil Tracy, "Padres Organizing for 'Chicano Power,'" National Catholic Reporter 18 (2 April 1971), quoted in Hurtado, Attitudinal Study, pp. 52-53.

[53]See Romero, Reluctant Dawn, pp. 27-33.

[54]Ibid., pg. 21. Martinez was a territorial representative in the pre-war years of 1830, 1831, 1836, 1837, 1845, and 1846.

[55]For example, see Hurtado, Attitudinal Study, pp. 34-40; PADRES newsletter, VII, No. 2, pp. 16-19, and VI, No. 4, pp. 14-15.

[56]"Willing" is used here with some reservation, since much of the immigration from Europe was caused by adverse economic and political conditions in Europe and not an active desire to leave one's homeland. The point being made here, however, is that the European immigrant came to the United States, while for the early Mexican, the United States came to him. For an essay on the "willingness" of the European immigrant, see Oscar Handin, The Uprooted (Boston: Little, Brown, and Company, 1951).

[57]Slavery at the time was not considered immoral according to Catholicism. As Ellis, American Catholicism, explains:

"Official Catholic doctrine held that slavery was not necessarily evil, it taught that slavery, thought of theoretically and apart from specific abuses to human dignity, was not opposed to the divine or natural law" (pg. 89).

This argument, of course, ignores the reality that slavery was and is per se a specific abuse to human dignity. Also, see Greeley, Catholic Experience, pg. 123.

[58]By homogeneity, I do not wish to imply a stereotype of the population. What is meant here is that a population with a continuous historical foundation existed in New Mexico. The population was for the greater part (although there were obvious exceptions, i.e., ricos) poor, Mexican, and at least nominally Catholic. In California, by contrast, the population was to become largely transient and Anglo with various European backgrounds.

[59]Clifton L. Holland, The Religious Dimension in Hispanic Los Angeles, A Protestant Case Study (South Pasadena, California: William Carey Library, 1974), pg. 72.

[60]John Bernard McGloin, S.J., "The California Catholic Church in Transition, 1846-1850," California Historical Quarterly 42 (March 1963), quoted in Leonard Pitt, The Decline of the Californios (Berkeley: University of California Press, 1971), pg. 214.

[61]Pitt, The Decline of the Californios, pg. 216.

[62]Ibid., pg. 222.

[63]See Herring, History of Latin America, pp. 314-315; and Parkes, History of Mexico, pp. 233-235.

[64]Herring, History of Latin America pg. 316.

[65]Cumberland, Mexico: The Struggle, pg. 185.

[66]Quoted in Robert E. Quirk, The Mexican Revolution and the Catholic Church 1910-1929 (Bloomington, Indiana: Indiana University Press, 1973), pg. 11.

[67]Parkes, History of Mexico, pg. 260.

[68]For accounts of the Diaz period and the Church collaboration see Parkes, History of Mexico, pp. 285-295; Herring, History of Latin America, pp. 325-334; and Quirk, Mexican Revolution and the Catholic Church, pp. 12-20, passim.

[69]Frank R. Brandenburg, "Causes of the Revolution," in Revolution in Mexico: Years of Upheaval, 1910-1940 eds. James W. Wilkie and Albert L. Michaels (New York: Alfred A. Knopf, 1969), pg. 19.

[70]See for example, John Womack, Jr., Zapata and the Mexican Revolution (New York: Vintage Books, 1968); John Reed, Insurgent Mexico (New York: Simon and Schuster, 1969); William Weber

Johnson, Heroic Mexico (Garden City, New York: Doubleday and Company, Inc., 1968); James Wilkie and Albert Michaels, Revolution and Mexico; and Stanley R. Ross, ed., Is the Mexican Revolution Dead? (New York: Alfred A. Knopf, 1966).

[71]See Cumberland, Mexico: The Struggle, pg. 240.

[72]Quirk, Mexican Revolution and the Catholic Church, pg. 17. The papal encyclical Rerum Novarum by Leo XIII and later social encyclicals will be examined in greater detail in Chapter IV.

[73]That the intelligentsia had generally abandoned the Church and religion did not necessarily translate into "enlightened" views and the championship of the people's causes. Intellectuals in Mexico, as elsewhere, were/are primarily subject to the economic depedence on others for their livelihood and risk punishment if their views seriously challenge those in positions of power. As Parkes, History of Mexico, noted in prerevolutionary Mexico:

> "The rule of bread or the club enable Diaz to win the support of the intelligentisia . . . the Mexican middle class were only too willing to serve the dictator in return for substantial and regularly paid salaries. (pg. 294)

[74]Quirk, Mexican Revolution and the Catholic Church, pg. 38.

[75]For events surrounding the writing and reaction to the Constitution of 1917, see Quirk, Mexican Revolution and the Catholic Church, pp. 79-112. Also see Robert E. Quigley, American Catholic Opinions of Mexican Anticlericalism 1910-1936 (Cuernavaca, Mexico: CIDOC Sondeos No. 27, 1969), pg. 39.

By August of 1914 the following members of the Mexican hierarchy resided in San Antonio: the Archbishops of Mexico, Michoacan, Oaxaca, Durango, and Linares, and the Bishops of Sinaloa, Saltillo, Aguascalientes, Zacatecas, Guadalupe, Tulacingo, Chiapas, and Campeche.

[76]Parkes, History of Mexico, pg. 384.

[77]Ernest Gruening, Mexico and Its Heritage (New York: The Century Co., 1928), cited in Blair, Spanish-Speaking Americans, quoted in Cortes, Church Views, pg. 133.

Parkes, History of Mexico, attributed the ability of the masses to operate religiously without the Catholic priest a function of the Mexican religion being "after four hundred years --more pagan than Christian" (pg. 384). Much, if not most, of the literature concerning the Mexican and the Church eventually makes the same point of the mixed religious "pagan-Christianity of the Mexican." The usual explanation is that the remnants of Indian beliefs are permeated throughout the Mexican Church. While there is a certain degree of validity to these assertions, this may not be sufficient to explain the seeming lack of "pure" Catholicism among the Mexican community. Ricard, The Spiritual Conquest of Mexico, is persuaded that much of the "paganism" that was to be found in the Mexican Church was the direct result of importation from Europe. He argues that the "mixed religion" argument is overemphsized since examples of such religious practices could also be found in European religious life. See pp. 278-279.

In a more recent study, Pedro Carrasco argues that the religious practices of the Tatascan Indians of Mexico compare favorably with the "folk religion" practiced by southern Europeans. As Carrasco notes:

". . . We must realize that within Roman Catholicism there are differences of belief and practices between Church hierarchy and the lay folk communities. It would be absurd to ignore this distinction and to compare the folk beliefs of the modern Tarascans only with the tenets of the faith as understood by Church theologians . . . . Tarascans will pass their Christianity test with honors if we compare their religion with the folk religion of Catholic Southern Europe." ("Tarascan Folk Religion, Christian or Pagan?" in Walter Goldschmidt and Harry Hoijer, eds., The Social Anthropology of Latin America [Los Angeles: Latin American Center, University of California, 1970], pg. 6.)

[78]For accounts of the Cristero uprising see Quirk, Mexican Revolution and the Catholic Church, pp. 188-214. Special attention should be drawn to Pope Pius XI's encyclical, Iniquis Afflictisque (1926) which decried the religious situation in Mexico. The Pope condemned the government and stated that Mexico was under the influence of "barbarism." The Mexican bishops used the Pope's encyclical as a defense of Catholicism in Mexico. Quirk quotes the bishops as saying:

"The defense of Christian civilization is based upon religion, the sanctity of matrimony, private property, and sane liberty, as against the

communistic utopians of socialism, free love,
and the subjection of religion to the state"
(pg. 195).

[79]For further details see Cumberland, Mexico: The Struggle,
pp. 281-282.

Morrow, not incidentally, also mediated in other aspects of
the revolution, including the all important issue of land reform.
He gave Calles a capitalist rationale for abrogating land distribution, effectively negating the primary reason for the revolution. See Parkes, A History of Mexico, pg. 391.

[80]The reaction of militant Catholics to the accord was
anticipated by the Pope. His representative in Mexico, Bishop
Ruiz y Flores of Michoacan issued a strong statement warning
Catholics not to criticize the agreement.

> "Once the pope has sanctioned the terms of re-
> conciliation, within the limits of the Catholic
> conscience, it is not right for any Catholic to
> rebel and constitute himself a judge of the
> supreme authority of his Church, for obedience
> to the Church is not limited to dogma, but
> reaches   to the fullest extent to administra-
> tive discipline. . . . Now is not the time to
> discuss, but to obey . . . ." Quoted in Quirk,
> Mexican Revolution and the Catholic Church, pp.
> 245-246 (emphasis added).

[81]Ellwyn R. Stoddard, Mexican Americans (New York: Random
House, 1973), pg. 88.

[82]An instance of petty harassment was the prohibition of the
Church in 1935 from using the mails for any materials of a religious nature. See Cumberland, Mexico: The Struggle, pg. 283.
For an example of the overzealous dogmatic anti-Catholicism that
existed among some state politicians, see Arnulfo Perez H.'s
(self-styled "Personal Enemy of God") article, "God Does Not
Exist," in Wilkie and Michaels, Revolution in Mexico, pp. 195-
198.

For the official Church reaction to the immediate post-
revolutionary period in Mexico see Pius XI encyclical, Firmissi-
man constantiana (On the Religious Situation in Mexico, 1937).
The encyclical, as with other papal proclamations conerning Mexico, is an appeal for order, obedience (to the Church), justice
based on Catholic Action, and the primacy of eternal salvation
over economic and social reform. See Terence P. McLaughlin,

C.S.B, The Church and the Reconstruction of the Modern World: The Social Encyclicals of Pope Pius XI (Garden City, New York: Image Books, 1957), pp. 403-421.

[83]Despite the claims of "socialism" by the eventual victors of the revolutionary struggle and/or the charges of "bolshevism" by the Church and other enemies of the revolution, the government of Mexico was never operated under Marxist principles. As Parkes, History of Mexico, notes, in 1934

" . . . an amendment to the constitution declared that the official viewpoint in all Mexican schools was to be that of socialism. Socialist education did not, in practice, have much connection with socialism. The word 'socialist' had in Mexico become almost meaningless: Calles still called himself a socialist-- nor did more than a small minority of the schoolteachers have the slightest knowledge of Marxist doctrine. What socialist education was generally understood to mean was education which combated clericalism by inculcating a scientific view of life" (pg. 398).

[84]See Quirk, The Mexican Revolution and the Catholic Church, pp. 215-247. Also see Robert E. Quirk, "Religion and the Mexican Social Revolution," in Religion, Revolution and Reform ed. William V. D'Antonio and Frederick B. Pike (New York: Praeger Publishers, 1964), pp. 59-71.

[85]See Patrick Hayes McNamara, "Bishops, Priests, and Prophecy: A Study in the Sociology of Religious Protest" (Ph.D. dissertation, University of California, Los Angeles, 1968), pp. 66-79.

[86]Joan Moore, Mexican Americans (Englewood Cliffs, New Jersey: Prentice-Hall, 1970), pg. 86. Also see Manuel Gamio, The Life Story of the Mexican Immigrant (New York: Dover Publications, 1971) for numerous examples of the immigrants' attachment to the symbols of Catholicism, while having a lack of commitment to the canons of Catholicism, passim.

[87]McNamara, "Bishops, Priests, and Prophecy," pg. 79.

[88]See Joseph H. Fichter, S.J., "The Americanization of Catholicism," in Anatomies of America: Sociological Perspectives, ed. Philip Ehrensaft and Amitai Etzioni (Toronto: Collier-Macmillan, 1969), pg. 124.

[89]McWilliams, North from Mexico, pg. 124, notes that there was an ethnic cleavage within the Church in New Mexico especially in the large community, where there were usually two churches-- one for Anglos and another for Mexicans.

While McWilliams' observation could be attributed to a failure by the Church to deal adequately with de facto secular segregation, a Church sponsored study of the Southwest in the 1920's indicates that segregation was often deliberate:

> "A young Spanish-American girl of good education told me [author of the article] that she and a number of her friends had organized a branch of a large Catholic fraternal organization in her community. She said, 'If the Americans had organized first we would not have been received.' There are even many Catholic Churches in which a Mexican cannot feel that he has a right to worship. In one Church attended by the English speaking people were two signs bearing the words, 'Mexicans Prohibited.' In another Church a sign hung on the very last pew in the Church reads 'Mexicano' interpreted by them to mean 'Mexicans, sit here.' This pew could accommodate at the most six persons." Linne E. Bresette, Mexicans in the United States (Washington, D.C.: National Catholic Welfare Conference, 1929), pg. 42, in Cortes, Church Views.

[90]For an example of how the local Church functioned as an integral part of the life of one New Mexican village, see "El Cerrito People, Land, and Culture," Journal of American Folklore 48 (April 1935): 1-72, passim.

For a brief and somewhat sketchy description of Mexican religious practices in the pre- and post- revolutionary period in Los Angeles, see Samuel M. Ortegon, "Mexican Religious Population of Los Angeles" (M. A. Thesis, University of Southern California, 1932, reprinted by R and E Research Associates, San Francisco, 1972).

[91]See Clifton L. Holland, The Religious Dimension, pp. 179-208; and McNamara, "Bishops, Priests, and Prophecy," pp. 74-76.

[92]See G. Bromley Oxnam, S.T.D., "The Mexican in Los Angeles from the Standpoint of the Religious Forces of the City," The Annals of the American Academy 93 (January 1921): 130-133. Also see Holland, The Religious Dimension, pg. 200.

[93]Grebler, Mexican-American People, pg. 487.

[94]Blair, Spanish-Speaking Americans, pg. 135 in Cortes, Church Views.

[95]For a narrative on family reactions to Protestant conversion see Beatrice Griffith, American Me (Boston: Houghton Mifflin Company, 1948), pp. 170-194, passim.

[96]The differences between Protestant denominations has been abundantly documented. For general reference, I refer the reader to two of the classic works on American religion: See Gerhard Lenski, The Religious Factor: A Sociologist's Inquiry (Garden City, New York: Doubleday Anchor Book, 1963), pp. 35-211; and Will Herbert, Protestant, Catholic, Jew (Garden City, New York: Doubleday Anchor Book, 1955, 1960), pp. 99-135.

Also see N.J. Demerath III, Social Class in American Protestantism (Chicago: Rand McNally and Company, 1965); and Dehainaut, Faith and Ideology, pp. 2/1-2/45. For a specific work concerning Mexicans in the United States, see Walter R. Goldschmidt, "Class Denominationalism in Rural California Churches," American Journal of Sociology 49 (January 1944): 348-355.

[97]See for example Griffith, American Me, pp. 181-195; and Robert C. Jones and Louis R. Wilson, The Mexican in Chicago (Chicago: Chicago Church Federation, 1931), pg. 23 in Cortes, Church Views.

[98]Blair, Spanish Speaking Americans, pg. 135.

[99]However, for further information on Mexican Protestants see in addition to the previously mentioned works of Cortes, Ortegon, Holland, Oxnam, Griffith, also Kyle Haseldon, Death of a Myth (New York: Friendship Press, 1964); Fernando Penalso, "Class Consciousness and Social Mobility in a Mexican-American Community" (Ph.D. dissertation, University of Southern California, 1963); R. Douglas Brackenridge and Francisco O. Garcia-Treto, Iglesia Presbiteriana: A History of Presbyterians and Mexican Americans in the Southwest (San Antonio: Trinity University Press, 1974); and Grebler, Mexican American People, pp. 486-512.

[100]McNamara, "Bishops, Priests and Prophecy," pg. 76.

[101]"The Business of the Church," The Tidings, 22 October 1937, pg. 8, cited in Grebler, Mexican American People, pg. 458.

[102]See Harold A. Shapiro, "The Pecan Shellers of San Antonio, Texas," in Chicano: The Evolution of a People, ed. Renato Rosaldo, Robert A. Calvert and Gustav L. Seligmann (Minneapolis, Minnesota: Winston Press, 1973), pp. 193-202.

[103]See Rev. William B. Killian, et al., eds., "Triple Jubilee of Archbishop Robert Emmet Lucey, S.T.D.," The Alamo Messenger Press (San Antonio), 1966, cited in McNamara, "Bishops, Priests, and Prophecy," pg. 73.

[104]In an article where the primary concern is Protestant proselytizing among Mexicans, Lucey is concerned that the Mexicans might be easily fooled:

> "Protestant preachers play on the poverty and ignorance of these (poor) Latin Americans. They exchange social services for religious faith.
>
> One might reasonably wonder how the preacher can hope successfully to impart to such people the intangible vagaries of Protestant unbelief. He can't; but he can appeal to their poverty and their emotions. The gentile Mexican is easily taken in." Robert E. Lucey, "'Christianizing' Mexican Catholics," America, 16 August 1947, pg. 542.

[105]In an article on farm workers, Lucey finds it "strange" the they are not included in labor laws:

> "The Congress of the United States, aided and abetted by certain powerful growers' associations, has seen to it that native-born American citizens in the migratory labor force have not even a minimum of protection by social legislation. It is passing strange that a little group of willful men can so sway the Congress of the United States."

In the same article Lucey advised one of his pastors to ask the mayor for his help in removing "illegal workers" who are supposedly taking jobs away from his parishioners. The pastor informed the archbishop that the mayor had fifty "wetbacks" of his own on his ranch. See Robert E. Lucey, "Migratory Workers," The Commonwheel, 15 January 1954, pp. 370-373.

[106]The bracero program provided for the importation of temporary workers from Mexico. The program started in 1942 and lasted until 1964. The workers often had poor working conditions and were sometimes used as strikebreakers.

[107]See Grebler, Mexican American People, pp. 462 and 482-483.

[108]Aaron I. Abell, American Catholicism and Social Action: A Search for Social Justice, 1865-1950 (Garden City: Hanover House, 1960), pg. 258; and Robert D. Cross, The Emergence of Liberal Catholicism in America (Cambridge: Harvard University Press, 1958), pg. 218; both cited in McNamara, "Bishops, Priests, and Prophecy," pg. 93.

[109]For an account of the development of Fathers McCullough and McDonnell's unionizing efforts, see Joan London and Henry Anderson, So Shall Ye Reap (New York: Thomas Y. Crowell Company, 1970), pp. 79-98.

[110]Reply of Auxiliary Bishop Donohoe of San Francisco to Fr. McDonnell's request to be a consultant to farm worker groups, quoted in McNamara, "Bishops, Priests, and Prophecy," pg. 116.

[111]Excerpts of these letters are in Ibid., pp. 120-121.

[112]London and Anderson, So Shall Ye Reap, pg. 97.

[113]Bishop Hugh A. Donohoe in an interview with McNamara, February 1967, "Bishops, Priests, and Prophecy," pg. 123. At the time of the interview Donohoe was ordinary of the diocese of Stockton, California.

[114]See Jacques E. Levy, Cesar Chavez: Autobiography of La Causa (New York: W.W. Norton and Company, 1975), pp. 89-91.

[115]See Eugene Nelson, Huelga (Delano, California: Farm Workers Press, 1966), pg. 49.

[116]The relationship between the Church and the United Farm Workers will be explored in greater detail in Chapters III and IV.

[117]See London and Anderson, So Shall Ye Reap, pp. 91-93.

[118]Norman D. Humphrey, "The Changing Structure of the Detroit Mexican Family: An Index of Acculturation," American Sociological Review (December 1944), pp. 622-626; Richard G. Thurston, "Urbanization and Sociocultural Change in a Mexican American Enclave" (Ph.D. dissertation, University of California,

Los Angeles, 1957); Sister M.J. Murray, A Socio-Cultural Study of 118 Mexican Families Living in a Low Rent Housing Project in San Antonio, Texas (Washtington, D.C.: Catholic University of America, 1954), pg. 64; and Most Rev. Jose I. Candeleria in an address to a National Council of Churches meeting on Spanish work (c. 1955)--all cited in Blair, Spanish-Speaking Americans, pg. 138, in Cortes, Church Views.

[119]Margaret Clark, Health in the Mexican-American Culture: A Community Study (Berkeley: University of California Press, 1959, 1970), pg. 110.

[120]Grebler, Mexican American People, pg. 459.

[121]See the Speech given in the 1950's by Monsignor Thomas J. O'Dwyer (exact date uncertain), "Catholic Charities and Mexican Welfare," cited in Ibid.

[122]Patrick H. McNamara, "Catholicism, Assimilation, and the Chicano Movement: Los Angeles as a Case Study," in Chicanos and Native Americans: The Territorial Minorities eds. Rudolph O. de la Garza, Z. Anthony Kruszewski, and Tomas A. Arciniega (Englewood Cliffs, New Jersey: Prentice-Hall, 1973), pg. 127.

[123]See Grebler, Mexican American People, pg. 475.

[124]See Ibid., pp. 460-461; 482n.

CHAPTER III

THE CONTEMPORARY CHICANO AND THE CHURCH

Choosing a starting date to examine the contemporary Chicano is somewhat arbitrary. One could choose several time periods - the sixty-year span since the beginning of the great migration from Mexico, the Second World War from which many Chicanos returned to become more vocal in asserting their rights as citizens, or the Chicano movimiento period of the 1960's and 70's. I have chosen this last period since it provides an appropriate political time frame for attempting to assess the current relationship of the Chicano and the Church, and the prospects for the future. The historical foundation for the present relationship is, of course, extremely important as evidenced by Chapter II. History has demonstrated that the Chicano-Church linkages have been formed both by the external factors (outside the Church and the Mexican/Chicano people) and the internal factors that are particular to the institution and the population under study.

In choosing the "movement" period of the 1960's and 1970's as a focal point, care should be exercised not to give the popular misconception that it exemplifies that Chicanos were finally awakening and/or merely engaging in individual activities to (as is often heard) "better themselves." As was demonstrated in Chapter II and has been documented more fully by others, there has virtually always been some "movement", or more precisely struggle, not merely to better oneself, but also to identify and resist sources of oppression. The focus on the the contemporary period should be viewed as the latest segment of continuous struggle and development, and not as the reawakening of a people.

We saw in the previous chapter that Catholicism's hold over the Mexican/Chicano has been a virtual ecclesiastical monopoly while often failing to elicit a strong commitment. How does this compare to the results of my interviews (described in Chapter I) with various members of the Chicano community? How are the historical relationships that have evolved being changed, especially by the organizations that have developed as a result of the political activities of the past two decades?

An examination of the information that I have gathered points to a variety of possible directions, and not to a homogeneous view of the Chicano. Of the thirteen people in the general population who were interviewed, nine identified themselves as Catholic, however, all of those who said they were not a member of any church identified the Catholic Church as the Church in which they formerly belonged. Of the thirteen only six stated that they attended mass on a regular basis, although not

necessarily weekly. Their commitment to the obligation of weekly
mass attendance and regular sacraments was rarely a dominating
facet of their lives. While the number of persons interviewed is
obviously too small for a quantitative analysis (and no such
claim is made), the proportion of religious practitioners vis-a-
vis non-practioners is very close to the historical studies cited
in Chapter Two,[1] and with the more contemporary works of Grebler,
et al. and Carrillo.[2] As shown in Tables 1 and 2, the percentages of Chicano Catholics who attend mass--an important obligation in the Catholic religion--is significantly lower than that
of the general United States Catholic population.

TABLE 1
FREQUENCY OF SUNDAY MASS ATTENDANCE,
MEXICAN-AMERICAN AND NATIONAL SAMPLE SURVEYS

	Percent Attending Once a Week or More	Percent Attending Less than Once a Week	Percent Never Attending	Total Number (=100%)
Los Angeles Mexican-American survey respondents 1965-1966	47	47	6	852
San Antonio Mexican-American survey Respondents 1965-1966	58	41	1	569 a
U.S. Catholics 1966 b	67	20	13	n.a.

a. Weighting procedures were used in the San Antonio sample. This means that total numbers cannot be used as a
direct indicator of error.

b. Gallup Survey, reported in the Catholic Digest, July,
1966, pg. 27.

Source: Adapted from Leo Grebler, Joan W. Moore, Ralph C.
Guzman, The Mexican American People (New York: The
Free Press, 1970), pg. 472.

TABLE 2

FREQUENCY OF MASS ATTENDANCE, BY SEX
MEXICAN-AMERICAN SURVEY, NATIONAL SURVEY, AND
SCHUYLER STUDY

	Percent Attending Once a Week or More		Percent Attending Less than Once a Week		Total Number (= 100%)	
	Men	Women	Men	Women	Men	Women
Los Angeles Mexican-American survey respondents 1965-1966	39	52	61	48	365	488
San Antonio Mexican-American Survey respondents 1965-1966	56	60	44	40	230a	339a
Schuyler Study 1960 b	73	82	27	18	7,354	

a. See note a in preceding Table.

b. Joseph B. Schuyler, S.J., Northern Parish: A Sociological and Pastoral Study (Chicago, 1960), pg. 2020.

Source: Adapted from Leo Grebler, Joan W. Moore, Ralph C.
Guzman, The Mexican-American People (New York: The
Free Press, 1970), pg. 473.

With the exception of one small category (College-educated Chicanas of San Antonio, Texas) Chicanos go to Church less than the United States Catholic and the non-Catholic population. This would indicate that the notion of Chicanos as highly religious people should be subject to considerable revision.

Of the leaders who were interviewed in my survey, the lack of religious practice was more pronounced and also more deliberate. Of the twelve leaders interviewed only three considered themselves practicing Catholics and one of those only attended services "about once a month." Of the remaining nine, only one could be classified as what is popularly known as a "fallen-away" Catholic, i.e., those who merely stop attending services, due to indifference, inactivity, etc. Eight of the non-attending leaders had made a conscious decision to quit or renounce the Church.

Later in this Chapter, I will elaborate upon the various levels of church participation mentioned above. For the sake of clarification, however, it is useful to delineate here and label these levels of Church participation:

Group A - Practicing Catholics. This group includes those members who label themselves as practicing Catholics and make reasonable attempts to conform to Church requirements. A few in this category could objectively be classified as Nominal Catholics[3] (i.e., attendance at services only monthly or less often), but who, in their opinion, make a good faith effort to meet Church obligations.

Group B - Those who Quit, Renounced, or otherwise made a conscious decision to leave the Church. This may have been for a political, intellectual or personal reason.

Group C - Fallen-Away Catholics. This group does not participate in the Catholic community but does not do so for any specific reason; i.e., they are similar to group B in that they do not participate in Catholic religious services but unlike Group B, they usually do not have a conscious reason for ignoring their former faith. Fallen-away Catholics usually recognize themselves as such although they still may consider themselves Catholic for identification purposes. Some still have a tenuous relationship to the Church and appear to fit, in a limited manner, Spitzer's model of a cultural Catholic; i.e., they attend baptisms, weddings, etc., but the Church and its formal teachings do not enter into their daily (and rarely yearly) existence.

Spitzer's definition of a cultural Catholic is important to this study since an analysis of cultural Catholicism in conjunction with the information presented elsewhere in this study, will illuminate reasons for the often mistaken impression that Chicanos/Mexicans are a highly religious, Catholic population. Cultural Catholicism is defined as follows:

> (1) The Church regarded as an adjunct of the total social organism and subordinate to it. (2) Identification with Catholicism, but the Church treated on a natural par with any other compartment of daily life. (3) The presence of the Church in society regarded as an expression of the cultural organization of the environment rather than as a path to spirituality.[4]

While we shall return to the concept of cultural Catholicism shortly, it is necessary to first identify the last group that emerged from the study.

Group D   Based on Spitzer's definition of Formal Catholicism,[5] this group is largely clerics (who will be explored in greater detail in the following Chapter), but not necessarily limited to the clergy. However, among those interviewed, only two persons who were not members of the clergy could possibly be classified as members of Group D. Criteria here included a close identification with the Church, a through knowledge of Church dogma and teachings (even above that of the standard practicing Catholic), and, in general, a life that is centered around the Church in more than a perfunctory manner, i.e,. one that demands an intellectual commitment.

The standard impression, both academic and popular, of the Chicano population is that they are devout Catholics and therefore, conservative, and the more Catholic (in practice), the more conservative. What was observed was that there is no one Chicano Catholic practice, nor is there one Chicano political ideology; even two categories are insufficient. Like the rest of society, Chicanos encompass the entire political spectrum from right to left. To find the impact of religion on the political beliefs is not purely a question of finding the portion of the political spectrum occupied by those with a Catholic background, since there are different degrees of Catholic awareness, upbringing, devoutness, and consciousness.

It appears too sweeping a generalization to assert that Catholicism is the main conservatizing factor among Chicanos. In that statement are many implications that may or may not be true, but that should not be asserted without collaborating evidence. The implications of such a statement are:

1) Chicanos can be thought of as a unified body.
2) Chicanos as a group are conservative.
3) The Church is a conservative factor.
4) The Church is the main conservative factor.

In reality Chicanos constitute an extremely heterogeneous group of nearly ten million persons. The input into their lives, ideology, and consciousness comes from a variety of sources other than the Church, such as social class, economic class, and the competing cultural influences of United States' society and Mexican society.

Compadrazgo

The cultural Catholicism of the Chicano population is one reason for the impression that Chicanos are a devout Catholic group. Cultural Catholicism in various levels of intensity cuts across the different groups. Events and activities that appear to have religious orientation often elicit little or no religious commitment. An illustration of this is to be found in the very estimates that over 90% of the Chicano population are Catholic. Basically, this means that virtually all are baptized as Catholics, a ceremony that is the foundation for compadrazgo, or being a Godparent/co-parent of a child. To become a compadre imposes religious and social obligations on the accepting party. While nearly all of the respondents stated that they were or would be a compadre, they did not necessarily consider the concomitant religious obligations to be of paramount importance. To those who felt an obligation in conjunction with the relationship, the obligation entailed a social focus--primarily between the adults involved, the natural parents and the Godparents--any only secondarily a religious bond between the adult Godparent and the child. During the research, I had the occasion to interview two persons (one formally and one informally) who had very recently become compadres. Neither of these individuals believed in God and both considered themselves to be politically radical. When I asked why they would go through a religious ceremony in which they basically did not believe, the answers were similar. They had an obligation to the parents and felt honored to be chosen by the parents as theoretically co-responsible for the child. In one case it was for a brother's child, and in another for a friend's. The formal religious aspect was unimportant--although they felt a moral responsibility to the child. What was important was the bond between the parents and the Godparents--a bond based on trust, respect and mutual dependency between the adults.

94

The emphasis that individuals put on the religious relationship vis-a-vis the social bond varied. However, very few people
whom I interviewed felt that the religious obligations were of
paramount importance. Some comments from the interviews would be
illustrative:

> Yes, (I'm a comadre) . . . it's more religious
> than anything else. I've never seen it happen
> but that's the way it's supposed to be.[6]

> Yes, soy madrina, it's a social responsibility,
> a poor people's responsibility. The Catholic
> Church started it. The Padrino and Madrina are
> responsible for raising the child as a Catholic
> . . . . and so they could help with finances and
> emotionally. The relationship is very strong .
> . . one of help.[7]

> Yes, it's a very moral relationship, not only
> religiously but financially and morally.[8]

> A religious responsibility to follow scriptures
> . . . . The compadre has an obligation of a
> parent but not anymore--everything has changed.[9]

> It's complicated. I'm a Godfather, but I feel
> ignored--have not developed the relationship
> even though we are neighbors . . . . As for
> taking care of the child, I think people would
> do that anyway even if the relationship didn't
> exist. I think that people that come to this
> relationship were good friends already. People
> are close but not because of religion . . . .[10]

> I think it's important, it's a way of bringing
> people together, it brings people into the
> family.[11]

> In my family, it has become essentially a rit-
> ual--a rite, . . it doesn't have religious
> importance.[12]

> I view it as both a social and religious rela-
> tionship . . . it places responsibility . . .
> the child needs religious guidance.[13]

> I am a compadre, to my brother and friends.
> Vestige of culture of Chicanos, Italians too and
> some Anglo Americans. It's not really religious

. . . . People are starting to see the contradictions.[14]

Well, I'm not a Godparent, but to me it's one of
the formalities of religion that is now imbued
within the culture of what is essentially the
Mestizo people, the Indian people that we are,
that the Chicano people are. It has taken on a
cultural meaning and significance. I don't know
one Godparent, my own included, who really has
any semblance of knowledge or understanding of
religion really . . . . It's internal family
politics. That's what it adds up to . . . . The
Godfather and Godmother themselves are about as
areligious as anybody who walks.[15]

It is social and has a religious aspect but
parents live longer--it's not primarily religious. (Chicanos) make it a point to ask
someone who is not a blood relative.[16]

The Godparent role is more important to parents
than to the children. Non-blood relations are
brought in. Most Godparents only play a social
role--an alliance in case the parents can't
afford to support children. It's more important
to the parents.[18]

Yes, I'm a Godparent, but not a good one, but
it's a socially demanding position. In Mexican
tradition it should be strong, but my job is
demanding and I don't have the time.[19]

Yes, it's a social and moral responsibility not
a religious one.[19]

While these answers vary in complexity and perspective,
there are some consistent themes. The religious role is becoming
less and less important--even to those who may lament its demise.
At the same time, it is a relationship that virtually all will
enter if asked--regardless of political or religious orientation.
It is, in fact, an important secular aspect of Chicano culture
rather than serving as only a religious one. It is an aspect of
Chicano culture that seems to be becoming more culturally symbolic than culturally utilizable. As indicated above in several
of the statements, along with the decline of the religious com-
ponent, there are also implications that the secular role of
mutual support based on compadrazgo as a formal bond and obligation, while still functional, it also decreasing in importance.

For example, the comments that the relationship has become "essentially a ritual" and that it incorporates non-blood relatives who in all probability would help anyway, indicate that the mutual commitment to each other is now based fundamentally on friendship rather than religious belief or material necessity and could become less intensive. This is especially true of those whom I interviewed who could be classified as middle class by occupation and self-description.

To understand why, we should look at the probable reasons that compadrazgo evolved into an important de facto secular bond for groups such as the Mexican/Chicano. Clark notes in her study of Chicanos in San Jose that compadrazgo is a significant social institution not only among the Chicanos but also in southern Europe and Latin America.[20] A probable reason that compadrazgo became important among the Mexicano/Chicanos is that they were/are fundamentally a poor people. Compadrazgo can be seen as more than just a method of bringing persons into the family for altruistic or religious reasons. For the poor--whether they be Mexican, Chicano, southern European or Latin-American--it can be viewed as another method of survival. When one enlarges the family and the resultant family obligations, risks of poverty are spread beyond the immediate and extended family--it is now extended to the "family" that had no blood ties. In time of need, compadres can be called upon and can be expected to help. This spreading of responsibility becomes, in effect, a form of insurance against the conditions of poverty Mexicanos/Chicanos have been forced to endure.[21]

As more Chicanos become acculturated into life in the United States (either as strongly culturally oriented Chicanos or Anglo-cized Chicanos, or variations in between), the rationale for a strong compadrazgo relationship diminishes. For the growing Chicano urban working class (the vast majority of Chicanos), the ruling ideas of society (individualism, etc.) also become anti-thetical to the rationale for a strong compadrazgo. The competing cultural influence of American society does not, of course, stop the relationship, but it does weaken it in comparison with the Mexican national population. I would suggest, based on the information presented but subject to further research, that as more generations evolve in the Chicano community in the United States the relationship based on Mexican national culture will become weaker.

Some may argue that reasons for this decline of a cultural element (i.e., a decline of strong compadrazgo) is based on a decision by some Chicanos to acculturate and assimilate and that a conscious attempt should be made to retain the old culture. While the intent of maintaining cultural integrity may well be noble, this view may be too subjective in that it ignores the material reality--the context--in which cultural features evolve. The transmutation of compadrazgo is not only because of United States cultural influences but also because the objective reality of urban Chicanos is different from that of a rural peasant. To lament the "loss of culture" or to try to transplant a culture in a different time and space is to duplicate in reverse the errors that the original missionaries made in attempting to transform the consciousness of the natives without changing their objective reality.[22] Here, cultural nationalists, for example, may be attempting to retain the consciousness of a people while their objective reality has been changed. Cultural integrity involves more than the protection of the old culture from the onslaught of a different culture (in this case United States culture superseding Mexican culture), but establishing the control of the culture in the population itself, while recognizing that changes will occur within a dynamic population. To deny that change will occur is to have a romantic idealized conception of culture and ultimately may lead to reaction.[23]

Chicano Diversity and Unity

Thus far, we have examined two major activities that give contradictory evidence regarding the religious practices of the Chicano--weekly church attendance and compadrazgo. Sunday mass is a serious obligation in the Catholic religion, yet Chicanos appear equally divided in their commitment to meet that obligation (and if this is used as one criterion for devoutness, Chicanos can be judged less devout than the general American population, especially other Catholics).[24] Compadrazgo, however, is a unifying force (albeit possibly diminishing) that would superfically indicate that Chicanos wish to fulfill their religious obligations (Baptism). A closer examination, however, indicates that the almost universal acceptance of compadrazgo is not based on religious fervor, but on establishing social networks.

What other evidence is there of Chicano diversity and/or apparent unity? What are some of the other religious practices that would give us clues of religion's potential impact on political ideology? How are the four groups I have defined (Groups A, B, C, D) established and what impact does their degree of religious commitment have on their members' political ideology?

The first group [(Group A (i.e., Practicing-Nominal)] that emerged from the interviews partially supported the dominant literature, but only to a limited extent. Some who can be described as practicing Catholics and those who are nominal

Catholics as defined by Spitzer appear to fall into the political range of conservative to moderately liberal, i.e., in the main-stream of dominant American ideology.

I use the term "mainstream" here as do Dolbeare and Dolbeare in their work, American Ideologies.[25] They delineate the various ideologies that compete for followers, including capitalist, liberal and conservative beliefs which constitute the mainstream --beliefs that raise no fundamental challenge to the functioning, characteristics, principles, and practices of the American pol-itical system.

The image of the American political process is that of pluralism. For Chicanos in Group A the view of the political system is not that it requires a complete change or restructuring but rather that Chicanos as a group need to become "part of the system" or "need to learn how to play the game." While virtually all expressed, in varying degrees, concern about the problems of Chicanos, their proposed solutions were well within the accept-able margins of the American political process. This group's criticism of American society was not systemic because their vision for improvement could not include a totally different society. The world-view (a beginning aspect of ideology as defined in Chapter One) of this group (A) was such that the problems of the society were elaborated upon as "defects" that could either be changed through laws (if they saw defects as primarily legal) or through countervailing forces against the Anglo (who some stated as being the fundamental problem). In other words, the primary method for political efficacy was the advent of Chicano interest group politics as it takes advantage of the pluralistic society. The political goals and values for this group coincided with the acceptable goals and values of the larger society.

In conducting the interviews, factors looked for were the degree of religious commitment judged by self-identification, knowledge of religious teachings and personalities, educational choices (parochial vs. public schools), level of Church partici-pation through mass and the sacraments, membership in religious organization, Church loyalty in secular matters--e.g., following Church attempts to influence public policy options.

Group A evolved as the dominant group among the general population (eight of thirteen). However, only one leader of twelve fit into this group. This group has the greatest degree of diversity internally of the four delineated. The reason for this is that I classified here, all who make what they consider to be a good faith effort to practice their religion. Thus the group includes those who practice weekly to those who are more lax in meeting their obligations, but who attempt to practice their faith.

The Reverend Albert Carrillo notes that Mexican-Americans who are lax in their religious duties often consider themselves still to be Church members and thus the fact that they have not been to Church in some time does not necessarily indicate that they are (in their opinion) outside of the Church.[26] Carrillo notes that the hierarchy of the American Catholic Church is primarily Germanic-Irish and thus has a different tradition of religious practices than the Mexican. (A more in-depth examination of the hierarchy and other clergy will be found in Chapter Four.) Carrillo states that the Germanic-Irish tradition is that of law-and-order while for the Mexican "religious expression is based on cultural expression."[27] The law and order that Carrillo refers to is not that of criminal justice but Church teachings. Thus a "good" Catholic in the Mexican tradition need not coincide with a "good" Catholic in the Germanic-Irish tradition. Unless a Chicano feels that he is outside of the Church, either due to inactivity (Group C to be discussed below) or feels that he deliberately no longer wants to be part of the Church (Group B to be discussed below), he should be considered a practicing to nominal Catholic.

The information presented thus far in this Chapter and Chapter Two tends to indicate that the formal bonds that tie the Mexicano/Chicano to the Catholic Church are not strong, and that these bonds may be weakening with the continual urbanization of Chicanos--and (as we shall see) the political awareness generated by the activities of the past two decades. While it may be possible to conclude that the trend is toward more secular activity, history cautions one to note that formal Catholicism was never an overwhelming facet of Mexican or Chicano life. Any apparent decline in Church participation must be viewed longitudinally. The last few years have seen a resurgence of religious activity among the American population in general, and this may or may not be reflected in the Chicano population in the future. Predictions based on transitory changes in active membership and participation may not reflect the evolution of Church-Chicano relationships.

Likewise, information obtained from the individuals regarding their political and religious views should not be used in a snapshot time-capsule manner. A person's framework for political ideology is formed over the life-time of the individual and the same is true, perhaps even more so, for their religious ideology. Therefore, I was most concerned with the process of development and change, both religiously and politically, and attempted to

have the interview reflect that historical development. Many of
the questions were open-ended for the purpose of trying to
evaluate that development. Also several of the questions, were
attempts to evoke directly the connection between religious and
political development, and to observe causality whenever
possible. At the end of the interview, I directly asked the
subject to personally analyze the primary question under study.
While the individuals, of course, have subjective views of themselves, it is often no less valid than the "objective" view of a
researcher. While I did not always agree with the self-analysis,
it was important to allow the subjects to speak for themselves.

Virtually all members of Group A states that they either did
not really know if there was a connection, or they did not think
that there was a connection. Although a few thought there might
be a connection in other Chicanos, they did not necessarily feel
that their religion caused them to behave and react in certain
political patterns. In a very real sense, they were possibly
correct, i.e., to most of these people the Church was a part of
being Chicano; it was a cultural aspect of life, not something
that needed to be intellectually explored. They were Catholic
because they were reared as Catholics, just as most adults in
this society who belong to a religious body belong because of
their upbringing. Freedom of religion--"religious choice"--for
most in our society is generally an accident of birth, and not a
painstaking task of choosing the truth. Thus, for Chicanos in
this groups (A), it may be overstating the case to look at the
information and conclude that the Church is a conservatizing
factor.[28]

While this may be true, the converse could also be inferred
--that being conservative to moderately liberal could influence
one to be a practicing or nominal Catholic (assuming, of course,
that one had had sufficient exposure to Catholicism). It is
unclear whether an absolute cause-and-effect relationship exists,
or if the religious-political views are merely mutually reinforcing. What can be said is that the dominant American ideology
is extremely compatible with the Church's influence on these
Chicanos. Those interviewed saw no contradiction between being a
concerned (in varying degrees) Chicano, accepting mainstream
American political ideology, and being a Catholic.

The group (C) that is known as Fallen-Away Catholics is
composed of those who are former practicing Catholics and former
nominal Catholics. The reasons given for leaving the Church were
rarely explicit and leaving was not a conscious decision. Attendance at services and reception of the sacraments generally

became less and less important until it reached the point where they did not necessarily consider themselves members of the Church.

What is significant about this group (C) is that their political views are similar to the first group (A), the Practicing to Nominal Catholics. Group C, as with Group A, fit the conservative-liberal paradigm of standard American politics. While the Church has little formal meaning to this group (C), they appear to have moral and political values that are similar to the first (A). This could be interpreted in at least two ways: 1) The Church has an impact on their lives because the concept of morality (minus the external trimmings) that they learned as a child is now ingrained in them; or 2) the culture of Chicanos is not dependent on the Church, and would be similar to what it is without the Church. However, this second point enters the realm of the historically non-verifiable, the "what-if," and it is unclear as to how far this hypothesis could be usefully expanded.

Of the thirteen persons in the general population, only three were identified as fallen-away Catholics. Of the leaders, only one was so identified. I interpret that the reason only one leader was fallen-away was that this designation entails a passive reaction. One does not choose to "fall away," one does so inactively. The strongest individuals interviewed almost always fit into one of the following categories: 1) Those who took their religious and political obligations and beliefs most seriously (usually clerics), and actively tried to implement these in their lives and the lives of others; and, 2) those who also took their religious and political obligations most seriously, but judged that their religion and their politics were in conflict, and therefore, chose to abandon religion in order to develop their politics. The former group--the formal Catholics (Group D)--will be dealt with mainly in Chapter Four; the latter group, Group B, will be explored next.

Group B is composed for former practicing Catholics and former nominal Catholics who quit or renounced the Church rather than merely stop attending services. Reasons for quitting included the existence of contradictions between their active involvement in the Chicano community and what they perceived as the Church's role in the community. The individuals of Group B often acknowledged the existence of contradictions which they observed in the Church and also within themselves. A contradiction that was observed by and among this group (B) was that they saw the Church as a conservative-to-reactionary force (especially the Los Angeles Archdiocese under Cardinal McIntyre) and yet they themselves were practicing to nominal Catholics. The resolution of

this contradiction for many was to become active in the formulation of a group--Catòlicos Por La Raza (CPLR)--and seek to reform
the local Church by forcing concessions to the Chicano community
through external pressure, but still working within the framework
of being Catholic and legal activities.

From my interviews and readings of the literature of the
time period of CPLR activity (1969-1970), it appears that CPLR
was not founded by radicals, but by persons who were very religious (including members of the clergy), somewhat religious, and
those who were not religious but who recognized the Church as an
institution which needed to be challenged in the Chicano community. Several of the persons in CPLR who were interviewed
supported this view, a view that was collaborated by some radicals (i.e., those who considered themselves Marxists). In most
cases these radicals declined the opportunity to help found CPLR.
They stated that while they were sympathetic with CPLR (sympathy
which grew as CPLR became particularly active, especially after
the events at St. Basil's Church, Christmas Eve, 1969), they were
not particularly interested in starting the organization because
they already considered the Church a "lost cause," or did not
want to be part of what they considered to be an essentially
liberal organization (i.e., CPLR) whose focus on the Church was
perceived as being too narrow and possibly unnecessarily divisive.

Who then were these people (CPLR) and why did they make the
Church a primary focus of attention? Why were they often the
most religious of Chicanos before the movimiento and why did the
majority eventually leave the Church?

As mentioned above, the Los Angeles Archdiocese under Cardinal James Francis McIntyre was a particularly fertile breeding
ground for Chicano-Church antagonism. Cardinal McIntyre has long
been noted as one of the most conservative prelates in the American Church--not only politically but also ecclesiastically. He
was one of the voices that protested the reforms of Vatican II,
and the Los Angeles Archdiocese was one of the last to implement
them.[29] Thus during the 1960's, a period of political and cultural upheaval in the United States, the Los Angeles Archdiocese
was headed by a man who refused to acknowledge the necessity for
change--even that which was considered legitimate and gradual.

In talking with the leadership of CPLR, it was clear that
the directions and magnitude of their movement grew in direct
response to Church refusals to help the then existing Chicano
movement, rather than an active desire for confrontation politics. When I asked the leadership why they helped to founded
CPLR, one stated that while he was a law student intern in

Salinas, California, helping to organize the United Farmworkers (UFW), he met Cesar Chavez. Chavez and the UFW were concerned that the Church had not publicly backed the grape boycott. The law student promised to see what he could do to get the Church's support. He stated that his actions were not done out of hero worship for Chavez, but that he also thought the Church should back the farmworkers. In addition, he had a more personal reason. He considered himself "a very mystical, very religious" person who thought that the Church should and would practice what it preached.

> [It] was my personal religion that made it clear to me that there was just no way on earth that the Church wouldn't, of course, get behind Chavez once they understood what was happening, with a little pressure.[30]

He soon found that it was not just a question of bringing injustice to the attention of the hierarchy.

At the same time that this type of organizing was occurring with the UFW, a group of MECHA students at East Los Angeles Community College were independently beginning to see that Chicanos should organize around the issue of the Church. The Church was another institution such as the schools, the health system, etc., that was beginning to be examined. In the words of the CPLR leadership:

> So a little coalition started developing of law students and college students and it ultimately led to laborers, welfare mothers, and brown berets. And the coalition grew and grew and ultimately organizers such as La Raza magazine and other people like that.[31] Really just people themselves--Immaculate Heart nuns. The coalition just spread like wildfire. It turned out that everyone was willing to look at the Church--especially, specifically, Cardinal McIntyre's domination of the Los Angeles Church.[32]

When a delegation from CPLR attempted to see Cardinal McIntyre, they were emphatically rebuffed. In interviewing a female member of the delegation (all of the former members of CPLR who were interviewed indicated that women were extremely active in CPLR, especially those in leadership roles), she stated that when the delegation attempted to see the Cardinal, the men in the group were physically prevented from seeing him by several priests. She stated that the delegation was rather dumbfounded because they had not come to have a physical confrontation with priests, and all of their religious training prevented them from attacking men of the cloth. (This researcher recalls that his religious training, especially in high school, taught that to strike a priest in anger was a grievous mortal sin.) Therefore, the group retreated.[33]

CPLR was able to meet with the Cardinal later, and rather than adequately deal with the problems of the Chicano community as outlined by the delegations, he responded, "We are aware of the militants and radicals in our society and are prepared and trained to deal with them"[34]

It was clear that the Cardinal did not consider the requests and subsequent demands of CPLR to be legitimate. Instead, CPLR as a group was considered to be the problem that needed to be dealt with. It is useful here to delineate the demands of CPLR:[35]

Education

1. The Church should cease the charging of fees for parochial schools at all levels.

2. It should subsidize educational expenses for all Chicanos in need of high school, college, graduate school.

Housing

1. The Church should establish a lending agency, controlled by the community, with the funds to approve loans or outright grants for building private homes or making repairs.

2. The Church should create a housing agency with the funds and power to build low cost housing for all those persons presently residing in the various housing projects.

Community Involvement

The Church should allow members of the community, democratically elected, to preside over its functions with respect to any charitable, educational or business program.

Public Commitments

The Church should make specific public statements in
support of the various issues which affect the Mexican
Americans:

1. The Farmworkers
2. Educational struggle of the Chicano, i.e.,
    walkouts
3. Racist Grand Jury in Los Angeles
4. Anti-war movement because of the fact that 20% of
    the Vietnam dead are Chicanos.

A focal point of CPLR protest and a symbol of the relationship between it and the Archdiocese of Los Angeles was the recently constructed St. Basil's Church at Wilshire and Kingsley
Avenue. While the Archdiocese claimed that it did not have the
resources to meet the demands of CPLR, it built St. Basil's at a
cost of 3.5 million dollars. Many within the Chicano community
felt that it was meant to be a monument to the Cardinal. The
Church was therefore the site for several demonstrations, the
most significant of which occurred at Midnight Mass, Christmas
Eve, 1969.

On that night a peaceful demonstration was planned. The
intent of the participants was indicated by the fact that the
demonstration at the Church began with a mass on the outside
steps of the Church. Three Anglo priests who were sympathetic to
CPLR conducted the services. After the mass the Chicanos
attempted to attend the scheduled services that had begun inside
the Church. To their surprise and chagrin they found that they
had been locked out.

For the demonstrators the evening was beginning to assume
surrealistic qualities that were soon to escalate. They had
never been refused admittance to a Church service, and they
shouted their demands to be let in. According to several accounts, an Anglo nun inside the Church came back to the vestibule
and asked the ushers, "Why don't you let the poor people in?"
Some Chicanos on the other side of the door took this up as their
cry and this became the chant of the now very angry group: "Let
the poor people in."

As is the custom in several cities, this particular midnight
mass was being televised as part of the Christmas season. While
the demonstrators were not shown on television, their chanting
was very audible. Some of the Chicanos in the group, in the
interim, had found a side entrance that had not been locked.
Upon entering they went to the back of the Church to let in their

106

compatriots. The protesters were immediately attacked by the ushers, who were off-duty, undercover Los Angeles County sheriff's deputies.

Several members of CPLR whom I interviewed referred to the night as an ambush. While they had intended to have a peaceful demonstration, what occurred was a riot that can be classified (as were many other riots of the 1960's) as a police riot.[36] The Chicanos upon entering the Church were attacked and beaten by the police ushers and the reinforcements that arrived almost immediately. While it is normal procedure for police to carry their firearms when they are off duty, the preparedness of the ushers--with night sticks, handcuffs, and mace--gives credence to the "ambush" suggestion.[37]

As mentioned above, the mass itself was being televised, which meant that the disturbance in the back of the Church was becoming embarrassingly loud. The congregation was therefore, ironically lead twice in a chorus of "O Come, All Ye Faithful." At the end of mass, Cardinal McIntyre, the principal celebrant, spoke to the congregation:

> We are ashamed of the participants and we recog-
> nize that their conduct was symbolic of the
> conduct of the rabble as they stood at the foot
> of the cross, shouting 'Crucify him!' Forgive
> them for they know not what they do.[38]

The Cardinal, however, did not forgive them since the Archdiocese pressed charges against twenty of the group, primarily the leaders.[39] While there was at first an attempt to book them on felony conspiracy charges, there was no evidence to support such a charge and they were tried for disrupting a religious service. Seven were convicted and served three months.[40]

For many in the group, the events of that evening forced them to confront the relationship of the Church to the secular world. The words of a CPLR leader are indicative here:

> So that night and later, the whole posture and
> approach of the parishioners, Cardinal, and
> police was that we were 'rabble'. It was a
> once-in-a-lifetime type thing. You don't always
> see the issues so clearly. Here you see Jesus
> being used like crazy, being used not by some
> flunky priest who's afraid of anybody, but by
> the Cardinal. It was a mind-blower, like seeing

some sort of fantastic painting, ... where
you could see theory, political action, philosophy, and religion all at once.[41]

The contradictions between the Church's teachings and its
actions became increasingly crystallized for many members of CPLR
and their supporters. This resulted not only from the events at
St. Basil's and Cardinal McIntyre's refusal to address the problems of Chicanos, but also from the results of the research that
CPLR conducted on the Church. For example, the group examined
the public records and found that the diocese had over one bil-
lion dollars in real property,[42] and further, that the Church,
while it had built Catholic schools in the barrio, treated the
"Mexican" schools as inferior,[43] and that there were a lack of
programs to attract Chicano college students to Catholic universities.[44]

For many in CPLR, the contradictions within the Church
became personal contradictions that needed to be resolved. They
were, after all, members who had often thought of themselves as
being very religious. Their subjective metaphysical training was
now in direct conflict with their objective world. As the contradiction became increasingly clear, most decided to leave the
Church. This, of course, was not an easy decision, but one that
became more palatable as they gained knowledge of the Church.
Some indicated that the situation was not pleasing to them; they
felt that they had not left the Church, but that the Church had
left them. Non-participation in the Catholic Church, however,
did not necessarily make them atheistic.

Based on the interviews I conducted with the individuals,
and also introspective analysis, I would disagree with the
evaluation that the "Church had left them." As we have seen in
the previous Chapter and as we shall note in the succeeding
Chapter, the Church does change but it invariably changes after
the society as a whole has transformed itself. To assert that
the primary movement is within the church is to deny history.
While it may give comfort to a person seeking to justify his
shifting consciousness, it does not accurately describe the individual who can no longer reconcile old religious concepts with
a growing political awareness. Therefore, I would assert that
those who left the Church did so as individuals, who created
and/or were caught in a shifting consciousness based on objective
conditions that no longer could be rationally justified.[45]

For many the break with the Church was a private affair.
For several of the members of CPLR, however, it took public
forms. For example, in the late summer of 1970, there was a
"Baptism of Fire." At this ceremony, baptismal certificates were

burned in much the same manner as the draft-card burning of the same era.[46] Activity such as this indicates that the Church is not the changing party--that to assert his independence the individual needed to break away from the institution that was recognized as personally non-viable.

Of those persons interviewed, virtually all who fit into Group B--i.e., those who chose to leave the Church--believed that the Church was a conservatizing factor in their lives before they left. All of the people in CPLR have had over a decade to reflect on their activity with that group, and all view it as an important event in their lives. Some, of course, give it more importance than others in the formation of their present political awareness; but their individual politics now range from what can be described as left-liberal to a former novice (student nun) who is now a member of a socialist party.[47] All indicated that religion was not beneficial to their political development and that the Church is a political retardant to the Chicano people.

They were not implying that the Church made them conservative in the right-wing sense of the term, but that when they were religious, options that they now consider progressive, leftist or otherwise, in the political spectrum were closed to them. In the words of a CPLR leader:

> Using myself, if I'm any example at all, the less religious I got, finally when I got rid of it, the more political I became. Any by political all I mean is power . . . . A direct relationship, the less religion, the more political. . . . Back to the words, 'blessed are the poor,' and 'the meek shall inherit the earth.' The meek don't inherit nothing, nothing at all. Maybe they sleep good and maybe they do add up to a very safe person; but essentially the meek are meek and the poor are poor . . . . So the less religion the better, if we see that there's a translation of power--political power for the people. But I don't think that can come about with everybody being super religious.[48]

This response was typical of many members of CPLR whom I interviewed, and of other persons who had made the decision to leave the Church before the formation of CPLR. Some examples would be illustrative. (These are excerpts from answers to the question. "Do you feel that there is any connection between your religious and political beliefs and/or the changes you have undergone? How about other Chicanos--From your experiences, would you say that there is a connection between Chicanos' religious and political beliefs? If yes, what is that connection?"):

> Yes. As I became more political, more scientific . . . it has lead me away from methaphysical acceptance.[49]

> Yes, the Church taught the status quo should be maintained and that protects them [the Church] and I don't want to anymore.[50]

> Yes. Politics is always important . . . . It all goes together [politics and religion]--it put me where I am now. I was more conservative, naive, and trustful. Yes, I think so. My relatives voted for Ford because of Carter's abortion issue, because of the Church's position. I don't want my mother to hear the bishop's off-the-wall statements.[51]

> When I separated from the Church I became more political. Faith has always given me the strength to endure but now I get that strength from my co-workers. Yes, a majority of Chicanos follow the Church blindly and it is therefore, a strong negative influence.[52]

> Yes, we've already answered the contradictions [in the Church and my participation]. Yes, yes, to me religion always permeates peoples' lives, whether you deny it or not, just like any other superstition. I do believe it permeates [Chicano] activities and goals.[53]

The interviews with several members of CPLR point to the conclusions, in their minds, that the Church is a political retardant for a rise in political consciousness, and active as a control mechanism regulating political options. Again, it should be emphasized that the conservative influence was not necessarily making one conservative in a right-wing sense, but rather--as expressed in the interviews--that one's attention could be diverted to ethereal concerns rather than secular necessities. Further, it is possible that the Church can support the status quo either actively or through proclaimed neutrality.[54] When the status quo that Chicanos lived under was that of an oppressed minority, the Church activity was seen as one of reaction.

CPLR, as an ad hoc group, had little formal structure, but rather it was a group, as indicated in the interviews, that was a coalition of persons and other groups that were often acting spontaneously in relation to the Church. While CPLR, for reasons discussed below, was not supported universally by the Chicano community, it did receive a broad base of support.[55] As with many Chicano groups of the era, it was led by activist who were often college students or college-trained professionals--as such it was a Chicano elite group. (Elite here is a relative concept. Since the average educational level of the Chicano community is eight years, the "elite" would probably not be considered part of an elite group if they belonged to an European ethnic group.) This young elite, however, was almost universally working class in background and thus could be considered representative of the Chicano community.

A fundamental difference between CPLR and the general community, however, was the CPLR was forced to call into question their religious beliefs as they examined the institutional structure. Before working with CPLR, many of the members had not seriously questioned their religion's compatibility with other beliefs. Other than the common philosophical questions that one often has in young adulthood, many of the members did not attempt to make the connection between "theory, political action, philosophy, and religion all at once," as they were forced to do at St. Basil's. When the members realized that they could not incorporate their new-found activism and growing radicalism with Church participation, they gave up the Church and attempted to assess the impact of religion on their thinking. For most of the non-activist population, the choice did not have to be made and thus there was not sufficient reason for total community rejection of the Church. However, the publicity generated by CPLR did serve to weaken even further the already weak commitment of many Chicanos to the Church--as they saw their people being beaten by the Church and the police. Indeed, as Gomez argues, the principal impact of CPLR was that the week after the events at St. Basil's, Chicanos were forced to think about, and argue with their families about, the Catholic Church and its impact on Chicanos. The fact that one had to defend or attack the Church set the "seeds" for critical thinking.[56]

Despite the fact that the events at St. Basil's could be considered a military victory for the Los Angeles Archdiocese, it was rather embarrassing for the Catholic Church to have televised beatings in the vestibule, "rabble" or not, while the congregation was singing, "O Come, All Ye Faithful." One immediate impact was the quick "retirement" of Cardinal MyIntyre after a visit by the papal nuncio.[57]

111

CPLR had other direct impacts on the Chicano and the Church, such as the start of the Campaign for Human Development. This fund began shortly after the events at St. Basil's. Gomez interprets this as conscience money being offered to the community, which also served to neutralize criticisms and divert criticism away from the Church.[58]

Another impact was the appointment of Chicanos and other Spanish-surnamed priests to the hierarchy of the Church. Before 1970, there were no Chicano bishops in the United States, despite the large Chicano Catholic population. Since that time, an average of one Spanish-surnamed bishop per year has been appointed. By 1985 there were seventeen Hispanic bishops in the United States, most of whom are auxiliaries. (The impact of the clergy-both priest and bishops will be discussed in the next chapter.)

Another impact was greater Church involvement in the United Farmworkers' grape strike. Richard Martinez, a member of CPLR, has been quoted as saying that Chavez recognized the group's contributions:

> Some of us talked to Cesar Chavez in Delano several months later and he said, 'If it wasn't for you people, although I may not agree with your tactics, the Church wouldn't have pushed so adamantly for a resolution.'[59]

While the relationship between the Church and the UFW will be examined immediately in the next section, it is first important to discuss the disagreement with the tactics of CPLR. This was a very common criticism of most of the individuals whom I interviewed who were not members of CPLR, and who knew of the organization. While virtually all agreed that CPLR had legitimate grievances (some of this agreement was in hindsight), they did not approve of their tactics. When asked to elaborate they usually referred specifically to the riot at St. Basil's. My investigation indicates that the tactics, and the resultant negative publicity that was generated, were in fact not the tactics of CPLR but the action of the Sheriff's deputies as planned by the Cardinal. Virtually all the evidence that I have explored reveals that CPLR did not plan, want, or expect a riot. Acuna states that many if not most Chicano Catholics reacted negatively to the events at St. Basil's. However, he notes that opinions have changed. After a meeting in a Mexican Catholic Church in East Los Angeles in 1972, Acuna reported that devout Catholics were defending CPLR before the papal delegate, Jesus Garcia, and

the Archbishop of Panama, Tomas Clavel. Many of the statements
Father Garcia made at the meeting echoed what CPLR had stated two
years earlier.[60]

The United Farmworkers

As noted in the introduction, the United Farmworkers (UFW)
is a rural-based organization and this study is primarily focused
on the urbanized Chicano. However, it is equally true that the
UFW has had a profound influence on the origins and perpetuation
of the movimiento within the urban Chicano population. This was
borne out by several of the interviews I conducted. The UFW was
the only group that was virtually universally known and supported. The degree of support ranged from active participation
in boycotts, etc., to merely stating that they had a good cause.
Six of the interviewees named the UFW as the best Chicano organization. No other organization received as much positive support.
Most of the rest of the leaders and people either did not wish to
single out any particular organization, or named scattered other
organizations. When I asked who were the three most important
Chicano leaders in the nation, the only name that was given with
any consistency was Cesar Chavez, mentioned by fifteen of the
twenty-five interviewed. Many of these emphasized that there
really are no Chicano leaders nationally, but that Chavez was the
one who came the closest to having a national constituency. This
was despite the fact that his formal leadership role is restricted to the farmworker movement.

When I asked why Chavez was considered a leader and the UFW
so important to the urban population, the answer given very
consistently was that the UFW gave Chicanos a sense of victory, a
sense that indeed Chicanos can organize and win their rights.
This sense of Si Se Puede can not be overemphasized. There were
a large number of Chicano groups that were organized during the
movimiento, as well as groups that have been on the national
scene long enough to have some degree of permanency. However,
the UFW was the group that captured the imagination and attention
(eventually) of the vast majority of Chicanos, as well as large
segments of the Anglo population. It is clear that the UFW is
more than just a fringe element of the Chicano movement.

One reason that the UFW stands out for Chicanos as a sup-
portable organization is that the issues that the UFW tackled are
often clearer for their potential supporters. It should be
noted, however, that the farmworkers and Chavez himself were/are
often romaticized (as well as vilified) in the popular and
Chicano press. However, it is quite clear that the UFW's influence extends well beyond the farm fields and areas of its

principal focus, and it is thus important to this study. The immediate task here is not a general overview of the UFW's history--there are a plethora of works that are available for that purpose--but rather an examination of the relationship between the Church and the UFW and the impact that it has had on the Chicano community, farmworkers and non-farmworkers alike.

While the UFW is not a one-man organization--no true organization is--the unmistakable leader and driving force is Cesar Chavez. It is necessary to briefly examine his political and religious development and assess that influence on the farmworkers and supporters.

Chavez's use of religious symbolism in organizing and strike activity is well known. This effort to utilize religion appears to be a quite genuine effort to incorporate his concepts of morality and right and wrong into the farmworkers' struggle. Chavez considers himself a religious person whose beliefs on social justice could not be based on economic or political ideas alone, but which also require faith.[61]

As with many Chicanos, Chavez in his youth often did not have the opportunity to attend services, or attend a great deal of formal religious instruction. When he was to receive his first Communion, the priest at first balked because of his lack of formal religious training. The priest was finally convinced however, after Cesar's mother insisted that the priest quiz him in order for Cesar to prove his religious knowledge.[62] As noted earlier in Chapter Two, Chavez's adult training in the Church teachings on social issues came from Father McDonnell when the priest came to the barrio of Sal Si Puedes in San Jose, in conjunction with the priest's work with the Mission Band.[63] Before that time, Chavez's theoretical knowledge of economics and the Church's position on the rights of the working men was not sufficient to build a successful organization.

This raises an important issue that goes beyond Chavez and the UFW. The Catholic Church has a full, rich, and complex body of dogma, rituals, teachings, and administrative rules. To understand the impact of the Church on the Chicano population, it is necessary to try to assess which teachings are emphasized, and which are not emphasized, to the Chicano population--not just to know the potential teachings that can be made available to the community. Chavez is a good example of the selective (often neglected) training that Chicanos receive. What Chavez learned from McDonnell led him to believe that the Church would support the farmworkers once it knew the facts. He was soon to discover that the support from the Church would not be automatic, but would have to be extracted under pressure.

114

Chavez's decision to utilize religious symbols was not merely based on personal preferences, but on his perception of the Mexicano/Chicano community as being "a religion-oriented culture."[64] Before proceeding in an examination of the Church in the UFW struggle, it is necessary to examine Chavez's perception. Do the campesinos have "a religion-oriented culture"? Horacio Ulibarri in an attitudinal study of Spanish-speaking migrants in the Southwest found that religion was not a strong factor in the migrants' lives.

> Rather a complacent contentment toward religion, where involvement in religious affairs was minimal, seemed to prevail among the migrant and ex-migrant workers in the sample.[65]

While there are differences in how these conclusions were reached (i.e., Chavez's impressions of primarily California migrants vs. Ulibarri's scaled attitudinal questionnaire in the other four southwestern states), this may not primarily account for the divergence. Chavez's impressions were a qualitative judgment based not only on his personal life, but also from his unique position as a leader and observer of part of the Chicano community. Ulibarri attempts a quantitative study that measures answers to his questions. He does not, however, present a proper historical framework to understand the phenomenon which he is discussing. The study of religious impact is inherently an interpretive undertaking, and over-quantification in scales of religiosity tends toward what Geertz discussed, and was noted earlier in this work, as attempting to escape making interpretations by

> . . . turning culture into folklore and collecting it, turning it into traits and counting it, turning it into institutions and classifying it, turning it into structures and toying with it.[66]

I would argue that both Ulibarri's and Chavez's assessments can be viewed as essentially correct, and do not present an irreconcilable contradiction. However, Chavez's impressions appear to capture a fuller meaning of the farmworker's religious orientation. It is equally true, however, that Chavez's statement is subject to misinterpretation in evaluating the campesinos' religion. To say that one has "a religion-oriented culture" is not to say that one has a religion dominated culture, or an institutional Church-oriented culture, as Ulibarri correctly notes, and as has been shown historically. Chicanos and Mexicans do go to Church less often than their Anglo counterparts, they do have less instruction, they do appear empirically to be "less"

115

Catholic. However, they do consider themselves Catholic, even when not attending regular services; and often, as shown with the Mission Band, the lack of regular attendance is due to a lack of opportunity and not a lack of desire.

In such a situation the inverse could be inferred from "a religion-oriented culture," i.e., that campesinos have a "culturally oriented religion." A synthesis of Spitzer's cultural and nominal Catholicism becomes apparent for much of the Chicano community, especially farmworkers. (Chicanos have only been a predominantly urbanized people since the end of World War II.[67]) This entails an identification with the Church, but not necessarily a subordination to it. There is some independence in the interpretation of a variety of Church practices, which becomes an expression of the cultural organization of the environment. In other words, the Church fits into the "hard surfaces of life" that Geertz delineates in his cultural analysis, and the material reality that Marx based his analysis upon.

A culture so understood is a culture that can utilize itself in political action; i.e., it is a culture that can see beneath the outward symbols--symbols that have significance beyond their obvious perceptibility. A non-religiously oriented union organizer described how Chavez explained using a fast of penance (for alleged union violence) without requiring the same beliefs from all sympathizers.

> When we visited Cesar in his little room at
> Forty Acres, Leroy says, he would point at the
> wall and say, 'See that white wall? Well,
> imagine ten different-colored balls, all jumping
> up and down. One ball is called religion, an-
> other propaganda, another organizing, another
> law, and so forth. When people look at that
> wall and see those balls, different people look
> at different balls; each person keeps his eye on
> his own ball. For each person the balls mean
> many different things, but for everyone they can
> mean something!'[68]

The organizer explained how he considered his ball propaganda and kept his eye comfortably on that. He understood the fast in those terms and it did not negate what he considered to be the other nine balls--organization.[69]

An important symbol that was (and is) utilized by the farmworkers was the Virgin of Guadalupe. As stated earlier, the Virgin has been used in the past as a uniquely Mexican symbol, not merely a religious symbol. This message was not lost on the

116

UFW leadership in its search for legitimate symbols for the farmworkers. This was by no means an unanimous decision by various leaders of the UFW--several of whom were non-Catholic and/or non-believers. However, the majority of the leaders approved the use of the Virgin and as Luis Valdez, Head of El Teatro Campesino, the Union's theatrical group, noted, it was not merely for religious reasons:

> The Virgin of Guadalupe was the first hint to the farm workers that the pilgrimage [1966 march from Delano to Sacramento] implied social revolution. During the Mexican Revolution, the peasant armies of Emiliano Zapata carried her standard, not only because they sought her divine protection, but because she symbolized the Mexico of the poor and humble. It was a simple Mexican Indian, Juan Diego, who first saw her in a vision at Guadalupe. Beautifully dark and Indian in feature, she was the New World version of the Mother of Christ. Even though some of her worshipers in Mexico still identify her with Tonantzin, an Aztec Goddess, she is a Catholic saint of Indian creation--a Mexican. The people's response was immediate and reverent. They joined the march by the thousands falling in line behind her standard.[70]

Such a statement illustrates a blend of culture, nationalism, and politics. For the various individuals involved the particular order of importance my be different, but it is, as with compadrazgo, a symbol of unity--one that can be effectively utilized. It has distinct non-religious meanings as well as being a symbol that would possibly give signals that could denote an overly religious population--a mispreception. A symbol that can be used can also be abused; but it would appear historically that the Virgen de Guadalupe elicits a particular reverence from, and has relevance to, the "poor and humble."[71]

It is clear that Cesar Chavez does use religion but he does not appear to use it in an unprincipled manner. He does not manipulate his or the farmworkers' beliefs into something that he or they do not feel is true. He uses it as a resource for--for lack of a better term--spiritual uplifting of the farmworkers when they are quite understandably discourage or confused over the lack of perceivable day-to-day progress. Long protracted struggles (especially with limited goals) do not lend themselves to qualitative daily leaps that can be a source of inspiration to the participants.[72]

117

Chavez also uses the Church for its potential material resources. That the Church as an institution has money, influence, and power is beyond dispute. Chavez in a speech in 1968 emphasized the actual and potential power of the Church, and that this power should be used for the farmworkers:

> The Church we are talking about is a tremendous powerful institution . . . . It is a powerful moral and spiritual force . . . . There is tremendous spiritual and economic powers in the Church . . . . We began to realize the powerful effect which the Church can have . . . . Therefore, I am calling for Mexican American groups to stop ignoring this source of power. It is just our right to appeal to the Church to use its power effectively for the poor.[73]

As mentioned earlier, Chavez expected to receive support from the Church although it was, as Dunne characterized, "less institutional clerical support."[74] He quotes Chavez as stating:

> This didn't start when the strike began. I've been making friends with the clergy for sixteen years, ever since I was with the CSO. How could the Catholic clergy stay out of this one? All the Mexicans are Catholic. And the Church is the one group that isn't expecting anything from us. They are not doing any politicking among us. All the other groups, the unions, the civil rights groups, they all want something in return for their support. Not the Church. I would have been surprised if I hadn't gotten their support after all these years.[75]

Chavez's statement is misleading in the sense that he was crediting the Church as an institution for the actions of the few priests and nuns on the picket line--just as the growers in an earlier time period blamed the Church for the actions of a few priests in the Mission Band for labor organizing. The "less institutional clerical support" that the UFW received was often minimal institutional support, especially from an important constituency, the local Catholic churches.

The priests who were actively involved with the UFW at the beginning of the Delano grape strike were primarily outsiders who were not under the direct control of the local Bishop (A.J. Willinger of the Monterey-Fresno diocese). The local priests in Delano were under heavy pressure from the growers (who were primarily Catholic) not to intervene. As the pastor of a predominantly Anglo parish succinctly stated, "If the growers have a poor year, the Church feels the effect of a poor harvest."[76] The same pastor noted that the local Church's position was one of neutrality, and that it was not a matter of primary concern to the Church's activities:

> We took the stand that it's not our place to take sides. It would be just as wrong to be on the growers' side as it would be to be on the side of the workers. The rightness or wrongness of the strike is something I can't answer. I think it's an economic issue. It's not a moral issues.[77]

Other priests, i.e., priests from outside the immediate area, saw the labor dispute as a moral issue. Among them were Father James L. Vizzard of the National Catholic Rural Life Conference (NCRLC) and Fathers Keith Kenney and Arnold Meagher of Sacramento. What is significant about these priests is that their participation was not as representatives of the institutional Church--certainly not the regional Church--but rather as individual clergy who had a certain degree of autonomy such as Fr. Vizzard, or as individual priests who were acting without official authorization such as Fathers Kenny and Meagher.

For example, Fr. Vizzard as Head of the NCRLC was not accountable to the local hierarchy. He also had contacts with the news media that would make public any institutional confrontations. This would be potentially very embarrassing for the Church.[78] Fr. Vizzard and Bishop Willinger did engage in public confrontation after Fr. Vizzard's arrival. Fr. Vizzard noted the Church officials often acted out of fear for their pocketbooks.[79]

The situations of Fathers Kenny and Meagher illustrate vividly that the historical pattern of priestly involvement in workers' movements is not a action that is condoned by the Church--as regulated by its hierarchy. When the priests were asked if they had asked permission from their Bishop, Alden J. Bell, to come and help the farmworkers, they answered, no, because it would have been refused if requested.[80]

The presence of the priests on the picket line was a source of irritation to the growers and Bishop Willinger. The two priests returned to Sacramento, however, before any official action could be taken. Bishop Willinger sent a letter to all of California's bishops asking that no priest from outside come to Delano.[81]

The priests, however, did go back to help the farmworkers in their struggles. But when they again returned to their home diocese, they were called into the chancery office and reprimanded. In a letter by Bishop Bell, who was then attending the Second Vatican Council in Rome, they were forbidden to make any statements concerning the labor strife, to have contact with persons associated with the strike, and to disclose that they had been disciplined.[82] As with other priests before them, who took a leadership role in attempting to actualize the gospel for the benefit of the workers (the most notable being Fathers McCullough and McDonnell), they were silenced.

The attitude of the local Church was not lost on the farmworkers. They became more alienated from an institution to which they belonged, and from which they expected support. During the first six months of the Delano grape strike, Chavez stated that his biggest worry was to keep the union supporters from picketing the Bishop, the local Church, or picketing during mass.[83]

Chavez also added that many strikers stopped attending church services. This is another example of the weak commitment that Catholicism elicits from the Chicano community (due to the Church's actions), while the community continues to have a strong attachment to Catholic symbols, e.g., the Virgin.

In the two decades since the beginning of the United Farmworkers, the Church has shifted its positions several times. It is currently thought to be highly sympathetic to the farmworker movement. How this shift came about and the mutual impacts of Chicanos on the Church, and the Church on Chicanos, will be explored in further detail in the following Chapter which focuses on the role of the Catholic clergy in the Chicano community. As we shall see, organizations that may appear diverse and unconnected have ties to each other.

The Migrant Ministry

Before proceeding with an examination of the Catholic clergy and hierarchy, it is important to take note of a religiously-oriented organization that has had a profound impact on the Chicano community through its association with the farmworkers. The Migrant Ministry is a Protestant organization that was started in 1920 to serve the poor, itinerant farmworkers, eventually in several states. It was funded by the United States interdenominational National Council of Churches of Christ. The scope of the national Migrant Ministry went well beyond Mexican farmworkers. The relationship between the California Migrant Ministry (CMM) and the farmworkers precedes the actual beginning

120

of the Delano grape strike. In an interview with Chris Hartmire, the Director of the California Migrant Ministry, he stated that his involvement with the farmworkers began in 1957-1958 when he and the Reverend Jim Drake, another CMM minister, began to train with Fred Ross and Cesar Chavez in the Community Services Organization (CSO). The Rev. Hartmire stated that Chavez recruited him and Rev. Drake. The relationship between the CMM and the UFW was well established. When the strike began there wasn't any question that the board of directors would support them.[84]

When the Rev. Hartmire was asked why he thought that the Catholic Church was not as receptive initially to the farmworker's cause as were his and other Protestant organizations, he made an interesting observation. He noted that the Catholic Church did not have a parallel institution such as the CMM. (The Mission Band had been dissolved.) Thus the Catholic Church had no one to draw it into the conflict. After the CMM became involved, the Protestant churches had to make a choice--either to support their agency or to disavow it. The Protestant churches were drawn into the strike. If the United States Catholic bishops would have had to make a choice to support or reject an official Church organization, then the situation at the beginning of the strike might have been different.[85]

It should also be pointed out that the lines of discipline are considerably tighter in the Catholic Church vis-a-vis an interdenominational Protestant organization. The CMM enjoyed structural freedoms that would have been difficult to match in the Catholic Church. For example, the CMM was unencumbered by (1) individual denominationalism, and (2) a local congregation.[86]

The aspect of localism is particularly important. The CMM was not without its critics. Among the most vocal were the local Protestant churches. Hartimire notes that:

> Early in the strike the Delano Ministerial Association unanimously passed and publicized a resolution criticizing visiting clergy-men and asserting that their [Delano clergymen's] competence was in spiritual affairs and that 'such controversial matters [as the Delano strike] should be handled through proper and established channels that justice and peace might prevail.' In a later public statement the Ministerial Association 'deplored the unethical tactics of the Migrant Ministry.' They did not supply details.[87]

The CMM eventually evolved, due to its close ties with the UFW, into the National Farm Workers Ministry (NFWM). It lost most of the financial support that it originally had while gaining other support, including different Catholic religious religious priests' councils and orders.[88]

Summary

What is perhaps of greatest significance is the considerable degree of diversity within the Chicano community. Chicanos are not shown to be a highly religious population that can be easily classified and analyzed. The information, both primary and the literature cited (including that of Chapter Two), shows Chicanos to be divided in their commitment to weekly church obligations-- with the preponderance of sources indicating a lack of church attendance. Chicanos as a religious entity appear to be less homogeneous in their religion beliefs and practices than are other Americans, especially other Catholics.

This does not mean, however, the Chicanos do not consider themselves to be Catholic. Evidence from compadrazgo, church attendance, the devotion to the Virgin of Guadalupe, is often contradictory and must be evaluated not independently but concurrently to present a more accurate religious picture of the Chicano.

At least four groups emerged from the study, which examined the Chicano community's relationship to the Church. Three of these groups were discussed in this Chapter, with the last group (D), primarily clerics, to be discussed in the next. The four groups were:

Group A - The Practicing to Nominal Catholics who constitute the largest group.

Group B - Former Catholics who Quit or Renounced their religion rather than merely stop attending services.

Group C - Fallen-away Catholics who stopped attending services, but not for a specific reason.

Group D - Formal Catholics whose lives center around the Church.

The diversity within the Chicano community was also evident within the groups, especially the largest group (A). In attempting to assess the political impact of religion on Chicanos it is not sufficient to categorize Chicanos by groups and state that the political ideology of the group is "X". The socio-political impact of religion on individual Chicanos appears to be proportional to the amount of time, study and energy they devote to religion and their overall political perspectives which is influenced by other factors. For conservative Church members, the Church can provide a rationale and purpose for their attitudes and behaviors. The same appears true for liberals (i.e., liberalism that is within the mainstream of American ideology); religion can also provide them a rationale and purpose for their ideology and behavior. To characterize the Church as having only a conservative political impact (in the right wing sense) is insufficient. Catholic belief and influence and the dominant American ideology of conservative-to-liberal politics can be said to be mutually reinforcing, but to state a cause-and-effect relationship appears to be too strong an assertion.

The fact that the Church's influence on Chicanos exerts itself in seemingly different directions should not be unexpected. As indicated in Chapter One, religion is a form of social control, and social control mechanisms are seldom perfect in their operation, nor are they usually the sole determinant of a person's actions, nor do they operate uniformly upon all groups.[89] When a group is a large, heterogeneous, and changing as is the Chicano community, the same mechanism does not and cannot be expected to operate uniformly within the group. This is especially true when the mechanism is of a more subtle persuasion than, e.g., physical coercion.

This was demonstrated in the examination of different Chicano organizations. The Church's attempts to influence the Chicano community are often thwarted by the existing political realities that come into conflict with Church practices, if not teachings. When the Church itself is the target of political activities by Chicanos, as with CPLR, contradictions are revealed that present personal dilemmas to the individual members. In the case of CPLR members, these individual contradictions often lead to the breakdown of the control the Church has previously exercised over them.

Some members of the UFW found themselves in similar positions, although the issues were not as clear as with CPLR. The UFW's conflicts with the Church were less intense and less direct than were the conflicts that CPLR had with the Church. In both cases it is evident, however, that the Church had an opportunity to increase its commitment from the Chicano community, if it had been responsive to the community. However, the Church did not permit itself to be of secular service without conflict.

Thus the overall commitment the Church has generated from the Chicano community has been weakened. In contrast to the Catholic Church, the CMM demonstrated that it was able to serve the interest of its constituency without the necessity for the conflict with that population. Significantly, however, this was accomplished not because of its institutional support, but despite it. We will examine the shifting institutional support for social change within the Catholic Church, both domestically and in Latin American, and its implications for Chicanos in the next Chapter.

[1]In addition to the historical evidence cited in Chapter Two, a study in Arizona reaches similar conclusions:

> "Ninety-one percent of the Mexican-Americans in South Tucson are Catholics, compared to 37.9 percent of the Others category [all non-Mexican Americans]. One National Opinion Research Center sample taken in January of 1964 found the American general public to be 26.0 percent Catholic. The commitment of Catholics in South Tucson to their church is not as great as you would find among Catholics in New England: 31.9 percent said they seldom or never attend church, and 37.7 said they are not strong Catholics." Donald Freeman, "Party, Vote, and the Mexican American in South Tucson," in Chicano: The Evolution of a People, ed. Renato Rosaldo, Robert A. Calvert, and Gustav L. Seligmann (Minneapolis: Winston Press, 1973), pg. 405.

[2]See Leo Grebler, Joan W. Moore, and Ralph C. Guzman, The Mexican-American People (New York: The Free Press, 1970), pp. 472-477. Also see Albert Carrillo, "The Sociological Failure of the Catholic church Toward the Chicano," The Journal of Mexican American Studies 1 (Winter 1970): 75-83.

[3]Allen Spitzer's difinition of nominal Catholicism is used here:

> "Nominal Catholicism: (1) Identification with and allegiance to the Catholic Church. (2) Perfunctory relationship with the formal Church. (3) Independent interpretations of a variety of Catholic injunctions and practices." In "Religious Structure in Mexico," Alpha Kappa Deltan 30: 54-58.

While Spitzer's study is located in Mexico, I found many of his classifications and insights useful in the present study.

[4]Ibid.

[5]Ibid.

> "Formal Catholicism: (1) Full and complete knowledge of the Catholic Faith, its expectations, and proscriptions. (2) A reasonably

thorough desire to practice this faith, and evidence that such a wish is being fulfilled. 3) A realization on the part of one's neighbors and associates that one is 'muy Catolica.'"

[6]Interview, December 17, 1976.

[7]Interview, December 28, 1976.

[8]Interview, January 13, 1977.

[9]Interview, February 5, 1977.

[10]Interview, February 9, 1977.

[11]Interview, August 30, 1976.

[12]Interview, September 14, 1976.

[13]Interview, September 16, 1976.

[14]Interview, September 24, 1976.

[15]Interview, December 8, 1976.

[16]Interview, December 10, 1976.

[17]Interview, December 12, 1976.

[18]Interview, December 31, 1976.

[19]Interview, January 5, 1977.

[20]Margaret Clark, Health in the Mexican-American Culture (Berkeley: University of California, 1959, 1970), pg. 157.

[21]For examples of how this was implemented, see Clark, Ibid., pp. 157-161; Joan Moore, Mexican Americans (Englewood Cliffs, New Jersey: Prentice-Hall, 1970), pp. 104-105; and Grebler, Mexican American People, ppg. 354-357 and pg. 374n.

One should take care in examining compadrazgo not to misinterpret the relationship. Arthur J. Rubel in Across the Tracks: Mexican-Americans in a Texas City (Austin: University of Texas, 1966), pg. 82, notes that "In any case, the importance which Chicanos attribute to the baptismal triad--padrino-adhijado-compadre--cannot be overemphasized." However, if one merely examines the surface relationship, it can be overemphasized to indicate a sense of religion that may not exist, at the expense of the material reasons that do exist.

[22]See Chapter II for examples of why missionary work is prone toward failure.

[23]An example of this evolutionary process may be found in the Rev. Juan Hurtado, An Attitudinal Study of Social Distance Between the Mexican American and the Church (San Antonio, Texas: Mexican American Cultural Center, 1976). He illustrates that there is considerable social distance between Mexican Americans in the San Diego area and the Church. Those who identified themselves as Mexicans were the closest to the Church. Those who identified themselves as Mexican-Americans had more social distance from the Church, and those who identified themselves as Chicanos were the furthest.

[24]Philip E. Lampe in a study conducted in San Antonio, Texas, on the degree of assimilation for those who attend parochial schools vs. public schools offers an interesting interpretation that notes that since Chicanos attend services less than Anglos, the most Anglocized Chicanos are those who are the most religious.

"Grebler, Moore, and Guzman, present the findings that Mexican Americans are less observant of religious beliefs and practices than Anglos. The more religious a Mexican-American is, therefore, the more he departs from the commonly found Mexican tradition, and the closer he moves to that of the Anglo. Any movement away from the 'Mexican'toward the 'Anglo' has implications for assimilation." Comparative Study of Assimilation of Mexican-Americans: Parochial Schools Versus Public Schools (San Francisco: R and E Research Associates, 1975), pg. 31.

In the main focus of Lampe's study he found that Chicanos who attended parochial schools were more assimilated into American society than Chicanos who attended public schools.

[25]See Kenneth M. Dolbeare and Patricia Dolbeare, American Ideologies: The Competing Political Beliefs of the 1970's, 3rd ed. (Chicago: Rand McNally College Publishing Company, 1976), pp. 1-89.

[26]Carrillo, "The Sociological Failure of the Catholic Church."

[27]Ibid., pg. 77.

[28]Certainly so if one means conservative in the right-wing sense of the term.

[29]See John Tracy Ellis, American Catholicism (Chicago: University of Chicago, 1969), pp. 175-177, 196. Also see references to Cardinal McIntyre in Chapter Two.

[30]Interview, December 8, 1976.

[31]The editors of La Raza newspaper (later magazine), a Southern California Chicano publication, were extremely vocal in their support of CPLR and critical of the Los Angeles Archdiocese.

[32]Interview, December 8, 1976. There was also a group in San Diego that was independent of the Los Angeles based organization. For accounts of the activities of the San Diego CPLR, see Hurtado, "An Attitudinal Study," pp. 3-4, 81-83, 106-107.

[33]Interview, CPLR member, December 12, 1976. A quote from Cardinal McIntyre needs no comment here to illustrate the type of resistance that CPLR received from the Archdiocese. The Cardinal is reported to have angrily told a group of Chicano students, "I was here before there were even Mexicans. I came to Los Angeles 21 years ago." Rodolfo Acuna, Occupied American: The Chicano's Struggle Toward Liberation (San Francisco: Canfield Press, 1972), pg. 257.

[34]La Raza (newspaper) c. 1970, Vol. II, No. 10, pg. 8.

[35]Abbreviated list of demands printed in Ibid. For a more complete list, see La Raza (newspaper) c. 1970, Vol. II, No. 2.

[36]For a survey of such riots involving the Chicano community see Armando Morales, Ando Sangrando (I am Bleeding): A Study of Mexican American - Police Conflict (La Puente, California: Perspectiva Publications, 1972).

[37]See David F. Gomez, Somos Chicanos: Strangers in Our Own Land (Boston: Beacon Press, 1973), pg. 162. Also see Eberado S. Hernandez, "Let the poor people in," Machete (newspaper) 8 January 1970, pg. 2.

[38]Gomez, <u>Somos Chicanos</u>, pg. 164 and Hernandez, "Let the poor people in."

[39]See <u>La Raza</u> magazine, c. 1970, Vol. 1, No. 1. A woman whom I interviewed (December 21, 1976), who had previously been a nun for twelve years, indicated that those who were later arrested and indicted were not necessarily those who had been engaged in any overt violent activity, but rather those whom the police and the Church considered the leaders. She was one of the members indicted--she was found not guilty.

[40]Gomez, <u>Somos Chicanos</u>, pp. 164-165. Also see <u>La Raza</u>, Ibid. Such was also indicated by interviews with CPLR former members.

[41]Quoted in Gomez, Ibid., pg. 164.

[42]Memorandum from CPLR, November 29, 1969, with attached documents from the Los Angeles County Assessor's Office.

[43]An interview conducted with an ex-nun (see footnote 58) produced testimony that to teach in the "Mexican" parochial schools was considered an undesirable teaching assignment, and such assignments were often used as punishment for nuns who angered their superiors. She also stated that at least when she began to teach in the Chicano parochial schools, they were largely staffed with ill-trained personnel.

[44]In addition to Cardinal McIntyre and the Los Angeles Archdiocese, the criticism generated by CPLR extended to other Caholic institutions in California such as the Universities of San Francisco and Santa Clara. See the bilingual newspaper of La Raza Students Association, <u>Justicia O...</u>, Vol. 1, Nos. 4, 7, 10, 11, c. 1971.

[45]For a theoretical elaboraion see Maurice Godelier, <u>Perspectives in Marxist Anthropology</u>, trans. Robert Brain (Cambridge: Cambridge University Press, 1973, 1977), pp. 169-185.

[46]See <u>El Popo</u> (newspaper), Vol. II, No. 1, c. 1970; and <u>La Raza</u>, Vol. 2, No. 12. The baptism of fire was mentioned in the interviews conducted with CPLR members.

In addition to the text in the newspapers mentioned (<u>El Popo</u>, <u>La Raza</u>, and <u>Machete</u>), these periodicals also contained excellent photographs of the events involving CPLR.

[47]Interview, January 5, 1977.

[48]Interview, December 8, 1976.

[49]Interview, September 24, 1976.

[50]Interview, December 12, 1976.

[51]Interview, December 21, 1976.

[52]Interview, December 22, 1976.

[53]Interview, January 5, 1977.

[54]See Gomez, Somos Chicanos, pg. 159, for examples of Cardinal McIntyre's proclaimed neutrality.

In interviewing the former nun (December 21, 1976), I was informed that she had been instructed by her superiors to vote for Nixon in 1968. As she had taken a vow of obedience, she was confused as to what course to take since she most definitely did not wish to vote for Richard Nixon. When she asked her confessor whether she must follow the Cardinal's order, she was informed correctly that the vow of obedience does not extend to taking orders in elections. When she informed her superior of the confessor's answer, her superior stated that while that was true, "A good nun would have followed the Cardinal's orders."

For an amusing, somewhat fictionalized account of the events at St. Basil's and the subsequent trial, see Oscar Zeta Acosta, The Revolt of the CoCockroach People (San Francisco: Straight Arrow Books, 1973). Acosta was the defense attorney for CPLR.

[55]One of the CPLR leadership estimated that in the year and a half of CPLR activity (mid 1969 through 1970),

> ". . . a minimum of between three to five thousand people related, whether they demonstrated or picketed, or wrote letters, or fasted or so many things that happened . . . . There was a midnight march from downtown--from the chancery itself, the headquarters of the Church--to where the Cardinal was living at the time. . . . I don't know who called for it and all of a sudden there were a thousand people there from all over West L.A. The cops couldn't believe it. I know we couldn't."

CPLR also had the support of the Congress on Mexican American Unity, an umbrella group of several Chicanos organizations in Southern California. Hernandez, "Let the Poor People In," and

130

Congress of Mxican-American Unity memorandum on CPLR, December 15, 1969.

[56]Gomez, Somos Chicanos, pp. 167-168.

[57]See Ibid., and Acuna, Occupied America, pg. 257.

[58]Gomez, Ibid., pg. 166. Also see Robert Allen, Black Awakening the Capitalist America (Garden City, New York: Anchor Books, Doubleday and Company, Inc., 1969), for a more elaborate analysis of the reasons for private and public funds being diverted to minority communities.

[59]Gomez, Somos Chicanos, pp. 166-167.

[60]Acuna, Occupied America, pg. 257.

[61]See Jacques E. Levy, Cesar Chavez: Autobiography of La Causa (New York: W.W. Norton and Company, Inc., 1975), pp. 25-27.

[62]Ibid.

[63]See Chapter Two.

[64]Cesar Chavez, "Peregrinacion, Penitencia, Revolucion," in Aztlan: An Anthology of Mexican-American Literature eds. Luis Valdez and Stand Steiner (New York: Vintage Press, 1972), pg. 385.

[65]Horacio Ulibarri, "Social and Attitudinal Charcteristics of Spanish-Speaking Migrant and Ex-migrant Workers in the Southwest," in Mexican-Americans in the United States ed. John H. Burma (Cambridge: Schenkman Publishing Company, Inc., 1970), pg. 31.

[66]See Chapter one, footnotes 57 and 60.

[67]See Grebler, Mexican American People, pp. 112-117.

[68]See Peter Matthiessen, Sal Si. Puedes: Cesar Chavez and the New American Revolution (New York: Random House, 1969), pg. 182.

[69]Ibid., pp. 182-183.

[70]Luis Valdez, quoted in Ibid., pp. 128-129.

[71]Note the importance of the Virgin in Mexican history. See Chapter Two.

An example that parallels the Virgin of Guadalupe and Mexicans is the St. Stephan's Crown of Hungary. This religious symbols is also a symbol of legitimacy for the Hungarian government—including an ostensibly communist government. The United States returned the Crown in the late 1970's to the Hungarian government after repeated requests.

[72]I asked The head of the National Farm Worker Ministry, why the UFW uses religious symbolism in its marches, strikes, etc., and he stated that "Cesar Chavez is a deeply Catholic person. He believes long struggles need spiritual vitality. people draw strength from the Catholic liturgy. It's more important to farmworkers but its also important to eveybody—even atheists." Interview, January 8, 1977.

[73]Cesar Chavez, quoted by Hurtado, "An Attitudinal Study," pg. 105. Emphases are Hurtado's. The full text of the speech can be found in "The Mexican-American and the Church," Voices: Readings From El Grito, ed. Octavio Ignacio Romano-V. (Berkeley: Quinto Sol Publications, 1973), pp. 215-218.

[74]John Gregory Dunne, Delano (New York: Farrar, Straus, and Giroux, 1967), pg. 81.

[75]Ibid., pp. 81-82.

[76]Ibid., pg. 82.

[77]Ibid.

[78]See Patrick Hayes McNamara, "Bishops, Priests, and Prophecy: A Study in the Sociology of Religious Protest," (Ph.D. dissertation, University of California, Los Angeles, 1968, pp. 137-159).

[79]See Grebler, Ibid.

[80]McNamara, "Bishops, Priests, and Prophecy," pg. 136.

[81]Ibid., pg. 137.

[82]Ibid., pg. 138.

[83]Grebler, pg. 465.

[84]Interview, Rev. Hartmire, Janauary 8, 1977.

[85]Ibid.

[86]See Grebler, Mexican American People, pg. 501.

[87]Wayne C. Hartimire, Jr., "The Church and the Emerging Farm Worker's Movement," California Migrant Ministry, mineo, July 22, 1967, pg. 24.

[88]See the National Farm Worker Ministry (NFWM) Newsletter, Vol. 6, No. 1, Spring 1977, pg. 3.

[89]For an elaboration of these points, see Joseph S. Roucek, Social Control (New York: D. Van Nostrand Company, Inc., 1947). See especially Chapter One, "The Nature of Social Control," and Chapter Thirteen, "Conceptual Means of Social Control."

CHAPTER IV

THE CLERGY

Thus far, we have examined the historical relationship between the Church and Chicanos, and have attempted to assess the current relationship between the lay Chicano Catholic and the institutional Church. There is another group which deserves close examination in this study--individuals whose lives are dominated by the Church. Not every individual whom I interviewed who could fit into Group D--i.e., Formal Catholics--was necessarily a member of the clergy. However, there were only two lay persons who could possibly be defined as such, and their complete domination by the Church is debatable. These individuals should not be ignored and will be discussed in the final Chapter which attempts to place them in an overall perspective. The Catholic clergy, whose function it is to oversee and inculcate the rank and file into believing members, is the focus of this Chapter.

The hierarchy and the priests play an important role in the definition of the Church as utilized in this study.[1] The Catholic clergy is a highly organized and (despite notable exceptions) disciplined force through which the Church as an institution functions. Without a clergy, an institutional church will cease to operate according to its own rules--it could dissipate into disorganized individual beliefs.[2]

The power of the clergy has long been recognized by the Catholic Church in its dealings with the Mexican/Chicano population. From the time of Montesinos to Hidalgo to Martinez to McCullough and McDonnell, the institution has sought to hold a tight rein on its clergy. In this study we have previously examined the actions of the above mentioned clergy (and others), but what of the current relationship of the Catholic clergy (both Anglo and Chicano) with the Chicano population? Just as importantly, if not more so, what are the current trends among the Catholic clergy that indicate possible future directions for the Chicano and the Church?

We will begin our discussion of the current relationship of the clergy and the Chicano with a further examination of the United Farm Workers (UFW). As explained in the previous Chapter, the UFW has had a profound impact on the current Chicano movement that extends well beyond the areas of its principal focus. This is especially evident in current Chicano relations to the Catholic Church. The UFW has acted as a catalyst (often indirect) in generating parallel Chicano organizations. Catolicos Por La Raza (CPLR) is a prime example. CPLR in Los Angeles centered a great deal of its initial orientation on attempting to mobilize UFW support. When the Church refused to give its support to the Chicano community, the contradictions of the Church became more apparent to many Chicanos, and the issues vastly expanded.

Chicanos belong to an institutional Church that is international in scope. They have thus been influenced in their relationship with the Church not only by the internal contradictions of the American Catholic Church, but also by external issues such as the internal contradictions of the global Catholic Church—especially in regard to Latin America. While the international influence is still at a nascent stage, it is, as will be shown below, of possibly great future significance.

The Clergy and the UFW

In 1973, the institutional Church (i.e., the Catholic hierarchy) began to officially back the farmworkers' struggles. At that time the Church supported the UFW in its conflict with the Teamsters. The head of the National Farm Workers Ministry noted that this was a critical period—comparable to the beginning of the Delano grape strike of 1965. When the Bishops gave their public backing, there was a great deal of public support which emerged with the bishops' approval.[3]

Had the Church experienced a one-hundred eighty degree turn in less than a decade—or was it following a pattern similar to its past? The Church had shifted its position, although it has not undergone a complete turn. It shifted its position due to the changing secular world—not as a leader but as a follower. By the middle 1970's, to support the farmworkers—by then a demonstrated non-radical trade union organization—was not as controversial or as daring as in the early and mid 1960's. Support for the farmworkers had become a relatively safe issue that was virtually a cause celebre among liberals. This is not to say, of course, that Church support for the farmworkers was unimportant. It was and is important and the farmworkers' union desires and needs the support. In examining the Church's position, its resources and talents that are utilized should not be minimized, nor however, should they be glorified. What is needed here is an analysis of how the apparent change has occurred and lessons for the future.

As noted in Chapters Two and Three, early attempts at farm union organizing were punished by the hierarchical Church (e.g., Fathers McCullough and McDonnell, and Fathers Kenny and Meagher), rather than rewarded. Historically, in Mexico and the United States clerical endeavors to improve the conditions of the various working classes have met similar fates.[4] Was the end of the 1960's and the 1970's a new era of Church leadership in hierarchical responsiveness to the Chicano working class? Apparently such a judgment may be erroneous if the United Farm Workers is used as an example.

When the UFW was first formed (1962) and was facing its greatest difficulties (i.e., 1965--the beginning of the grape strike), the Church's actions could at best be described as non-responsive. Those members of the Church who tried to intercede on behalf of the farmworkers were either punished, or as in the case of Fr. Vizzard, immune from punishment because of organizational insulation. Hierarchical negative reaction to Chicano activities extended beyond their control over the clergy. When the Church itself became a target of protest activities from the Chicano community--much of it related to the Church's insensitivity to the farmworker movement--the Church's response was at first repressive. But finding its position embarrassing the Church attempted a reconciliation.

The attempted reconciliation of the Church and the Chicano population after the activities of CPLR is important. As noted in the previous Chapter, the gains made by Chicanos were not made (ironically) by moral persuasion from the rank and file upon the hierarchy, but through political activism--disruptions--"tactics" that brought disapproval not only from the targeted institution but often from the population who would benefit. The situation between Chicanos and the Church and the gains made is in many respects similar to that of liberal reforms granted by Western societies to their working classes. As Piven and Cloward note, "a placid poor get nothing, but a turbulent poor sometimes get something."[5]

The something that was received included, as indicated in the previous Chapter, the commitment of Church funds, Cardinal McIntyre's retirement, Chicano dialogue about the role of the Church in the community, the appointment of Spanish-surnamed bishops (a point we will return to below), and an apparent resolution of the grape boycott with a committee of the National Conference of Catholic Bishops acting as liaison between the growers and the union. This last point is the object of our immediate attention. Members of the committee included Bishops High Donahoe of Fresno, Joseph Donnelly of Hartford, Connecticut, and Archbishop Timothy Manning of Los Angeles. Monsignor George G. Higgins of Washington, D.C. headed the committee staff.[6] Without the intervention of this committee in 1970, the timely resolution of the strike would have been much more difficult.

The Church's involvement with the farmworkers can thus be traced in a time sequence:

1962 - The beginning of UFW: no strike actions, little or no institutional Catholic Church support; protestant church support from the CMM (later NFWM).

1965 - Beginning of Delano grape strike, "less institutional clerical support," proclaimed neutrality from local and diocesan Church, full support of the CMM.

1969-70 - Bishop committee acts as liaison between the growers and the UFW. Pressure had been mounting on the Church by Chicanos to support and/or intervene in the dispute.

1973 - The Church backs the UFW in its dispute with the Teamsters as to who should be the legitimate trade union of the farmworkers. Eight years after the union began its public struggle, the Church lends its support.

While Chavez sought, courted, and eventually received support, he recognized that it was somewhat cosmetic. In an interview with the Rev. Mark Day, a Franciscan priest who had been appointed Chaplain to the UFW, Chavez noted:

You know there are many changes in the church today. But many of these changes, like the new ritual of the Mass, are merely external. What I like to see is a priest get up and speak about things like racism and poverty. But even when you hear about these things from the pulpit, you get the feeling that they aren't doing anything significant to alleviate these evils. They are just talking about them.[7]

Fr. Mark Day was one of the priests who early in the farm union struggle did more than just talk about the conditions of the farmworkers. He was appointed chaplain to the UFW in 1967. While his appointment ostensibly gave notice that the Church was actively concerned early in the strike, he indicates that it was primarily through the workers' struggle, rather than the Church's benevolence, that he was appointed.

138

Day, who had been working unofficially with the union, indicated that then Bishop Manning didn't like his "style or politics," and told him to leave the farmworkers. Manning intended to appoint another priest to work with the farmworkers-- one who would be less political and who would confine his duties to ecclesiastical affairs. Day stated that a group of farmworkers, principally women, demanded and received a meeting with Manning. The meeting turned into a sit-in which lasted all day. The result was that Fr. Day was appointed union chaplain.[8]

Chavez's United Farm Worker movement was not the only modern labor dispute into which the Church was drawn. Archbishop Lucey of San Antonio, a bishop who has previously been noted as being considered very liberal and sympathetic to Chicano workers,[9] also has made decisions that have had adverse effects on Chicano workers and their clerical supporters. In 1966-67, there were farm union organizing activities in South Texas similar to the events that were gaining national attention in California. The diocese of Brownsville was, at the beginning of that time period, without a resident bishop, although Bishop Humberto Medeiros of Fall River, Massachusetts was scheduled to assume responsibility in mid 1966. Two priests, Father William Killian and Sherill Smith, from the San Antonio Diocese had personally traveled to the Rio Grande Valley to aid the union organizing. When they were subjected to criticism from local clergy, Archbishop Lucey gave them his public support.[10]

Bishop Mederios sent word that he was assuming a neutral position in the labor dispute and that he did not need "outside priests," as the diocese could "handle its own problems,"[11] Archbishop Lucey told his priests (who had since returned to their home diocese) not to return to the Brownsville diocese. The priests, however, were concerned about the fate of the farmworkers and did return. To Lucey, this constituted an act of deliberate disobedience. He ordered the pair to a mandatory retreat. While they did not protest their punishment, four other priests did so publicly. These other priests public protests were also a challenge to the authority of the Archbishop, and Lucey suspended the four priests from their posts.[12]

In this instance it is again demonstrated that priests who do not enjoy what has been termed "organization insulation" (such as did Father Vizzard) can and will be punished for organizing activities on behalf of workers. This is so, especially if their superior defines the official Church position as one of neutrality and finds the clergy's actions detrimental or embarrassing to the diocese. Detrimental and embarrassing here do not necessarily refer to illegal or malicious activities, but to actions that may anger other sectors of the Church's constituency, such as growers and/or other clerics and hierarchy.

Public punishments such as those endured by Frs. Killian and Smith are not the only deterrents to political activism among the clergy. A Chicano priest whom I interviewed in Los Angeles stated that he was punished for his work with the United Farm Workers and for being peripherally associated with CPLR (he attended a few meetings but did not participate in the major demonstrations). He stated that he had been due to be promoted to principal of his high school, but that he was not given the post because of his political views.[13]

These situations in which activist priests find themselves illustrate that one must always be careful to distinguish between the Church as an institution and the conduct of individual clerics whose political activities can at times bring more censure than praise from the institutional Church itself. The possibility of displeasing one's superiors, can have the immediate effect of making one's position, at the minimum, uncomfortable; but more importantly, it can have a chilling effect on one's career through the resultant denial of promotion. This can be a very effective channel for control of the clergy. The clergy soon learn, if they were unaware before, how power can be used in the Church and what issues should be avoided.[14]

Chicano Priests

The reader will note that, with very few exceptions, the priests mentioned in this essay in the United States are predominantly Anglos. Of the 58,300 ordained Catholic clergy in the United States, only an estimated 185 are Chicanos. There are also another 400 other Spanish-surnamed priests, largely immigrants from Latin America and Spain. These figures are taken from a 1978 report by PADRES (a Hispanic clergy group that will be discussed below). According to this source, the demography of Hispanic Catholicism in the United States is as follows:[15]

> *Of the 49 million Catholics in the U.S., 13,123,000 or 27% are Hispanics.

> *Of 350 Bishops in the U.S. only 8, or 2% are Hispanic. Of these only 3 are Ordinaries, Bishops with jurisdictional power. (In 1985 there were 17 Hispanic bishops.)

> *Of 58,300 priests, 585 or 1.04% are Hispanic. Of these only 185 are U.S. born.

*Of 130,800 Women Religious, 14,000 or 11% are Hispanic.

*Of the 27% U.S. Hispanic Catholics, 20% are Mexican American.

*According to the U.S.C.C. Southwest Regional Office for the Spanish Speaking, these are the percentages of Hispanics among the Catholic population:

Diocese of Amarillo, Texas		76%
" " Brownsville, Texas		85%
" " Corpus Christi, Texas		86%
" " El Paso, Texas		73%
" " San Angelo, Texas		73%
" " Tucson, Arizona		75%
" " San Bernadino, Calif.		65%
" " San Diego, California		52%
" " Gallup, New Mexico		75%
Archdiocese of San Antonio, Texas		72%
" " Sante Fe, New Mexico		80%
" " Los Angeles, Calif.		70%
" " New York, New York		55%

In addition to the above dioceses cited with over 50% Hispanic population, the Diocese of Orange (County) has an Hispanic population of approximately 60%,[16] and the Archdiocese of Chicago has an Hispanic population which is increasing rapidly.[17] It is estimated that by the year 2000, over one-half of the U.S. Catholic population will be Hispanic.[18]

These figures are very revealing and also challenging. It is apparent that among United States Catholics, the largest single ethnic group is Chicanos, with other Hispanics becoming increasingly more visible. Why then are there not more Chicano priests? Chicanos are, of course, under-represented in virtually all professions; but this particular under-representation demands an explanation. (If Chicano priests were proportional to their population, there would be about 10,000--far greater than the 185 actually ordained.)

I asked individual members of the clergy why they thought there were not more Chicano priests, and received various replies. Mentioned by several priests were the cultural differences and adjustments that young Chicanos, who feel they have a vocation, would face if they should enter a seminary. Mentioned were such concepts as "educational deficiencies," "cul-

141

tural clash," and "the different environment" that Chicanos face in seminaries, as well as "inadvertent segregation." A list of complaints of Chicano seminarians compiled by the Rev. Juan Hurtado, a Chicano priest, is illustrative:

> . . . because of our culture, traditions and spirituality, we are different. The following are some of the daily problems we meet in the Seminary:
> 1. Attitude of others, e.g., mimicry.
> 2. Lack of comprehension of Mexican ways.
> 3. We have an impression of being ignored.
> 4. We are accused of forming a clique because we often get together at meals.
> 5. They complain about our speaking Spanish.
> 6. There is lack of interest in trying to understand us.
> 7. We have a different attitude toward the Seminary.
> 8. We emphasize a living spirituality which will allow us to maintain a link with our people.
>   a. Education: The University does not offer programs for Chicanos.
>   b. Economic: We feel an economic difference because of our lower family income.
> 9. Our food is a subject of jokes.[19]

Some of these complaints may appear to be minor--but they are not to the young men attending an institution where they expected more exemplary behavior than the secular racism outside of the seminary. One priest with whom I talked stated that he had not encountered discrimination "until adult life and oddly enough it was from among other priests that I began to feel discrimination and get the message. It was quite a shock."[20] Several other priests also mentioned that they considered the Church to be either a former or contemporary racist institution. They often mentioned that historically the Church through its hierarchy, clergy and membership reflected the surroundings in which it existed.[21] As such it exhibited a great deal of racism found in the Southwest where the Chicano population principally resides. For example, one priest noted that a seminary in Colorado do not accept Chicanos as a matter of policy until two decades ago.[22] The racism was also noted by Anglos who were sympathetic (or to be more precise, had solidarity) with Chicanos. An anglo priest who worked with farmworkers noted:

142

I remember going through the seminary. If you were not doing very well--if you were a C student or a borderline B student--if you were not one of the more brilliant students, it was suggested that you go work with the Mexicans. It was very racist. It was not as a punishment but because it was felt that that was where you were best suited.

The clerical caste system is oriented toward the individualistic WASP Horatio Alger myth. Education is to prepare people to be winners. The poor are poor because they are lazy. Before Vatican II, that was the attitude. You didn't go into the priesthood to change society . . . .[23]

The priest's last few comments are important here; and they are alluded to in the seminarians' complaints, especially #8 a.b. Chicanos generally come from a different economic class than do Anglos who attend seminaries. This does not mean that Anglo seminarians are the elite or upper class of society, but many are reared in the middle class while Chicanos are poor, or of the working class.[24] According to Lenski's classic religious study, Catholic clergy tend to be more conservative on political issues than even their own middle class parishioners.[25] Thus the world in which the Chicano seminarians and clergy function is largely different from the barrio from which they may have emerged. Virtually every Chicano priest whom I interviewed recognized this dichotomy. They knew that they wanted to identify with the working class, but that they now lived a middle class existence. Being a priest often gave them a position in which they could serve the community, but it had also separated them from the people by putting them above the masses and making it difficult to live with the people.[26]

One priest who is very active in the Chicano community stated in a "confession" during the interview that he had been a regional officer for a large order and thus conducted business on an expense account that permitted him to live a very affluent life style, both in the United States and abroad:

I live a double standard as a cleric and I guess, as a Mexican American. One of the greatest things that has happened to me, as to my involvement with the United Farm Workers, is an awareness as to where life really is. The things that are of value to farmworkers give you a totally different perspective. You start

143

seeing the dimensions of the gospel. [It has had] a tremendous influence on me.[27]

The reader may be questioning why the above individual needed to work with the farmworkers to experience much of the poverty and life style of many Chicanos. While the exact class background of Chicanos who _did_ become priests is not available, many clerics and lay persons whom I interviewed thought the Chicano clergy were often from a middle class background and did not experience many of the problems of poorer Chicanos.

The Rev. Virgilio P. Elizondo, a Chicano activist priest in San Antonio, notes that the successful Chicano priest candidates were often (but not always) those who had the least solidarity with the Chicano community:

> Many of the native-born, Spanish-speaking priests are rediscovering today that they were forced to sell out their heritage to be ordained. Therefore some of the priests who have completed seminary training are the ones who least identify with their own people.[28]

Bishop Flores, the first Chicano bishop, notes that it is alarming to him the even though there are so few Chicano priests, about half _do not_ want to work in the Chicano community because they do not feel that the training they received in the seminary equips them to work in their community.[29]

This relates to questions that I asked my respondents in regard to their preparation and training to serve their constituency. Most answered that their training was almost wholly philosophical, theoretical, and theological, and that they had for the most part been ordained without being trained to deal with the everyday problems of their parishioners--problems such as unemployment, exploitation, and of persons without proper papers (undocumented workers).[30]

This relates very closely to an issue raised in the previous Chapter, i.e., of which teachings and policies of the Church are emphasized to the Chicano community. My informants indicated that aside from the minimal practical training received in the seminary, they had had little exposure to the social encyclicals other than as part of the routine reading assignments of many papal encyclicals. They had little training on how to relate those encyclicals to the outside world. This is especially true for those whose training came before, or during, Vatican II--and in Los Angeles, sometimes after Vatican II.[31]

144

This information agrees with that reported by Grebler, et al. Seventy-three percent of the pastors of Los Angeles reported that they had no exposure to the social teachings of the Church in the seminary. In San Antonio, only 8% said that they had had no exposure.[32] Knowledge of the social encyclicals, of course, does not mean that the priests will necessarily preach them. Grebler notes that the majority of priest do not speak on topics of social justice. In Los Angeles, the reasons given for not emphasizing the social teachings of the Church were that other topics were more pressing, plus the lack of suitable occasions. In San Antonio the pastors thought the people "not ready" to utilize the social teachings.[33]

Chicano priests recognized that the Church has been, at best, lax in teaching the social messages of the Church. They also recognized that when the clergy were forced to speak out on specific issues, the pastors' proclamations of neutrality were often detrimental to Chicanos. This was noted by several priests whom I interviewed. They stated that the Church had been remiss in teaching its messages of social justice, that the Church had become an "enclave of a certain class of people."[34] It was stated that this was not due to a lack of communication or a desire by the Church not to get involved in political issues. The example most often cited was that the Church's anti-abortion stand was well known and that the Church does try to influence the voters and politicians. One active Chicano priest stated that while he agreed with the Church's position on abortion, it made him very angry when the Catholic bishops appeared to give their unofficial backing to Gerald Ford over Jimmy Carter in the 1976 presidential election based on the abortion issue.[35]

It is significant that when I asked the Chicano priests whether they would give weight to the political opinions of other priests in general (predominantly Anglo), the answer was often a qualified "no." Hurtado notes that there are differences in ideologies that separate the Anglo priest from many of the Chicano priests. For example, the institutional Church is geared toward the tradition salvation theory which emphasizes a narrow conception of spirituality and salvation of one's soul, while Chicano religious are becoming increasingly attracted to the Theology of Liberation which emphasizes that personal and insti- tutional oppression must be eliminated as an aspect of salva- tion.[36] Although those priests who were familiar with the Theology of Liberation said that it possibly had more immediate relevance to Latin America than to the United States, they con- sidered it a development that deserved close attention. (We will explore the Theology of Liberation below.)

The 1960's saw the advent of many Chicano and non-Chicano political activist groups, some of which have been previously discussed in this essay. Chicano priests suffered from many of the same forms of alienation that engendered many of the minority protest groups or "caucuses" which are formed in other institutions and organizations. As a unique minority group they often shared their frustrations and anxieties when they met each other. The need and desire for more formal organizational activity became evident. Father Ralph Ruiz contacted other Mexican American priests in 1969 to meet and to discuss their mutual concerns. In February of 1970 in Tucson, Arizona, twenty-five Chicano priests and other interested parties gathered. The organization which they formed was limited to Chicano priests, and was named Padres Asociados para Derechos Religiosos Educativos y Sociales (PADRES) [Priests Associated for Religious, Educational, and Social Rights]. Others who were not Chicanos or priests could be affiliated as associates or honorary members.[37] As the name of the group implies, it is concerned with more than pastoral duties, but ventures also into secular matters.

From its beginning PADRES has been influenced by the Theology of Liberation, and the concept of "conscientization," a pedagogical device for liberation elaborated upon by Brazilian educator Paulo Freire.[38] PADRES, although an in-house Church organization, has been highly critical of the institutional Catholic Church in its treatment of Chicanos. It seeks to make the Church more accountable to its large and ever increasing Chicano population. A principal program of PADRES has been to increase the number of Chicano and Hispanic bishops in order to increase the number of Chicano priests. Bishop Flores is of the opinion that more Chicano bishops are needed first, then it will be easier to augment the number of priests.[39]

It is, however, unlikely that the number of Chicano/Hispanic bishops will continue to increase rapidly. The availability of Chicano priests vis-a-vis Anglo priests is too small to sustain the present rate of appointments until any degree of parity is reached. Before 1970, there were no Hispanic bishops. In 1985 there were seventeen--an average of about one appointment per year. If the current rate were to be maintained, by the year 2000 there would be nearly 30 Hispanic bishops. It is, however, unlikely that this trend will continue even if it reaches this plateau.[40] Other priests, especially the Irish, presumably will not stand by quietly while Hispanics assume the positions of leadership in some of the more prestigious dioceses of the country. The potential for very divisive internal politics is present.[41] There is no foreseeable possibility that enough clerical vocations will be generated to establish proportional representation for Chicanos in the clergy (at least 10,000 would be needed), or in the hierarchy (if the estimate of one-half of the American Catholic Church being Hispanic by the year 2000 is correct, approximately 170 new Hispanic bishops would be needed to serve the population).

Chicanos will in all likelihood continue to be a population in a virtual missionary status rather than one with a native clergy. (To this point, one issue has not been explored which needs debate, and which should not be decided a priori--i.e., should Chicanos want to become priests; is this in the best interests of the Chicano population as a whole? We will address this larger question in Chapter Five.)

PADRES, as a group, appears destined to be a minority organization in racial, social, and political terms. It is also a group which explicitly recognizes the relation between religious and political development. In this group there is an obvious connection between the individual's religious beliefs and political beliefs. Most saw this connection themselves. They realized that their moral beliefs influence their political direction and parameters. The influence was not that of preferring one candidate over another, but rather of how one views political systems--i.e., how systems could be moral or immoral. Unlike their counterparts in CPLR, who also recognized that there may be a connection between their religion and politics, the clergy did not view religion as personally conservatizing but as politically progressive, or having a high potential for progressive politics. They were not implying that they were conservative before, but rather that the Church and religion guide their activities; and their often left-of-center political beliefs were given direction by their religion. The evidence here is somewhat contradictory because they often noted that other Chicanos (and as previously noted, non-Chicano Catholics) could and do interpret the application of the Church's messages differently. Comments by the clergy would be illustrative. (These are excerpts from answers to the question--Do you feel that there is any connection between your religious and political beliefs--and/or the changes you have undergone? How about other people, especially Chicanos, do you feel that there is a connection between their religious and political beliefs?)

> To me religion and politics are very tied in. I've told you how I view Christianity. I believe Christianity is a revolutionary force in the world. It could lead to violence [not killing] in the extreme. To our people, the old

religion has been an impediment--it's still being preached [that way] by some.[42]

Connection? Sure, no doubt, my position is influenced by religion and it has to be. I think that it is necessary in the structure of our lives that we have some meeting in our positions and beliefs, otherwise we will be divided.[43]

Yes [personally], not generally in other people--not in fact in many cases; there should be. I think that's the problem--some people fail to see the link.[44]

Yes, I'm traditional but leftist. . . . I'm for having a priest left. My involvement has made me more sophisticated--not naive about power.[45]

[A priest from Spain noted.] I wasn't exposed to political thinking in Spain. My approach to political issues comes from my Christain life-- it commits myself to social issues.[46]

It is mostly in social issues that I have seen the greatest change [personally]. Attitudes influence one or the other--they both influence each other. There've been political issues that have made me consider religion and vice versa.

[In regard to other Chicanos.] Some yes, some no. It can be seen obviously in Cesar Chavez--the politics and religion. I would say no in general--I wouldn't say that there is a connection. I wish there were, but that doesn't make it so.

I see a dichotomy where the Chicano community who are pious disassociate themselves from the political in their minds. They think that there shouldn't be the connection. That distresses me. I run into Chicanos who are politically active who have written off religion. I would like to unite. Being religious means giving a damn about what happens.[47]

No, [personally]. Not necessarily [in other Chicanos].[48]

The influence that most priests see is of their morality guiding their vision of justice. While there was not a definite consensus on the impact of the Church on other Chicanos, the trend that was noted was that the Church appears to be conservatizing rather than liberalizing. In other words, the Chicano priests were often in a political vanguard, not only among the Anglo priests, but also among Chicanos with whom the priests have contact (i.e., those who attend services most frequently).

While the term "liberalizing" has been used here--and while essentially correct--it may well be too weak to fully capture the views of about half of the priests I interviewed.

Many whom I interviewed saw modern capitalism as morally inferior to socialism. This view of socialism, however, was not primarily based on Marxism, but rather on an interpretation of the social encyclicals and other social teachings of the Church. One priest mentioned that he had no problem with Marxist economics, but rather with "atheistic communist prescriptions." In the discussions with the Chicano priests it was clear that the dominant political ideology ranged from moderately liberal, to a left liberalism that sometimes contained elements of socialism.[49]

It needs to be reiterated that the limited number of formal Catholics (primarily clergy) who have left-liberal and socialist tendencies appear to be strongly influenced by their interpretation of the social encyclicals, social teachings of the Church, and the new theologies, such as the Theology of Liberation.

The Social Encyclicals

While it is outside the present scope of this study to give an exhaustive critique of all the social teachings of the Church, it is necessary to present a brief review and analysis of the major documents--lest a misconception be inferred regarding the concept of "liberation." The possible mispreception is that this promotion of Church-generated liberalism or liberation can or will lead to actual liberation. As one examines the Church documents, the case for liberation becomes less and less clear. An analysis of the documents suggests that there are limits in both theory and practice that may necessarily preclude the successful systemic transformation of society. If such is the case, then the Church can be said to be an effective form of social control of the left.

For example, Pope Leo XIII's 1891 encyclical, Rerum Novarum, the first of the great modern labor-oriented social encyclicals, is consistently cited as a document stressing the right of the working man to organize. It does state that workers have the right to organize, but it does not emphasize the right of the workers to struggle, and it does emphasize the right of the owners of property (including capital property) to own and accumulate private property. The encyclical negates class struggle and emphasizes worker-owner cooperation. Socialism is specifically rejected.

The rationale of the right to private property is carried to the point of making it a precept of justice and a part of being human.

> . . . the remedy they propose [they=socialist, remedy=community of goods] is manifestly against justice. For every man has by nature the right to possess property as his own. This is one of the chief points of distinction between man and the animal creation.[50]

A second major social encyclical, Quadragesimo Anno, by Pope Pius XI was written in 1931 on the fortieth anniversary of Rerum Novarum to echo and amplify its message. It called for the creation of Catholic unions, while at the same time stating that strikes and lockouts should be forbidden. Noting the failure of laissez-faire economics to achieve justice in the capitalist world, it called upon the state to regulate the economy to insure a just distribution, including "just wages" to the working man. In response to a growing "Christian socialist" movement, the Pope stated that even if socialism did not engage in class warfare and was not repressive, it would still be unacceptable to the Church. The Pope's message is explicit and unmistakable:

> We pronounce as follows: whether socialism be considered as a doctrine, or as a historical fact, or as a 'movement,' if it really remain socialism, it cannot be brought into harmony with the dogmas of the Catholic Church. . . . 'Religious socialism,' 'Christian socialism' are expressions implying a contradiction in terms. No one can be at the same time a sincere Catholic and a true socialist.[51]

Social encyclicals by John XXIII, the father of the Second Vatican Council, demonstrate a humanitarian concern for the world's poor, as well as a desire for justice. Justice, however, includes the continuation and perpetuation of the "divine wisdom"[52] of private property, including capital property. In his works, Mater et Magistra and Pacem in Terris, John XXIII continues and elaborates upon the themes of Rerum Novarum and the changing condition of the world since that seminal social encyclical. While calling for greater justice (evolutionary not revolutionary) he makes it quite clear that the

> . . . unregulated competition which so-called liberals espouse or the class struggle in the Marxist sense, are utterly opposed to Christian teachings and also to the very nature of man.[53]

While calling for state intervention in the economy when necessary, he does not envision a welfare state but one based on the principle of subsidiarity. Quoting Pius XI in Quadragesimo Anno, John XXIII defines subsidiarity:

> It is a fundamental principle of social philosophy, fixed and unchangeable, that one should not withdraw from individuals and commit to the community what they can accomplish by their own enterprise and industry. So, too, it is an injustice and at the same time a grave evil and a disturbance of right order, to transfer to the larger and higher collectivity functions which can be performed and provided for by lesser and subordinate bodies. Inasmuch as every social activity should, by its very nature, prove a help to members of the body social, it should never destroy or absorb them.[54]

Pope Paul VI's encyclical, Populorum Progressio, published in 1967 continues with the theme of the need for world-wide justice espoused by John XXIII's Pacem in Terris. In Paul VI's work, he calls for greater distribution of resources and development of the poorer nations by the richer nations, through direct transfers of wealth, trade relations that benefit underdeveloped nations, and a world body that will oversee and regulate the distribution.[55] With Populorum Progressio the Church has developed fully its vision of the relationships of capitalist society. From its seminal works dealing with employer-employee relationships to those attempting to have global implications, the Church proposes to reform advanced capitalist relationships. While condemning the abuses of capitalism and stating the consistent Church theme that ownership of property entails social obligations, it affirms the right to private ownership of the means of production.

While reaffirming also that Marxism was not an acceptable philosophy,[56] there was one ambiguous passage in Pope Paul VI's encyclical that many in Latin America took as a sign that revolution may be acceptable. Noting that many of the world's population are destitute, and might be led to violence to "right these wrongs to human dignity," Paul VI stated:

151

> It is clear, however, that a revolutionary up-
> rising--save where there is manifest, long
> standing tyranny which would do great damage to
> fundamental personal rights and dangerous harm
> to the common good of the country--produces new
> injustices, throws more elements out of balance
> and brings on new disasters. A present evil
> should not be fought against at the cost of
> greater misery.[57]

While the thrust of the entire encyclical and this passage
is that evolutionary not revolutionary change is desirable, the
underlined portion of the above (my emphasis) caused Latin Americans on the right to view the encyclical with alarm and distrust,
while some on the left viewed the encyclical as possible justification for revolution.

The Pope did not intend to lend his approval to violent
revolution and he later clarified his statements to emphasize the
portion above that was not underlined. That is, while there
could be some justification for revolutionary violence, the
aftermath would probably be continued repression or worse.
Therefore, the preferred course in dealing with suffering is that

> We will be able to understand their afflictions
> and change them, not into hate and violence, but
> into the strong and peaceful energy of construc-
> tive works.[58]

All of the encyclicals and clarifying statements of the
popes share certain similarities. The consistent theme is social
justice--defined by the liberal capitalism of the particular era
in which the document was written. These are documents that are
not meant to overthrow capitalism but to save, humanize, and
liberalize capitalism. John XXIII in Mater et Magistra is explicit on this point. He notes that during the period of release
of Rerum Novarum--1891--

> On the one hand, the economic and political
> situation was in the process of radical change;
> on the other numerous clashes were flaring up
> and civil strife had been provoked.[61]

Europe and the New World had been in a continuous flux of spora-
dic class warfare for half a century. Rerum Novarum should not
be viewed as a new breakthrough in political ideology (although
it was in religious theology) that was ahead of its time (as I
heard a few times during the course of my interviews), but rather
an attempt to stop and redirect the existing class struggles.

Quadragesimo Anno reiterates the messages of Rerum Novarum for the Depression era. If one were to re-write Quadragesimo Anno without reference to the deity, to "divine truths" and religious obligations, one would find an almost faithful reproduction of the New Deal era proposals to salvage the capitalist order. As with its predecessor, this encyclical was not radical but reflective of the minimum necessities of the times.

John XXIII's and Paul VI's encyclicals follows a similar pattern. Without ethereal references they resemble the policies of liberal capitalism of the Kennedy-Johnson era, complete with programs of international trade unionism, progressive taxation, foreign aid, rural aid, economic development of the Third World, and the establishment of an international monetary fund.

The social encyclicals can thus be seen as a liberalizing influence, but not a radical one (if one defines radical as envisioning a Marxist interpretation). The judgment and analysis of the actual and potential impact on the Chicano community (as well as on others) therefore rests on the more fundamental debate regarding political perspective. Using a liberal analysis, the encyclicals present an opportunity to change the balance of power between the bourgeoisie and the proletariat. The goal for the workers would not be the assumption of power, but the establishment of a trade union, just wages, and a more equitable distribution of resources based on the mutual obligations and rights of both management and labor. This has been essentially the type of application of the social encyclicals attempted by the UFW and Cesar Chavez. As mentioned earlier, Chavez's first encounter with social justice theory came mainly from Father McDonnell's teaching of the social encyclicals.[60] The impact of the encyclicals, of course, is not direct for most of the Chicano community, but tangential and indirect, e.g., through the political support raising that has occurred in the Chicano community due to the UFW activities.

It must be remembered, however, that the teaching of the encyclicals, especially to the lay population, is not a normal occurrence and it is only through the extraordinary efforts of such men as Father McDonnell that the encyclicals were disseminated.

A radical analysis, however, may assert that the encyclicals are emphatically anti-socialist and therefore should not be considered as progressive--but as conservative. Such an analysis may well be incomplete, however. When examining the encyclicals, one does perceive their anti-socialist direction, and in noting the time period of their issuance, could interpret their impact as diverting actual and potential revolutionary activity. However, it is possible that the encyclicals could be used as a liberal means to a radical end. When examining the concrete application (in this case with the UFW) one finds that in the previous absence of successful organizational activity--especially with a population that has a "religious-oriented culture"[61]-- the utilization of these encyclicals may well be effective in organization, education, and propaganda. This is not because the implementation of the encyclicals should be the final goal (within a radical analysis), but that it is useful, if properly applied, in demonstrating contradictions while in the interim possibly alleviating some adverse conditions.

This does not mean that the social encyclicals are progressive in the abstract, but rather in a situation as described above. It is entirely possible, however, to interpret the encyclicals in such a manner that they retard social change. Again this interpretation would depend on its concrete application. In a situation where reforms instituted at a secular or clerical level are moving beyond the intent of the encyclicals, they could then be used to restrict the political parameters. For example, Atilio Garica Mellid, in his book, Revolución nacional o comunismo, states that those who favor land reform in Latin America have misinterpreted the intentions of Vatican II. In addition, he uses the encyclicals, Rerum Novarum and Quadragesimo Anno, to prove that the Church is the initiator of social ideas and "hasn't asked for the help of liberalism or socialism."[62]

Religious teachings that directly address secular concerns (e.g., labor relations) through application of "eternal truths" are, of course, actually dealing with changing variables beyond the particular religion's control. If one is interested in political change, the decision on whether to utilize the Church's teachings should be made on their concrete application, not on their ideological incompatibility with preconceived notions. This decision to utilize Church resources is a question of tactics, which should be flexible to meet the existing situation.

The Theology of Liberation

The encyclicals then are potentially liberalizing or conservative, depending on their application. But what of other Church teachings that purport to be liberating, such as the Theology of Liberation? What is its present and potential impact, especially for the Chicano population? It should first be noted that the Theology of Liberation lacks the authority of the papacy. A principal theoretician of theology of liberation is Gustavo Gutierrez,[63] although there are others, including lay persons who

expound upon this theology.[64] It is more the theoretical creation of professional theologians than an attempt to influence
ecclesiastical and secular policy from the Vatican.

In fact, by the mid 1980's, it had become increasingly
apparent that the Vatican's position under Pope John Paul II was
becoming anti-Theology of Liberation. In his travels to Latin
America and from the Vatican, the Pope has envolved from a position in 1979 that Liberation Theology per se is not necessarily
incorrect, but it is misguided, to questioning its theological
worth by 1984.[65] The Pope has not yet officially condemned
Liberation Theology, but that may well be the direction in which
he is headed. Liberation Theology remains popular among many in
Latin America and a serious battle looms over its future. The
international implications of that battle will be the focus of
future studies.[66] For our purposes here its is important to note
that PADRES is highly influenced by the Theology of Liberation.
The individual members whom I interviewed range from an enthusiastic commitment to one of limited support.[67]

Fundamentally, the Theology of Liberation attempts to link
society and the Church, not as separate entities but as interre-
lated phenomena. It states that the Church must simultaneously
promote human society and the gospel. There is no dichotomy
between spiritual and temporal existence. Eternal salvation is
linked to secular liberation. Liberation has various levels of
meaning,

> . . . the political liberation of oppressed
> people and social classes; man's liberation in
> the course of history; and liberation from sin
> as [a] condition of a life of communion of all
> men with the Lord.[68]

It thus calls for the liberation of man from sin, not narrowly
defined as only offenses against God, but greatly expanded to
include activity in society that prevent the individual, the
community, and the spiritual entity from realizing fully their
potential. It accepts a partial Marxist analysis but usually
stops far short of revolutionary activity.

In Latin America those who advance to revolutionary tactics
and activity, such as Father Camilo Torres, do so eventually
outside of the official Church,[69] as well as outside the group
who are in the forefront of the Theology of Liberation.[71]

The issue of tactics is of prime importance to this essay.
That is, what are the tactics that are acceptable to those who
believe in Liberation Theology? It would be possible to debate

the merits of Liberation Theology from a theological perspective, but that controversy is more appropriately the focus of another work--one that would be primarily concerned with theology and philosophy. It should be noted, however, that the number of clergy and other formal Catholics who constitute the followers of Liberation Theology are in a minority, both in the United States[71] where Liberation Theology is still in its infancy, and in Latin America where it is slightly better organized.[72]

For the purpose of this study, it is assumed that the followers of the Theology of Liberation have some basis in fact for their argument that the Theology of Liberation is a viable, workable theology qua theology. If we were to argue here that it was not theologically valid, then the Church (based on its history in Latin America) could be dismissed out of hand as a politically liberating force. From a political point of view, the most important question is, as a liberating philosophy, what are its directions and goals, and ultimately what is its usefulness?

Since the Liberation Theology influential among Chicano priests is of a Latin America variation, it is perhaps useful to explore briefly its attempted utilization in South America before discussing its applicability in the United States. As mentioned above, those Christians who become revolutionary or militant, not just liberationist, do so outside of the Church, and usually without the approval of those in the forefront of theoretical Liberation Theology. Thus a major criticism of Liberation Theology should be in regard to tactics. When one has a "more or less Marxist inspiration,"[73] one is more likely than less to be inclined to view the potential for revolutionary (including defensive) violence with a particular abhorrence. (The argument here should not be interpreted that revolutionaries are by nature violent or favor violence--rather that if one is in a politically revolutionary situation, one must be prepared for self-defense.) An abhorrence to violence can create a situation that makes effective liberation activity improbable, and may worsen an already dangerous situation.

In Latin America, where there are revolutionary situations, revolutionary groups, fascist coups, etc., to speak of liberation in metaphysical terminology without preparing for realpolitik is to engage in counter-revolutionary activity. I use the term counter-revolutionary here as does David Harvey--not to denote reactionary politics but that which obfuscates reality. According to Harvey, counter-revolutionary theory is

> A theory which may or may not appear grounded in
> the reality it seeks to portray but which ob-
> scures, beclouds and generally obfuscates

(either by design or accident) our ability to comprehend that reality. Such a theory is usually attractive and hence gains general currency because it is logically coherent, easily manipulable, aesthetically appealing, or just new and fashionable; but it is in some way quite divorced from the reality it purports to represent. A counter-revolutionary theory automatically frustrates either the creation or the implementation of viable policies. It is therefore a perfect device for non-decision making, for it diverts attention from fundamental issues to superficial or non-existent issues. It can also function as spurious support and legitimization for counter-revolutionary actions designed to frustrate needed change.[75]

The literature on the role of the Church in Latin America supports the contention that as attractive and appealing as the Theology of Liberation may appear, it tends to obscure many of the real issues in the political arena, such as imperialism, exploitation and the fundamental questions of power and class and struggle.[75] This is true even of the literature which is highly sympathetic to the Church's progressive wings.[76] The Theology of Liberation may well present goals and some values isomorphic with socialist (including Marxist) analysis. But without tactics that are based on concrete reality, its political efficacy is problematic.[77] Attempts at liberation often become a declaration of human decency rather than the struggle for political power.

It is perhaps significant that in a country (Cuba) where the Theology of Liberation would appear to have fertile ground for growth, it is not seen as viable. Archbishop Francisco Oves of Havana was a former classmate of Gustavo Gutierrez and is familiar with the Theology of Liberation. However, a PADRES member who visited Cuba notes that "Liberation Theology is not seen as applicable in Cuba where socialistic liberation has already been achieved."[78]

But what of the United States? What impact can theology of liberation have in a country that does not appear to have the domestic repression of Latin America? Does it have the same apparent counter-revolutionary tenets that are potentially applicable in Latin America? I would argue that this may not be the case for the United States. It is quite possible that an "aesthetically appealing" theory, that turns out to be counter-revolutionary because it is in a revolutionary situation, may well play a progressive role in a nation where there is currently limited revolutionary potential. Note that "progressive role" is

mentioned rather than "revolutionary role." It is unrealistic to
expect that Chicano priests, or PADRES, will engage in revolutionary activities. However, they have been engaging in secular
activities well beyond their normal priestly duties. A current
example of this activity is seen in organizations such as COPS
and UNO.

Both of these organizations, while not started by the Church
per se, have been greatly influenced by the Catholic clergy.
Both are organized on the community action organization principles of Saul Alinsky, and attempt to involve grass roots citizens who may not normally become community activist (e.g., non-
youth, permanent community residents). The people who belong to
these organizations are not recruited as individuals, but as
members of pre-existing groups. The prior groups most effectively recruited are Church congregations--principally Catholic
parishes.

The Communities Organized for Public Service (COPS) is based
in San Antonio, Texas, and consists of thirty-seven local units,
of which thirty-two are Catholic parishes.[79] COPS estimates that
it had 5000 people participating at various times. COPS is able
to attract followers and active participants by concentrating on
grass roots contemporary issues rather than on vague promises.[80]

United Neighborhoods Organization (UNO) is based in Los
Angeles and consists of thirty-two different church organizations, of which twenty-two are Catholic. UNO has followed the
example of COPS and concentrates on grass roots issues such as
pedestrian cross walks and response time from the police. The
group focuses upon issues that can be won in a reasonable amount
of time and have a direct impact on the community. An issue the
group has confronted, and won, is that of the high automobile
insurance rates of East Los Angeles. By focusing its attention
and efforts on the insurance issue, it was able to lower the
rates up to 38%.[81] While the organization itself operates on the
concept of individual self-interest, it is also concerned with
improving conditions collectively:

> Our whole objective is the empowerment of peo-
> ple. You ought not to be subjected to any kind
> of domination--whether from the church or pol-
> itical systems or economic structures.[82]

Neither of these groups is considered radical, but they
could be described as progressive. They are not, to any large
degree, incorporating the young who in the recent past have led
many of the more radical protest movements--but rather the older,
middle-aged resident. This may possibly make them a politically

useful element in the Chicano community. The incorporation of the politically disenfranchised (not narrowly defined by voting) means that people who may not otherwise be organized have the opportunity to become active, to participate and to learn political organization. It is doubtful that most of the goals of the organizations can be realized—as is no doubt recognized by the leaders. However, the potential exists for developing grass roots organizational skills—skills that would not have been generated without the Chicano clergy's active involvement in the community.

Summary

Before proceeding to the final assessment and conclusions of the next Chapter, it is useful to examine briefly some of the highlights of this Chapter. The institutional Church's relationship to the Chicano population has changed somewhat dramatically in the last two decades, and its influence and potential influence on the Chicano is shifting both in intensity and direction.

The changes in the relationship are dramatic because of the previous dearth of institutional commitment. In regard to the UFW, the Church has shifted from de facto localized opposition and proclaimed neutrality to one of open support that includes the utilization of resources—monetary and personnel. In regard to hierarchical representation, the Church has shifted from having no Chicano or Hispanic bishops to the point where it currently has seventeen, a few of which are ordinaries.

As we have seen, the changes in the Church's position have been largely through the critical activities of the Chicano population. This activity has been indirect, e.g., through the pressure generated by the United Farm Workers, or direct, i.e., through the pressures of such groups as CPLR. Both of these groups are outside of the Church. While the Church is changing, it is following patterns that were discussed in Chapters Two and Three; i.e., the Church is responding to outside pressures rather than initiating and leading its "flock."

A significant issue that emerges from this Chapter is that of activist priests. It was shown that priests who are actively involved in political, economic, and social issues are on the periphey of the Church and do not constitute the core of the Church. Priests who are in the forefront of political activity are often punished by the Church precisely for that activity. This was demonstrated not only in this Chapter, but also in the two previous Chapters.

159

While we have already discussed the hierarchy of the Church in regard to the Chicano, more importantly, on a daily basis, is the clergy in the field. The most striking thing about the Chicano priests is their numbers. Considering the number of Catholics who are Chicano, the fewer than two hundred Chicano priests make Chicanos a virtual missionary population. The reasons for the lack of Chicano priests vary from overt institutional racism (historical and contemporary) to the lack of desire for most Chicanos to become priests. The discrepancy between the number of priests that would be expected proportional to the population (10,000) and the actual number (185) cannot be attributed solely to racism in the seminaries, but also to the entire spectrum of relationships that have created the weak commitment among Chicanos to the institutional Church.

Given the changing demographics of the membership of the Church, the effects of the lack of Chicano priests may well be more dramatic on the Church than on Chicanos. In the Southwest, currently, and the nation in the near future, the Church may need the Chicano more than Chicanos need the Church. The lack of Chicano priests (and no real possibility for parity) will be an issue that may well haunt the institutional Church in the years ahead.

Chicanos who are currently priests contribute greatly to the criticism of the Church, and are working on methods to increase the numbers of priests (a question we will discuss in the next Chapter) and simultaneously attempting to improve the secular conditions of Chicanos. As discussed in the body of this Chapter, the theological concepts that guide many Chicano priests and their organization PADRES have political limitations and uses depending on their concrete application. The same principles used in the nations of Latin America may well be counter-revolutionary and therefore, be of negative value if one foresees the need for revolutionary change and the potential for revolution. The application of these principles in the United States, however, is more ambiguous. With the lack of mass revolutionary activity these principles may play a progressive role, especially since they are targeted at a population that is not radical to begin with--Church members. The progressive role, of course, is not a revolutionary one.

There is always the possibility (if not likelihood) that Church sponsored organizations such as UNO and COPS could become counter-revolutionary if indeed a potentially revolutionary situation evolved. At the present, however, these organizations could be said to play a progressive role that is similar to the UFW, i.e., they organize the heretofore unorganized portion of the population, they concentrate on grass roots issues, and improve slightly the living conditions of their constituency. Like the UFW, however, they have limited goals, are not radical, but have the potential to radicialize individual members.

In summary, the political function of the Church is not only that of promoting conservatism. In some cases, it does promote liberalism. What must be discussed further is whether this liberalism is compatible with Chicano liberation. If there are contradictions, and there appear to be many, they must be examined.

[1]See the definition of the Catholic Church in Chapter One.

[2]For an illustration of this see, especially in regard to the Mexicano, the instance of the Church strike in Mexico in Chapter Two.

[3]Interview, January 8, 1977.

[4]See numerous examples in Chapters Two and Three, passim.

[5]Frances Fox Piven and Richard A. Cloward, Regulating the Poor: The Functions of Public Welfare (New York: Vintage Books, 1971), pg. 338.

[6]See Joan London and Henry Anderson, So Shall Ye Reap (New York: Thomas Y. Crowell Company, 1970), pg. 163.

[7]Cesar Chavez in an interview with Mark Day, February 1973, in Sam Kushner, Long Road to Delano (New York: International Publishers, 1975), pp. 120-121.

[8]Interview, January 18, 1977.

[9]See Chapter Two.

[10]See Patrick H. McNamara, "Bishops, Priests, and Prophecy," (Ph.D. dissertation, University of California, Los Angeles, 1968) pp. 148-149.

[11]Ibid., pg. 151.

[12]Ibid., pg. 155. Stan Steiner in his book, La Raza: The Mexican Americans (New York: Harper and Row, 1969), notes that Lucey's actions caused discontent and frustrations among the Chicano community. Steiner quotes Paul Rodriquez, an 'elder of the barrios of San Antonio' as stating,

> "I feel that the Church in San Antonio has been grossly derelict in its Christian duty. Especially I condemn Archbishop Lucey, I wish I could do it in person. Sometime, maybe, the Lord will give me the opportunity. he has persecuted the few priests who have fought for the poor, who have sacrificed their priesthood. In my own parish the priests say: We can't get

involved in politics. The Archbishop doesn't like it. It's not politics. It's religion. It's Christianity" (pg. 350).

It is somewhat ironic that Archbishop Lucey has been singled out "especially" for criticism, since he is one of the few bishops who have demonstrated concern for Chicano problems.

[13]Interview, November 6, 1976. This priest indicated that during the Proposition 14 campaign of 1976, i.e., to give California farmworkers stronger organization opportunities, the Archdiocese discouraged the clergy's active participation. He also stated that the pastor did not let him put up a big sign supporting Proposition 14, although a smaller sign was approved. The priest said that he agreed to settle for the small sign since, "I have to live in peace with the people I live with."

For an example of how the Union used religious symbolism in the Proposition 14 drive, see the Los Angeles Times, May 1, 1976. Bishop Arzube, auxiliary of Los Angeles, publicly supported Proposition 14 in a letter to the Los Angeles Times, September 15, 1976.

[14]The situation could be compared to what Peter Bachrach and Morton S. Baratz discuss in Power and Poverty (New York: Oxford University Press, 1970). That is, the bishops of each diocese have the latent power to punish priests for activities that are not technically wrong. The bishops can make the activities (e.g., organizing) wrong and then punish the perpetrator. By the time the activities are defined as illegal, the priest may be too involved to merely obey the bishop and leave his chosen task. Comments by several priests in the previous readings indicate that they recognize that the bishop is legislator and judge, and therefore, it is best not to get involved. A non-decision as such is neutral--or, in other words, to do nothing and act as if the situation was not within their domain. The priests have learned--to use a metaphor used by Robert Paul Wolff and Ira Katznelson--which issues and actions are on the political plateau of acceptability and which one not. The result is that most priests will not engage in actions that actualize social justice principles which they may discuss. Katznelson borrows from Robert Paul Wolff, "Beyond Tolerance" in Wolff, Barrington Moore, Jr., and Herbert Marcuse, A Critique of Pure Tolerance (Boston: Beacon, 1965), pg. 44ff, in Ira Katznelson, Black Men, White Cities (Chicago: University of Chicago, 1973), pg. 139.

The objective impact of such priestly "non-action" is support of the status quo.

[15]Hermanas - PADRES National Encuentro News Release, August 15, 1978, San Antonio, Texas.

[16]Los Angeles Times, March 31, 1976, pg. 1.

[17]See Fr. Manuel Martinez, OFM, "The Perspective of the Hispanic Community" in Entre Nosotros: Informes de Hermanas y Padres 1 (Fall 1978): 10. Martinez notes that in the last ten years the number of Hispanic parishes has increased from seven to seventy-five in the Archdiocese of Chicago.

[18]Two of the priests I interviewed so indicated. The estimate is very reasonable when one considers that the fastest growing minority in the United States is Chicanos and other Latinos. Latinos are expected to be the largest minority in the United States before the end of the 1980's, and California is expected to have a majority of third world residents before the beginning of the 21st century.

[19]Juan Hurtado, An Attitudinal Study of Social Distance Between the Mexican American and The Church (San Antonio: Mexican American Cultural Center, 1976), pp. 30-31.

[20]Interview, March 2, 1977.

[21]Several interviews with the clergy. Various examples are cited in Chapter Two, passim.

[22]Interview, December 10, 1976.

[23]Interview, January 18, 1977.

[24]For a profile of United States priests see Andrew M. Greeley, Priests in the United States (Garden City, New York: Doubleday, 1972).

[25]Gerhard Lenski, The Religious Factor (Garden City, New York: Doubleday, Anchor Books, 1961, 1963), pg. 307.

[26]Various interviews.

One priest especially noted that even though he lived in the middle of an East Los Angeles barrio, his lifestyle as a priest meant that he lived differently. When I discussed his salary, he stated he only made about $4000, but that the figure was meaningless because of his office, room and board, housekeeper, etc. Interview, November 6, 1976.

[27]Interview, November 19, 1976.

[28]Rev. Virgilio P. Elizondo, Christianity and Culture (Huntington, Indiana: Our Sunday Visitor, Inc., 1975), pg. 139. David Gomez, a former priest, makes the same point more forcefully and on a personal level in his Somos Chicanos: Strangers in Our Own Land (Boston: Beacon Press, 1973), pp. 14-27.

Albert Carrillo, who is also a priest, states in "The Sociological Failure of the Catholic Church Toward the Chicano," The Journal of Mexican American Studies (Winter 1970), that the Chicano priest must often be willing to "live in a semi-schizophrenic state" because the methods he must use are often irrelevant to the Chicano people (pg. 80).

[29]Transcript of "Mexican...And American" telecast, National Broadcasting Company, Inc., airdate, February 15, 1976, pg. 14.

[30]Several interviews. The comment of Bishop Flores in Ibid. is illustrative here:

> "I know that I took many courses in the seminary for which I have never had any need, that really did, in no way, prepare me to be effective with my apostolate be it in the barrio, the jail or other institutions. And I personally feel that the seminary courses have to be oriented toward the service that the future priest is going to be expected to render" (pg. 14).

[31]One former seminarian (for two and one-half years) whom I interviewed noted that he received some "social problems training" from a Jesuit but that he was an "exception to the rule." This individual pointed out that in Los Angeles under Cardinal McIntyre there was very little social training in the seminaries. Interview, December 10, 1976.

[32]Leo Grebler, Joan W. Moore, and Ralph C. Guzman, The Mexican American People (New York: The Free Press, 1970), pg. 470. The knowledge of the social teachings of the Church is also evident among the laity. Andrew M. Greeley and Peter H. Rossi in The Education of Catholic Americans (Garden City, New York: Anchor Books, 1966, 1968), note that only 34% of those whose entire education was in parochial schools could identify the social encyclicals. The figure drops to 10% of those Catholics who had no parochial schooling (pg. 256).

[33]Grebler, Mexican American People, pg. 471.

[34]Interviews with several priests.

Nathan Glazer and Daniel Patrick Moynihan in Beyond the Melting Pot (Cambridge, Massachusetts: The M.I.T. Press, 1963), illustrate that the social encyclicals of John XXIII met opposition within the Catholic community:

> "The reaction of some conservative Catholics was disbelief bordering perilously [for a Catholic] on irreverence, as in the celebrated gibe 'Mater si, Magistra no' which appeared in the conservative National Review. The first reaction to the later encyclical of John XXIII, Pacem in Terris, was even more unusual. The Commonweal described the general attitude as follows: 'Of all the responses that Pope John's encyclical, Pacem in terris, could have been expected to arouse, perhaps none has been more startling than the general paralysis which has gripped American Catholics in the fact of its implicit "opening to the left." For once it seems impossible to find any significant support for an important part of a major encyclical'" (pg. 285 [emphasis added]).

[35] Interview, December 10, 1976.

[36] Hurtado, An Attitudinal Study of Social Distance, pg. 31.

[37] For more information on the beginnings of PADRES see the report of the "PADRES National Congress", February 25, 1975, San Antonio, Texas, pp. 1-9.' Currently other Hispanic priests and brothers are allowed to join as full members.

[38] For elaboration on Paulo Freire and his methods see Paul Freire, Pedagogy of the Oppressed (New York: Herder and Herder, 1968, 1972); and the LADOC 'Keyhole' Series #1, Paulo Freire (Washington, D.C.: Division of Latin America-United States Catholic Conference, n.d.)

[39] Bishop Flores in "Mexican...And American," pg. 13.

[40] Assuming that Hispanic clergy, including Chicano clergy, will be recruited and will therefore double to 1000 (a very generous assumption considering that the total number of seminarians is decreasing--the Denver Post, July 26, 1985, reported that were only 11,655 seminarians in 1983, down from a peak of 49,000 in 1965), then one of thirty-three Hispanics will be bishops while (if the total number of priest remain constant-very unlikely) only one of 150 Anglos will become bishop.

[41]Being a bishop is, of course, a highly prestigious and important position in the Catholic Church. Potential candidates for important posts are groomed (just as in many other professions), and individuals promote themselves for these positions. This is perhaps best stated in a lenghty passage by Andrew M. Greeley, a conservative priest, in his Priests in the U.S., pg. 112:

> "it is frequently said that my argument advocates the 'politicization' of the Church, and I am told that all kinds of terrible things will happen when men begin to campaign for episcopal office. This is all to laugh. Only the most incredibly naive would think that the Church is not politicized now, or indeed that any human organization can avoid politicization. Only the most ignorant can think that men do not engage in active campaigns for episcopal appointment and promotion; indeed, it was said of one very prominent American hierarch that his campaign for the office he presently holds was a brilliant and classic example of how one obtains power in the Church, a campaign begun when he was still a seminarian. The question is not whether we will have politics in the Church and in the nomination of bishops, it is rather what kind of politics will we have? Will they be the relatively open and relatively honest politics of democratic processes, or will they be the shadowy, degrading, and frequently corrupt politics of cronyism?"

Hurtado, An Attitudinal Study of Social Distance, cites Robert Anson, "The Irish Connection," New Times 2 (10): 29-33, to show where the distribution of power currently lies in the American Catholic Church. The United States Catholic population is currently 17% Irish, yet they have 35% of the priests and hold 51% of the posts of Bishops (pg. 30).

[42]Interview, November 6, 1976. In anwer to a previous question, the priest stated that the political role of the Church was "not necessarily to get at specific issues but to have guidelines to clairfy ideology. It should be obvious on morality, but shouldn't tell people to vote yes or no on specific issues."

[43]Interview, November 9, 1976 A.

[44]Interview, November 9, 1976 B.

[45] Interview, December 10, 1976.

[46] Interview, December 14, 1976.

[47] Interview, March 2, 1977.

[48] Interview, January 10, 1977. This was the only cleric who stated that there was no connection. He was also the one who appeared to have been in the past the least active in Chicano political activities.

[49] A few of the priests were quite explicit in their desire for a kind of "socialism:"

Interview November 6, 1976; December 10, 1976; and December 14, 1976. These and other priests mentioned praise for the Chilean government of Salvador Allende and his attempts at peaceful change.

[50] See Pope Leo XIII, "Rerum Novarum (The Condition of Labor)" in Seven Great Encyclicals with an Introduction by William J. Gibbons, S.J. (Glen Rock, New Jersey: Paulist Press, 1939, 1963), pg. 3.

[51] Pope Pius XI, "Quadragesimo Anno (Reconstructing the Social Order)" in Ibid., pp. 158, 159. Pius XI also wrote a ringing condemnation of Communism in "Divini Redemptoris (Atheistic Communism)" in Ibid., pp. 177-215.

[52] See Pope John XXIII, "Mater et Magistra (Christianity and Social Progess)," in Ibid., pg. 242. John XXIIIs "Pacem in Terris (Peach on Earth)" in Ibid., repeats a similar message, pg. 293.

[53] John XXIII, "Mater," Ibid., pg. 224.

[54] Ibid., pg. 230.

[55] See Pope Paul VI, Populorum Progressio (On the Development of Peoples) (New York: Paulist Press, 1967).

[56] While not mentioning Marxism per se, Pope Paul VI appears to be making reference to it in a passage that contains the Church's characterization of Marxist philosophy: "All social action involves a doctrine. The Christian cannot admit that which is based upon a materialist and atheistic philosophy, which respects neither the religious orientation of life to its final end, nor human freedom and dignity," Ibid., pg. 51.

[57]Ibid., pp. 47-48.

[58]Pope Paul VI, "Address to new priests and deacons,"
Bogata, 22 August 1968, quoted in The Church in the Present-Day
Transformation in the Light of the Council-Medellin Conclusions
(Washington, D.C.: Division for Latin America-USCC, 1973), pg.
63.

Also see the Pope's comment on Latin America in Alain
Gheerbrant, The Rebel Church in Latin America (Baltimore:
Penquin, 1974), pp. 80-117.

[59]John XXIII, "Mater," pg. 222.

[60]See Chapter Two.

[61]See Chapter Three.

[62]Quoted in Raymond K. Dehainaut, Faith and Ideology in
Latin American Perspective (Cuernavaca, Mexico: CIDOC, 1972),
pg. 6/9. For further examples of conservative Christian interpretations of Catholic and Protestant documents, including the
social encyclicals, see pp. 6/6-6/13.

[63]See Gustavo Gutierrez, A Theology of Liberation
(Maryknoll, New York: Orbis Books, 1973).

[64]See Alistair Kee, ed., A Reader in Political Theology
(Philadelphia: Westminister Press, 1974); and The Theology of
Liberation, The LADOC 'Keyhole' Series #2 (Washington, D.C.:
Division for Latin America-USCC, n.d.).

Archbishop Helder Camara of Recife, Brazil, is a most influential figure among liberation theologist. His work can be
found in Dom Helder Camara, Revolution Through Peace (New York:
Harper and Row, 1971); and Helder Camara, The LADOC 'Keyhole'
Series #12 (Washington, D.C.: Latin America Documentation-USCC,
n.d.). Also, the works of Paulo Freire are influenced by and
influence liberation theology.

[65]See news reports from the Los Angeles Times between
January 27, 1979-February 25, 1979 and reports from the Denver
Post March 6, 1983, May 15, 1981, September 4, 1984 and September
7, 1984.

[66]See, for example, the NACLA Report on the Americans, Vol.
XIX, No. 5, Sept./Oct. 1985 special issue "Visions of the
Kingdom: The Latin American Church in Conflict."

[67]Besides the interviews with the individual clerics, there is abundant evidence of Liberation Theology support in the PADRES newsletter, published quarterly, and the "PADRES National Congress" report, February 2-5, 1975. The interviews with the clergy as well as with those few leaders who were aware of liberation theology uncovered an interesting note. Some who were attracted to the Theology of Liberation were attracted not only by the theology itself, but by the fact that they perceived it as a Latin (i.e., Hispanic) theology rather than a European theology, where most Church theology originates.

[68]Gustavo Gutierrez, "Notes for a Theology of Liberation" in The Theology of Liberation, LADOC #2, pg. 18.

[69]Father Camilo Torres, who eventually became a revolutionary in every sense of the term, was relived of his priestly duties on June 24, 1965, two days after he requested that such be done. Earlier in the year he had issued a "Platform for a Movement of Popular Unity" to call for greater social equality in Colombia. The Columbian Cardinal, Luis Concha Cordoba, stated that certain points of the document (he never stated which, even in a personal interview with Torres) were "irreconcilable with the doctrine of the Church." Camilo Torres eventually joined the National Liberation Army, a guerrilla organization. On February 15, 1966, he was killed in action. For an account of Camilo Torres' activities see Richard Gott, Rural Guerrillas in Latin America (Middlesex, England: Penguin Books Ltd., 1970), pp. 321-355. For essays by Torres see Father Camilo Torres, Revolutionary Writings, edited with an introduction by Maurice Zeitlin (New York: Harper Colophon Books, 1969).

Camilo Torres is admired by some in the Catholic Left and Marxist Left in Latin America. Among his more famous quotes is, "A Catholic who does not become a revoutionary is living in sin." See Community Action on Latin America (CALA) newsletter, Vol. 4, No. 4, April 1975, pg. 2.

As Camilo Torres was an embarrassment to the hierarchy who attempted to forget him, so too were priests such as Father Francisco Lage of Brazil who resisted the military coup of 1964. See James Petras and Maurice Zeitlin, eds., Latin America: Reform or Revolution? (New York: Fawcett Publications, 1968), pg. 334n.

[70]Camilo Torres emerges from the Liberation Theology literature usually as a sort of folk hero, a myth, who is somehow admirable and seen as principled, but whose tactics are questioned. He is also sometimes portrayed as naive, while still being sincere. For example, see Helder Camara, LADOC #12, pg. 5.

In the interviews with the clergy, similar patterns emerged. Torres was seen as sincere and one whose activities could be understood, but not necessarily one whose revolutionary tactics should be followed.

[71]As indicated earlier, Chicano priests are wary of the political opinions of other priests. One priest indicated that the social encyclicals were ahead of 80% of the American Clergy. The reader should also remember that not all Chicano priests are left-liberal nor do they all work or desire to work in the Chicano community. The impact on the Chicano community of the liberalizing effects of the Church are greatly reduced by the limited number of Chicano priests available, willing, and politically committed.

[72]For accounts of the size and effectiveness of liberation theology, activist priests, and other progressive forces in the Latin American Catholic Church, see Leo Alting von Geusau, "Revolution and Religion: The 'Radical' Church in Brazil," Dialectical Anthropology 2 9February 1978): 21-42; Ivan Vallier, Catholicism, Social Control and Modernization in Latin America (Englewood Cliffs, New Jersey: Prentice-Hall, 1970); David E. Mutchler, The Church as a Political Factor in Latin America (Chapel Hill: University of North Carolina Press, 1971).

[73]See Gutierrez, "Notes for a Theology of Liberation" in The Theology of Liberation, LADOC #2, pg. 18.

[74]David Harvey, Social Justice and the City (Baltimore: John Hopkins, 1973), pp. 150-151.

[75]See, in addition to previously mentioned works by Mutchler, The Church as a Political Factor; Turner, Catholicism and Political Development; and Dehainaut, Faith and Ideology; Lawrence Littwin, Latin America: Catholicism and Class Conflict (Encino, California: Dickenson Publishing Company, 1974).

[76]An excellent source of various current writings on the Latin American Church is the journal LADOC, published by Latin America Documentation of the United States Catholic Conference. See particularly Vol. VII, #6, July/August 1977, pp. 31-56; and LADOC 'Keyhole' Series #13, Latin Americans Discuss Marxism-Socialism (Washington, D.C.: Latin America Documentation-USCC, n.d.).

[77]Metaphysical forms of socialism are of course not new. They precede Marxism and persist today. Marx and Engles critiqued these social ideals and demonstrated their incompatibility

with their analysis--as they themselves defined it. One form of socialism that Marx criticized strongly is remarkably similar to much of the Theology of Liberation literature. In The German Ideology (New York: International Publishers, 1947), Marx and Engles note that German or "True" Socialism of their era was

> ". . . concerned no longer with real human beings but with 'man,' [it] has lost all revolutionary enthusiasm and proclaims instead the universal love of mankind. It turns as a result not to the proletarians but to the most numerous classes of men in Germany, to the petty bourgeoisie with its philanthropic illusions and to its ideologists, the philosophers and their disciples; it turns, in short, to that 'common,' or uncommon, consciousness which at present rules in Germany" (pg. 81).

For further critiques of True Socialism see Ibid., pp. 79-193; Karl Marx, The Eighteenth Brumaire of Louis Bonaparte (New York: International Publishers, 1963), pp. 132, 148; and the Communist Manifesto in Robert C. Tucker, ed., The Marx-Engels Reader, 2nd ed. (New York: W.W. Norton and Company, 1972, 1978), pp. 493-497.

[78]See Rev. Antonio M. Steven Arroyo, "A Padre in Cuba" in PADRES VI:3, Fall 1976 (newsletter).

While the Church does not enjoy the privileges it had in pre-revolutionary Cuba, there is little indication that it suffers from overt repression. See Cuba Review: Church, Theology, and Revolution Vol. V, #3; Alice L. Hageman and Philip E. Wheaton, eds., Religion in Cuba Today: A New Church in a New Society (New York: Association Press, 1971); and CUBA, LADOC 'Keyhold' Series #7 (Washington, D.C.: Division for Latin America-USCC, n.d.).

[79]La Luz Vol. 7, #10, October, 1978, pg. 36.

[80]The Wall Street Journal, July 13, 1977, pg. 1. Among the grass roots issues tackled and won by COPS have been the lowering of a proposed water-rate increase; a $47 million drainage bond issue, zoning victories, and voter registration drives.

[81]See the Los Angeles Times, July 23, 1978, pg. 12, and SOMOS Vol. 1, #1, April/May 1978. For related information on UNO see articles in the Los Angeles Times, September 20, 1977, pg. 8.

[82]Los Angeles Times, July 23, 1978, pg. 12.

CHAPTER V

CONCLUSIONS

In the summary of the previous Chapter, it was stated that this concluding Chapter would be the "final assessment." That was perhaps too strong an assertion. This is rather the beginning of an attempt to understand a complex and continuing historical relationship and process. The Catholic Church has existed for almost two thousand years; Chicano history extends almost five hundred years (if one begins with the conquest of New Spain). Both the institution and the people will exist far into the future. The relationship between them will also continue to exist, but in changed form. One clear message that emerges from the preceding pages is that of change. What the Church purports to deal with is eternal truths and salvation. What it most definitely deals with is people--and that entails changing relationships.

In order to assess the changes that have occurred and the prospects for the future, it is necessary to bring the Church from its metaphysical perch from which it asserts to operate, to the material setting in which it conducts its operations.

This essay is (hopefully) a call for debate on the issues raised in work. As I have noted earlier, there has been very little research conducted on the relationship between the Chicano and the Church. Virtually all that has been done is either by priests or ex-priests.[1] The tone of their writings has usually been that of apologist, loyal opposition, or sometimes bitterness. While these perspectives are useful, they are not sufficient to grasp the complexities of the relationship between a megainstitution and a people whose growing size and concentrated location make them increasingly important to the religious institution and the secular society. To allow only the priest to speak of the institution is akin to allowing only military officers, present or former, to analyze the military.[2]

The works by the clergy show a natural reluctance to criticize the core of the institution, its doctrines and teachings, and prefer to concentrate criticisms on perceived defects of the hierarchical personnel who administer the teachings. Indeed at least two priest-authors note that the doctrines are not subject to criticism, but rather one should criticize the failures of individuals--the "human element."[3] It is apparent that certain subjects remain "sacred cows" in research.[4]

Needless to say, the perspective of this author is different from that of the priests. There are no "sacred cows" in this research and the goal is to bring the ethereal to earth. The point however, is not to engage in captious criticism, but to present an accurate overall picture of the relationship under study. It is not particularly novel, insightful, or courageous to focus on and criticize the human failings or perceived immorality of the Church and/or its clergy. The Church should be examined when it is in its best light, i.e., those teachings that are considered progressive and/or would tend to support progressive movements. Although human failings cannot be ignored, it is not enough to judge the impact of a religion on its worst merits.

As explained in the Introduction, it is also not enough to parrot Marx's "religion is the opium of the people" and to expect that to suffice. Opium and its derivatives have many uses and abuses. The various derivatives of religion also have many uses and abuses. As indicated earlier, Marx saw religion as a fantastic reflection of the real world in the minds of men. He also saw it as serving a dual purpose--both an escape and a protest against the misery of the world.

> Religious distress is at the same time the ex-
> pression of real distress and also the protest
> against real distress. Religion is the sigh of
> the oppressed creature, the heart of a heartless
> world, just as it is the spirit of spiritless
> conditions. It is the opium of the people.[5]

Religion thus serves not only to obscure reality but also to protest it. The religion of the Mexicano/Chicano has been shown historically, and in the present, able to serve as a protest against conditions of real distress. The Church has also been shown to be one of the conditions of the distress. This is not as contradictory as it first seems--the Church is the institution, the religion is the practice of the people. The goal of the Church is to have the two merge, but historically this has not occurred. A Chicano priest who is active in San Antonio notes that:

> Popular piety otherwise know as 'popular
> religiosity' runs deep in Hispanic peoples . . .
> Family religion [as opposed to the official
> ritual of the Church] can, at times, be seen as
> a subtle and quiet, yet strong protest against
> what a minority group may be tolerating in an
> atmosphere of oppression.[6]

174

The "popular religiosity" is similar to what has been termed in this essay the strong attachment to things Catholic (as noted earlier). It is not the same as having a strong commitment to the doctrines and teachings of the institutional Church. The Catholic Church is a complex organization, and a normative institution that demands an intense commitment from its members. In regard to the aggregate Mexican/Chicano population, the Church has failed to establish the strong commitment. As a normative institution it is somewhat ineffective. When one examines the history of the Church from the conquest of Mexico to its present circumstances, it becomes evident why the weak commitment exists. Despite the influx of clergy from Spain to Mexico, the conversion process often entailed minimal instruction but mass baptisms. While this swelled the ranks of Catholics, it did not ingrain in the masses the beliefs of the institution as their own; and the outward forms that were adopted by the neophytes were often duplicates of their former religions.[7]

Historically in Mexico the Church's conduct in regard to the masses was detrimental to their material well-being, and judging from the insurrections, rebellions, and protest that occurred, the people could see the contradictions. The accumulation of Church wealth, the unification of Church and state, the opposition to the revolutions by the Church, the conduct of the mission system, and the conflict between Bishop Lamy and Padre Martinez were not the types of activities that engendered an intense commitment to the institution.[8]

The Bishop Lamy-Padre Martinez dispute is indicative of the relationship between the institutional Church and the Chicano. Throughout its history, and continuing till today, the Church has been almost totally lacking in its desire and commitment to the recruitment of native clergy.[9] This creates a situation where the Chicano population was at first officially, and remains unofficially, a missionary population. After five-hundred years, it is perhaps the most compelling evidence of the absence of mutual commitment between institution and population.

The contemporary missionary designation is important. If indeed it is correct, it contradicts the often held assumption that Catholicism (as an institutionally self-defined religion) is an inherent part of Chicano culture. As defined in Chapter One, culture reflects a people's reality.[10] Religion, according to Marx, is a "fantastic reflection" of the real world. It is clear that Catholicism is a superimposed reflection--one historically imported and maintained by the elite of Spain in Mexico, and one currently maintained by a predominantly Irish hierarchy and overwhelmingly Anglo clergy in the United States.

Anthropologically there are numerous examples where the particular religion can be shown to "reflect" the reality of people[11]--as a "fantastic reflection" to Marxists.[12] These examples, however, are native religions of native cultures. Mexicans/Chicanos as mestizos (less than 10% of Mexicans/Chicanos can be considered Spanish), belong to a Church which does not reflect the real world of their day to day lives. What Catholicism, as an institution, reflected at the conquest was the reality of the missionaries--of cultures that were foreign to the natives of Mexico, and were/are foreign to the Chicanos of the United States Southwest before and after the great periods of migration.

Howard Selsam and Harry Martel in their introduction of Marx, Engels, and Lenin's works on religion note the complexity of Marxist analysis--that religion is seen as a "many-faceted reflection of the real world, including deep-seated human needs for security, consolation, and beauty."[13] We have seen that for the masses of Chicano society the institutional Church did not always provide "security, consolation, and beauty" but often insecurity, confusion, and discrimination. It is not surprising then that historical studies, both secular and ecclesiastical, Catholic and Protestant, saw the Mexicans/Chicanos as "unchurched." Most Mexicans/Chicanos in fact did not attend regular services nor participate in the institutional Church--i.e., according to the Church's own principles.

Mexicans/Chicanos are of course, not homogeneous but heterogeneous. Care must be taken not to replace one myth--that Chicanos are a pious, devout Church-going population, with another myth--that they as a group are not devout or do not attend services. It is obvious that many do. The preponderance of evident, however, indicates that at least half do not attend regular Church services (a conservative estimate). In this regard, Chicanos are thus similar to their Latin American counterparts. Turner notes that most countries of Latin America are over 90% Catholic, yet only 20% attend Mass regularly where priests are available.[14]

As we have seen throughout the body of this work, and as will be expanded upon below, culturally Chicanos do identify themselves as Catholics, but the range of their commitment to the institution and the religion differ--as does the Church's religious impact on Chicano political ideology. Thus far Groups A, B, C and D have been identified separately--also an assessment has been made of the impact of Catholicism on each group's current political ideology. It is now important to attempt to link the groups--not to stereotype the Chicano, but rather to demonstrate the diversity and how it occurs.

Before the synthesis it is perhaps useful to restate how political ideology as a concept is used in this study.[15] Political ideology consists of:

1) A world view. As used here it means an "image of power and process"; i.e., one's understanding of what is happening in the world and why. The understanding may be correct or incorrect but it is the general perspective of the individual who holds the particular ideology.

2) Values and goals. Every ideology has values that are central to its continuation. Some values tend to be more important and critical than others.

> The crucial questions are the way in which such values are understood or defined by the ideology, and how they are ranked in priority when they conflict with each other.

The goals become the specific guideposts, often interim, that attempt to bridge the gap between the values of the society and the present conditions as defined by the world view. A combination of world view, values, and goals, provides a sense of scope and direction of social change to achieve the goals and values that emerge.

3) Tactics for social change. Based then on the world view, the goals and values and the scope and direction needed, certain tactics become acceptable and some do not. Is violence necessary? Does the desired change require or forbid certain activities? Even if some tactics could work, would the cost be too high?

With this conceptualization of ideology, we will attempt to synthesize the material from Chapters Three and Four. Figure 1 is a visual summary of the interviews.

The top line is the political spectrum from left to right--from those who consider themselves radical[16] to the most conservative. The bottom line is the religious spectrum from not religious to the very religious or very devout. The solid arrows from the circle at the left end of the political line to the non-religious end of the religion line; and the circle at the very religious end of the religion line to the right end of the political line indicate what should have been expected from the literature. For example, Madsen portrays the religious Chicanos as conservative,[19] and left polemics expects those who are leftist not to be religious.

FIGURE 1

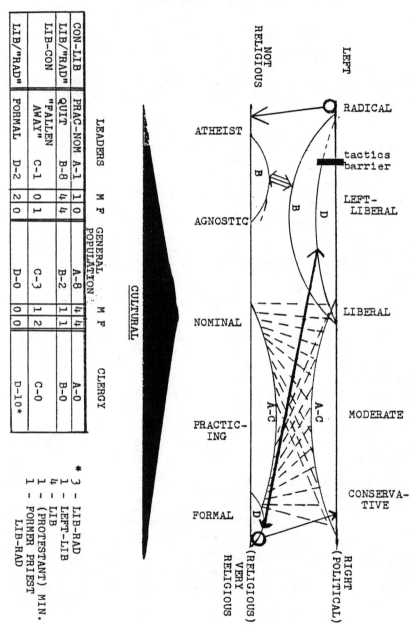

A-C: As indicated in Chapter Three, Group A (Practicing-Nominal) and Group C (Fallen-Away) are overlapping in the political spectrum and also overlapping in many concepts of morality and religion. Group C, of course, does not attend services or participate in the Church's outward manifestations. The lines that are drawn between the A-C religion line and the A-C political line are broken and scattered to indicate that the effect of the Church cannot be stated to be a particular cause of political beliefs. What can be stated is that these individuals see no contradictions between being Catholic, and the politics which they espouse. They rarely see the connections that may exist. As previously noted, however, they fall into the mainstream of American politics and ideology with visions, goals, and tactics that are compatible with the American political process. At times they are critical of the results, but not of the general socio-economic order itself.

B: Group B comprises those who have made a conscious decision to Quit the Church. The reasons given for quitting were often political contradictions with the Church. This group contains many former members of Catolicos Por La Raza, including some individuals who were very religious before their confrontations with the Church. The politics of Group B ranges from liberal (mainstream) to radical.

D: This is the group that was most religious--the Formal Catholics. This group is primarily clergy, but it also includes two leaders whose commitments to the Church go beyond the normal practicing Catholic, but yet are not quite as strongly committed as the clergy. Members of Group D fall on the left end of the political spectrum from liberal to that approaching radicalism.

For most Chicanos, whom I interviewed, the relationship between Catholicism and political ideology is neither direct nor simple. Catholicism does have an influence in the Chicano community, but this influence is not automatically identifiable in its impact by an analysis of Catholic doctrine and a perfunctory observation of the Chicano community. The only consistent impact of Catholicism is as a cultural expression. I use the term consistent here with great reserve. As I attempted to illustrate with the cultural line under Figure 1, the intensity of religious influence on the formal aspects of culture (as used by Hernandez[18]) is not uniform. While virtually all (including Marxists) participate in some outward aspects of Catholicism, such as compadrazgo, use of the Virgin of Guadalupe, weddings, baptisms, etc., this if often performed as cultural Catholicism (as defined by Spitzer[19]). It is important to note, as does Lampe, that Chicanos who come closest to following the norm of Chicano religious behavior are those who are not the most devout

179

(or the least), but those who only marginally follow the established procedures of the Church.[20] Chapters Two and Three
illustrates that such is the case.

In assessing the political impact of the Church, it is
evident that it is <u>not</u> a linear progression such as in Figure 2.

FIGURE 2

LINEAR PROGRESSION

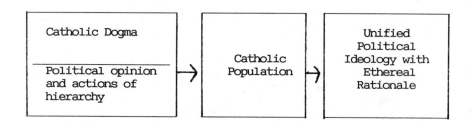

| Catholic Dogma

Political opinion and actions of hierarchy | → | Catholic Population | → | Unified Political Ideology with Ethereal Rationale |

To state the relationship in such a manner not only stereotypes and simplifies both the religion and Chicanos, but also
neglects the webs of influence that shape the individuals' political <u>development</u> and ideology. The impact of the Church must
be evaluated with the many concurrent factors that could
strengthen or weaken the commitment of individuals at certain
periods of time.

Note the emphasis on the concept of <u>development</u>. Virtually
all whom I interviewed felt that they had undergone some changes
in both their political and religious lives. Religiously they
experienced changes as they passed through youth and through
various stages of adulthood. Most remembered changes that the
Church had undergone because of Vatican II. Politically they had
lived through a time of domestic and international turmoil, which
left them with negative or positive impressions, but which could
not be ignored.

It should be noted that while the categories of A, B, C and
D have some endurance, their consistency in size and membership
is not stable. The members of Group B were at one time or
another members of Group A or D. Members of Group D and C used
to be A's. The possibility for shifts (although usually not
sudden) is ever present. The religious evolution that is
occurring among Chicanos is the accumulation of the individual

180

changes that are often reactions to the objective conditions outside the Church as well as individual subjective reflections, and this was apparent among the individuals with whom I spoke and whose organizations I examined. These changes and developments occurred not only through individual reactions to religious teachings, but to secular influences (the webs of influence mentioned above) in which Chicanos are entwined. Figure 3 is indicative of connection between some of these influences, religious and political, and their connections with Chicanos.

As each entity (in Figure 3) changes, it has a potential impact on religious-political views of the individuals. It has the greatest impact on those who have the greatest awareness of the changes outside the Church. I found that those whose level of political awareness was greatest were those of Groups B and D. Groups A and C, while not unaware of events and their causes, were less aware of the processes of change in the larger society. The awareness that is spoken of here is not judged on subjective agreement with the author, but rather one that is cognizant of situations that are occurring (e.g., domestically--protests, leaders, events; internationally--revolutions, U.S. foreign policies) and having the ability to formulate theories of why these events occur. Group A tends to feel less affected by events that have an indirect impact on them, and they have the ability to rely on their faith. (Blind faith is too strong a term here for most, although it has validity for some.)

Those who took their religion beliefs most seriously (Groups B and D) tended not to be accepting of events as being the work of some invisible hand. Group B and Group D, groups who are farthest apart on the religion spectrum, tend to be most personally affected by changes in the larger society. The changes that occurred drove them furthest apart in regard to religion, but drew them together in regard to politics. I found this to be one of the most interesting aspects of the study--that those who are on the opposite ends on the religious spectrum are often the closest politically, and whose religious-politicial ideological linkages are <u>clearest</u>.

The members of Group B virtually all felt that the Church had not allowed them to advance politically and had been a discriminating institution against Chicanos as well as a political retardant to the Chicano community. They felt that it was only <u>after</u> they had left the Church that they were able to develop themselves politically. The members of Group B were often among the most seriously (i.e., intellectually) religious individuals. They included students from Catholic colleges (e.g., law students from Loyola of Los Angeles), and then current priests and nuns. Their original intention in forming CPLR was not to rid the

FIGURE 3

RELIGIOUS AND SECULAR WEBS OF INFLUENCE

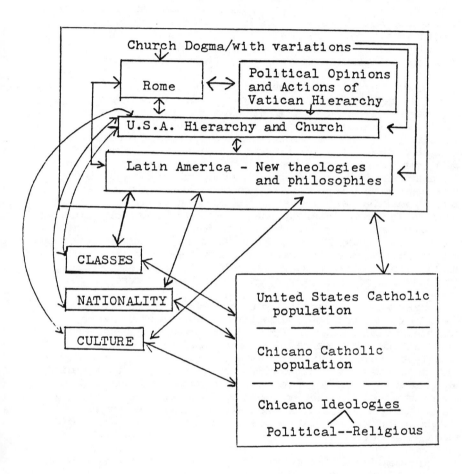

Chicano community of the Church, but to make it more responsive to the community. CPLR was a reformist organization that essentially believed in the principles of the Church but which felt that those individuals guiding it locally needed pressure in order to be of better service to Chicanos. What many CPLR members found was that the local institutional Church's repression and their own independent research compelled them to examine their religious beliefs. The events of St. Basil's, which forced them to confront "theory, political action, philosophy, and religion all at once," was a situation that most Chicanos have not experienced.

This was one of the distinguishing characteristics between Group B and Groups A-C. Most Chicanos (as well as most other Catholics) are not forced to make a choice between their religion and their political lives. For those who are engaged in what we have termed "mainstream" politics, the Church's teachings present no real conflict. CPLR in its formation could be described as the "margins of the mainstream"[21] that could well have become more mainstream oriented if Cardinal McIntyre had been a better tactician. It was when this group faced repression and non-reconciliation of their demands that they were seriously confronted with hard choices in regard to their religious beliefs. After they (Group B) had left the Church they moved steadily leftward. Not all are radical but as a group they are well to the political left of the Chicano population as a whole, and to the left of practicing to nominal-fallen away Catholics. It was not that Group B's politics were formed by Catholicism, but rather that leaving the Church has freed them to clarify their politics. Their world view, goals and values, and tactics for social change were in a state of flux. From an ideological viewpoint, their images of reality were being drastically altered. Their world view of how and why things operate was thrown into turmoil. Before their world view had been a metaphysical reality--now they could explore other alternatives. This does not mean that the members of Group B switched from one ideology to another overnight. When their metaphysical concepts were challenged, they found themselves in states of confusion that permitted them to develop politically to the points at which they are today.

It is perhaps significant that among the most radical and critical comments on the Church came from those who had the most to reconsider--the former nun and novice whom I interviewed. They both indicated that they had gone through considerable soul-searching to reach their present state of politcal awareness, but that they were still not free of all of the vestiges of religion --including the former novice who is now a member of a socialist party.

It is also significant that Group B was the predominant group among the Chicano leaders.[22] Of the twelve leaders interviewed, eight fit into Group B, one into Group A, one into Group C, and two into Group D. While this is not an essay on the qualities of leadership, it is clear that one characteristic is the ability to make active choices rather than to remain passive. To be a member of Group B or D requires a firm commitment to analyze and evaluate one's previous moral beliefs to the point where they will be either rejected or fully practiced and utilized. The decision that most leaders made was to reject the Church.

Some of the leaders, however, who had quit the Church before the formation of CPLR were reluctant to publicly criticize the Church for fear of alienating some of the Chicano community. Hence some of the more radical leaders declined to join CPLR at its beginning. As CPLR developed and generated both a great deal of support and dissent, this evaluation by some radicals not to overtly criticize the Church may have had some merit if they had fully expected that all Chicanos could be united politically without tackling the issue of the Church. However, I would disagree with the premise that all Chicanos can be united on the basis of a non-materialist view of culture, or some other perceived commonality. There have been many examples noted above in Mexico and the United States which illustrate the divisive nature of class interests <u>within</u> the Mexican/Chicano community. Those who prefer to ignore the issue of the Church because of its possibly divisive nature are ignoring the reality that the community <u>is already</u> divided on this issue. Possible resolution lies in open debate rather than in ignoring the situation.

It is not novel to state that religion can be used to justify any action or belief. However, it is useful to discuss how religion (in this case Catholicism) can influence political beliefs that may be similar but which also have profound differences.[23] Group D, as stated earlier, had political beliefs that are similar to Group B. Group D is largely clerics, men of the cloth, who as described in Chapter Four were often confronted with conduct contradictory to their expectations when they entered the seminary. For many of these priests the transition from barrio parish to an overwhelmingly Anglo seminary was not an easy one to make.[24] Those Chicano seminarians who survive have often been forced to adjust to an alien environment, and thus at ordination have often had the least in common with the community at large. However, the activism of the 1960's and 1970's did not escape the Church. Activism such as the UFW affected the Church and was a catalyst for CPLR and Chicano priest involvement with the community. As shown in Chapter Four, the Chicano priests often stated that their intellectual concepts of liberation politics come from the Church's teachings, and that the Church and religion give life to their hopes for Chicanos.

It would be possible to end this essay with concluding remarks about the changing Church and the possibility for liberalization and liberation. However, as noted in Chapter Four, there are deep questions on the possible political impact of the Church's liberal and left teachings. In the final analysis--from a political viewpoint--Theology of Liberation or other Church philosophies of liberation must be judged on their liberating effectiveness past, present, and potential. In other words, does it work--does it liberate?

A judgment could be made that perhaps the people of Group B overreacted--that since they have a political orientation similar to Group D, they could have reached the same point within the Church. This, however, would only be partially correct from an ideological standpoint. The primary overlap of Groups B and D is in regard to goals. Group D and sections of Group B have liberal to social democratic goals that call for greater worker and community power and organization. They do, however, have different world-views, in terms of how and why events occur. While there are some convergences, the overtly metaphysical views of Group D are largely in conflict with the primarily materialist views of Group B, especially the more radical members. As with the world-view, there are also conflicts in values. This is evident when considering that Formal Catholics (Group D) are, of course, concerned with salvation as part of liberation and rank that ultimately very high in priority, while some members of Group B do not recognize "salvation" as a valid concept. These are largely philosophical issues which perhaps influence the greatest difference between B and D--the question of tactics.

An ex-seminarian whom I interviewed noted that much of the Marxist-Christian dialogue that is gathering attention does not always discuss important political issues, but has become "intellectual sleight of hand," that becomes "metaphysical hairsplitting."[25] The dialogue deals with philosophy in regions (such as Latin America) where political action is necessary. The ex-seminarian noted that Liberation Theology is primarily concerned with revelation and philosophy, whereas Latin America revolutionaries are concerned with philosophy, tactics, and practice. The figure below illustrates a political problem with liberation theory.

FIGURE 4

THE MARXIST-CHRISTIAN DIALOGUE

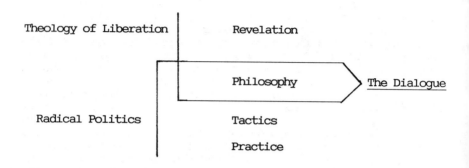

The significant split is between theory and practice, i.e., which tactics are acceptable to implement the goals and values of the different ideologies. Liberation Theology appears to be genuinely concerned with the liberation of the workers. However, it does not appear to allow for tactics (such as revolution in Latin America) that will be needed to implement this goal. Figure 1 has a thick line that appears as a tactics barrier to Group D. This line is to illustrate a significant difference between Groups B and D even if the stated goals are similar.

An evaluation--a judgment--of the Church's liberation teachings rests ultimately on one's political perspective. If liberal, one can see a new hope for the Church, not as a defender of the status quo but as potentially a leader of reasonable social change. The liberal would argue, with justification, that the Church should not be considered only as conservative and reactionary, but as a significant force for future change. If radical, the judgment may be that the Church is counter-revolutionary (as defined earlier); it diverts energy and goals and thus can objectively serve the side of reaction. This does not mean that one need consciously be a reactionary, but rather in a revolutionary situation the objective impact may be to serve reaction.[26]

Before proceeding with an evaluation of the liberalizing or liberation influences of the Church in the United States in regard to Chicanos (a continuation of the discussion begun in Chapter Four), it is necessary to address one final issue concerning activist priests in the United States and Latin America. Political labeling--radical, liberal, conservative, etc.--is a notoriously slippery task. I have attempted to avoid this problem by limiting "radical" to mean self-described Marxist (although I realize that there are many variants of Marxism), and liberal and conservative to include mainstream American politics as defined by Dolbeare and Dolbeare.[27] This is not because they have the only correct definition but rather that their work is logical, consistent and relevant to this study. As Geertz states in reference to his attempt to define culture, it is not that there is "only one direction in which it is useful to move, but because there are so many, it is necessary to choose."[28]

A term which needs to be discussed, however, is that of the "left," especially the Catholic left. There is a profound conceptual problem--it is not merely one of semantics--when one includes in the Catholic left those whose prime political activities are the opposition to the gross excesses of fascist and repressive regimes. It is true that many of priests and other religious of Latin America (e.g., El Salvador, Brazil, Chile, Ecuador) as well as other Catholic nations such as the Philippines have spoken out against the torture and imprisonment of dissidents. Some of these individuals, especially lower ranking priests, have themselves been imprisoned and murdered. However, this many not warrant the labeling of these religious protesters as part of the "Catholic left." To do so gives legitimacy and credence to dictatorial regimes who label all dissent as "leftist" or communist inspired. While protest against torture is necessary and in fact admirable, it is not the sole possession of the "left." To be more precise, one must examine the politics of protesting Catholic groups and not merely accept the regimes' definitions. To do otherwise is a disservice to both the revolutionary left and religious protesters who do not want to be considered part of the revolutionary left, but who are nevertheless concerned with oppression. To accept the regimes' definitions that such religious protest is always "leftist" negates any meaningful attempt to categorize political ideologies (an already arduous task), since by the regimes' definition anyone to the left of the leaders of these countries (e.g., former dictator Somoza of Nicaragua) is a "leftist"--an obvious absurdity. This would include prelates who have spoken out publicly against communism and socialism, but who are also averse to the more blatant acts of fascism--e.g., detention without cause, torture and murder.

Chicano priests in the United States do not appear to be faced with the same situations as their Latin American counterparts. As noted earlier, the contemporary United States situation is obviously not that of revolution. Therefore it is probable that Chicano priests and their organization (PADRES) have the potential to play a progressive role in the American Church.

This progressive role could be similar to that of the California Migrant Ministry (CMM) at the beginning of the UFW grape strike-- the leading edge of the Church.

The pronouncements and publications (such as the PADRES newsletter) of some Chicano clergy are developing a strong anti-capitalist orientation. The interviews I conducted indicate that the membership wishes to retain this orientation. Whether the leadership will is problematical. Although the Hispanic bishops are not automatically the formal leaders of PADRES, their position in the Church hierarchy places them in an influential role, both morally and practically.[29] The bishops are chosen by a predominantly Irish-Anglo hierarchy. Thus there is a great deal of opportunity, although no certainty, of compromising the leftward orientation of PADRES.

Based on the past experience in the history of Mexicans and Chicanos and the Church, there is a high probability that if the Church is caught in a political dispute it will cut its losses rather than allow itself to be pulled in deeper. This however presents a problem for the Church if PADRES remains progressive or becomes more so. It is an organization that is likely to grow in prestige and influence over time--if its leadership remains committed and strong. It is not an ad hoc group that merely responds to momentary crises, but one that has long range goals. It is also a group that will be hard to ignore by the dominant Catholic society, as it is composed of visible and vocal individuals who have met the standards of respectability and intellectual activity acknowledged by that society.

A radical argument could be made the PADRES, and Church-sponsored organizations such as UNO and COPS, are groups that divert people from "correct" (i.e., radical) political activities. This argument would have a great deal of validity if the audience which the Church appeals to were inclined toward radical activities. However, this does not appear to be the case. As stated earlier, Chicano radicals (Marxists) are not normally attracted to the Church. Some, however, recognize that the Church is a resource that can be utilized when the individuals they are trying to mobilize are religiously oriented.[30] In Latin America, the institutional Church, even its progressive wing, may play a counter-revolutionary role (although individual revolutionaries such as Fr. Camilo Torres do exist). In the United States, it is more difficult to state that the progressive Church is counter-revolutionary where there is little revolutionary activity. It may in fact be possible that the progressive Church may actually expose contradictions in capitalist society and the institutional Church. While not revolutionary, this could create what Marx has termed a "revolutionary point of departure."[31]

There is, however, a deeper issue which should be addressed. While this is not primarily an essay on the philosophy and teachings of the Church, any study that seriously examines the secular (in this case political) impact of the Church must inevitably confront the basic philosophies of religion. The Introduction and Conclusions have attempted to do so. The impression given is that the Church is a complex alienating force whose history in relation to Chicanos has often been one of repression. At the same time there are current indications that parts of the Church are changing toward liberalism and/or "liberation." If such changes are occurring, should Chicanos be encouraged to become more active in the Church?

PADRES, as should be expected, feels that Chicanos should be encouraged to return to the Church. A major goal of the organization is to increase the numbers of Hispanic Bishops and clergy. Presumably these clerics will become more active in the community. It is assumed a priori by most who have studied Chicanos and the Church in the past that more Chicano priests are needed.[32] Such an assumption should be subject to serious debate. Chicanos as a group attend services less, and devote less time to the institutional Church than do other United States Catholics. To the Catholic Church this is a problem to be solved. To others it may be a sign of hope and a foundation on which to build.

Even though there are instances of progressive individual and minor Church organizational activities, it may be a mistake to assume that the Church can be the force for liberation purposes. For individuals to be influenced by the Church for liberation requires an extraordinary interest in Church affairs, and the time to study and reflect upon the Church's teachings on social justice (which are available but not emphasized). One must also interpret and internalize these documents in such a manner that one feels compelled to take political action. Finally, it takes the resolve to continue this action not only in the face of possible secular oppression but also (and of equal importance especially for the devout and the clergy) Church hierarchical repression which, while certainly not universal, is an every present threat.

Proponents of Liberation Theology, of course, are firm in their belief of its potential positive impact. With the growth of "Basic Christian Communities" in Latin America, there are indications that lay peasant leaders can emerge as liberation leaders. One of the more eloquent works on Christian participation in revolutionary activities is Phillip Berryman's The

Religious Roots of Rebellion.[33] However, as Berryman illustrates elsewhere the quantitative impact of the basic communities is problamatic.

> "In Brazil, there are an estimated 80,000 such groups, involving up to four million people, between 1% and 2% of the population. Elsewhere the percentage is considerably less."[34]

An important question, of course, for our immediate purposes in discussing the liberating potential for the Church is: who speaks for the Church? Cumberland in his history of Mexico ask this question in his analysis of the Church's role in the revolution of 1810 and the same question needs to raised today.[35] Deborah Huntington ask the same question in regard to the confrontation inside the Central American Church:

> "[W]hose Church is it? Archbishop Romero (Archbishop of San Salvador who was murdered by right-wing death squads) was fond of saying, "I am not the Church; the hierarcy is not the Church; The Church is the people." The Pope and most of the Central American bishops believe that they have been chosen by God to make moral decisions for the laity. They view themselves as the Church, and see the laity as foot soldier for carrying out orders. This goes against the participatory concept of Vatican II.[36]

This, of course, is a continuing debate, one which will be subject to future research, including by this author. What can be stated with certainty at this time, as previously noted, is that Liberation Theology is still a minority position within the Church and does not have the backing of the Vatican.

Summary

In summation, the Catholic Church is an immensely complex institution of 800,000,000 world-wide, and 50,000,000 in the United States. Chicanos are not homogeneous but are a complex, dynamic, growing population. The relationship between Chicanos and the Church is not simple, nor is it unidirectional.

As noted in Chapter One, religion has historically been a form of social control. This has been demonstrated in Chapter Two to be the case regarding Mexicans/Chicanos. At the beginning of the relationship between Mexicans and the Church, the Church relied on both overt physical and subtle coercion. As conditions

190

changed, the subtle forms overtook the physical in terms of practicality and respectability. This does not mean, however, that the control is necessarily weaker. To be able to legitimize one's conditions or actions with ethereal justifications can be more of a social control (and certainly more cost-effective to those in power) than the more overt forms of control.

The Church can be seen as a form of social control because it conditions one to accept the dominant ideology and limits the political options to those that are perceived as religiously "moral," the effect of which is to reinforce and justify the present socio-economic order. The fact that one may desire "reforms" may not necessarily lessen the acceptance of the over-all system itself.

Religion, or more specifically the Catholic Church, can be seen as a form of social control not because it forcibly stops actions, but because it limits action and options.

The Church is, however, changing--as it has before in its two thousand years of existence. It has shown a remarkable ability to adapt to the objective conditions that surround it. During the transitions from slavery to feudalism to capitalism, it has not only endured but prospered. Its zenith was undoubtedly in the Middle Ages, before the Reformation, but its influence is still significant today. The present trend in many countries toward socialism is not an insurmountable barrier to the Church's continuation as a viable institution. While the Church has rarely been an innovator in regard to social movements, it does know when to become an imitator, especially when the Church as an institution is under attack. Irving Louis Horowitz has observed that

> . . . the prime impulse of Church organization in Latin America is not toward reform, revolution, or reaction, but toward something far more prosaic--survival.[37]

As a minority segment of the Church adapts to progressive forces and ideologies, it could be argued that the control mechanisms are not being lessened but more likely being strengthened or at least preserved. Any religion that rejects advances in human knowledge or refuses to change with the objective conditions of its setting will undoubtedly lose significant portions of the influence that it possesses. A religion that is intellectual and practical enough to study political trends and conditions and adapt to them will be able to survive and possibly strengthen its influence.

This is not to question the integrity or the motivation of those members of the clergy and/or other formal Church members in regard to their desire for systemic change, nor to assert that political action by those of a religious nature serves no useful liberation purposes. Rather, it is an analysis of the objective impact that such religiously oriented protest can have on political conditions. The Church's social control is seen here as a control of a much more subtle nature than on those whose interpretation of religious doctrine justifies the acceptance of the present socio-economic system, but it is a control nevertheless.

¹See Juan Hurtado, An Attitudinal Study of Social Distance Between the Mexican American and The Church (San Antonio: Mexican American Cultural Center, 1975); Rev. Virgilio P. Elizondo, Christianity and Culture (Huntington, Indiana: Our Sunday Visitor, Inc., 1975); David F. Gomez, Somos Chicanos: Strangers in Our Own Land (Boston: Beacon, 1973); Patrick Hayes McNamara, "Bishops, Priests, and Prophecy" (Ph.D. dissertation, University of California, Los Angeles, 1968); and Alberto Carillo, "The Sociological Failure of the Catholic Church Toward the Chicano," The Journal of Mexican American Studies 1 (Winter 1970): 75-83.

²It has been noted that war is too important to be left to the generals. Likewise the study of religion is too important to be left to the clergy.

³See Hurtado, An Attitudinal Study, pg. 207; and Carrillo, "The Sociological Failure," pg. 75.

⁴Hurtado, Ibid., states that his research would not have been possible ten years ago because "the people would not have been ready to analyze and criticize the Church." He also notes (pg. 211) that some whom he did interview were still hesitant to vent personal criticism of the Church—that it may have been seen as "disrespectful or irreverent."

Henry Flores, in "Worker Citizen Participation in an Ethnic Community: Some Interconnections," paper presented at 1977 Annual Meeting of the Western Political Science Association, Phoenix, Arizona, March 31 through April 2, 1977, notes that his research efforts to understand political tolerance among the workers were stymied when "the pertinent questions were stricken from the survey by the workers' committee. The committee felt that any questions which were anti-religious or dealt with communism would offend the community" (pg. 13).

⁵Karl Marx, Introduction to Contribution to the Critique of Hegel's Philosophy of Law in Karl Marx Frederick Engels, Collected Works, Vol. 3 (New York: International Publishers, 1975), pg. 175.

⁶Ricardo Ramirez, C.S.B., "La Familia, Channel of Faith and Culture," La Luz 7 (October 1978): 20.

⁷See Chapter Two for information on how missionary work is prone toward failure.

[8]The characterization of weak commitment is somewhat of an understatement in Mexico. Mexico, in fact, developed a strong anti-clerical and anti-Church movement that was able to become a dominant political force.

[9]It is not necessary here to posit that clerical racism was the only or even main reason for the Church's activities regarding the Chicano. Attempts at Americanization were also the policy with European immigrants. The impact of such a policy could, however, be seen to have detrimental effects on Chicanos. See Chapter Two, pp. 23-26.

[10]See the elaboration in Chapter One. Also see Raul A. Fernandez, The United States-Mexico Border: A Politico-Economic Profile (Notre Dame: University of Notre Dame Press, 1977), pp. 1-35; 149-157. Fernandez utilizes culture as such:

> "A definition of culture that is concerned with emphasizing the social content can thus be considered as having two mutually dependent aspects: formal and material. The formal aspects of culture would include such things as ideas (art and science), values, rules of personal behavior, social institutions, and , fundamentally, a given set of social relations in the process of production. The material aspect of culture, on the other hand, would be composed of all artifiacts and material goods resulting from human activity in a given society. These two aspects are not separate but interdependent" (pg. 152).

[11]See for example, Charles Leslie, Ed., Anthropology of Folk Religion (New York: Vintage Books, Random House, 1960); marvin Harris, Cows, Pigs, Wars, and Witches: The Riddles of Culture (New York: Vintage Books, Random House, 1974); William J. Goode, Religion Among the Primitives (New York: Free Press, MacMillan Co., 1951, 1964); William A. Lessa and Evon Z. Vogt, eds. Reader in Comparative Religion: An Anthropological Approach (New York: Harper and Row, 1958, 1965); and Annemarie de Waal Malefijt, Religion and Culture (New York: The MacMillan Company, 1968).

[12]See Maurice Godelier, "Toward a Marxist Anthropology of Religion," Dialectical Anthropology 1 (November 1975): 81-93; and Maurice Godelier, Perspectives in Marxist Anthropology (Cambridge: Cambridge university Press, 1977), see particularly Chapter 7, "Fetishism, religion and Marx's general theories con-

cerning ideology." Also see Stephan Feuchtwang, "Investigating Religion," in Marxist Analysis and Social Anthropology, ed. Maurice Bloch (New York: John Wiley and Sons, 1975), pp. 61-81.

[13]Howard Selsam and Harry Martel, eds., Reader in Marxist Philosophy (New York: International Publishers, 1963), pg. 224. The editors continue with,

> "They do not want to take away from people the solace, confort, or beauty that religion brings into their lives. They do want to do away with the need for this particular form of achieving these satisfactions by abolishing the conditions that require the 'illusions' religion offers" (pp. 224-225).

[14]Frederick C. Turner, Catholicism and Political Development in Latin America (Chapel Hill: University of North Carolina Press, 1971), pg. 42.

[15]The following is the utilization of ideology as used by Kenneth M. Dolbeare and Patricia Dolbeare in American Ideologies: The Competing Political Beliefs of the 1970's, 3rd ed. (Chicago: Rand McNally, 1976), pp. 5-11.

[16]I define "radical" here to mean those who self-define themselves as some variant of having a Marxist analysis.

[17]See William Madsen, Mexican Americans of South Texas (New York: Holt, Rinehart and Winston, 1964), see particularly Chapters 3 and 7.

[18]See the previous discussion in Footnote 12.

[19]See the definition of "cultural Catholicism" by Spitzer as noted in Chapter Three.

[20]See the previous discussions in Chapter Three.

[21]See Dolbeare and Dolbeare, American Ideologies, pp. 13-14.

[22]Alberto M. Camarillo in "Research Note on Chicano Community Leaders; The G.I. Generation," Aztlan 2 (Fall 1971): 148, also found that Chicano leaders could not be classified as practicing Catholics and that some were very critical and had "at early stages in their lives, severed all ties with the Catholic Church."

[23]Gary T. Marx notes in a study of the Black community that the political effect of religion is not homogeneous. Religion has been used as a strong form of social control as well as a vehicle for social protest. As Gary Marx Christianity contains many themes, which if not in contradiction, are certainly in tension with each other." Protest and Prejudice: A Study of Belief in the Black Community, revised edition (New York: Harper and Row, 1967, 1969), pg. 104. Chapter Four is of particular importance to this issue: "Religion: Opiate or Inspiration of Civil Rights Militancy."

[24]It is highly likely that minority priests come from highly minority congregations. A Gallup poll indicated that the Sunday morning church hour is "the most segregated hour of the week." While the pool was primarily concerned with Blacks and Whites, it is evident that de facto segregation exists in church congregations. See Los Angeles Times, 9 April 1977, pg. 6. It is also clear that secular variables (e.g., housing patterns) have a strong impact on the congregational separation.

[25]Interview, December 10, 1976. A close reading of the dialogue literature gives credence to these types of characterizations. See Herbert Aptheker, ed., Marxism and Christianity (New York: Humanities Press, 1968); and Joseph Petulla, Christian Political Theology: A Marxian Guide (Maryknoll, articles published in LADOC are particularly valnerable to the characterization; see particularly Latin Americans Discuss Marxism-Socialism, The LADOC 'Keyhole' Series #13 (Washington, D.C.: Latin American Documentation-USCC, n.d.). For an excellent short critique of Christian socialism, see Frank Teruggi's analysis in Chicago Area Group on Latin America - CAGLA 2, no. 4 (1972): 7-10.

Marx's own writings on religion are scattered throughout his works. They have, however, been collectged for easy use. See Selsam and Martel, Reader in Marxist Philosophy, edited and translated by Saul K. Padover (New York: McGraw-Hill, 1974); and Karl Marx and Frederick Engles, On Religion (Moscow: Progess Publishers, 1957, 1975).

[26]The potential for the liberal activities of the Church as counter-revolutionary is apparent to some who look favorably on the Church's role. John J. Johnson in his Political Change in Latin America: The Emergence of the Middle Sectors (Standord: Stanford University Press, 1958) notes that:

> "The Church and Catholic lay organizations in
> league with the middle sector political leader-
> ship might inject into politics a moral force

for the most part lacking at present. They also
might be highly effective in discouraging workers from deserting to the extreme Left Wing
organizations, especially to the Communists, for
many workers have a deep and abiding loyalty to
the Roman Catholic Church" (pg. 192).

[27]See Dolbeare and Dolbeare, American Ideologies, pp. 1-89.

[28]Clifford Geertz, The Interpretation of Culture (New York:
Basic Books, Inc., 1973), pg. 5.

[29]The Spanish-surnamed bishops are the "Episcopal Moder-
ators" of PADRES. While these bishops have influenced in the
Hispanic community, there is a serious question of how influen-
cial they are in the Church. As previously noted, most Hispanic
bishops are auxiliaries. As one Chicano priest stated:

"So when we create an auxiliary bishop from a
minority, we run the risk of creating a powerless token from an equally powerless people. We
will have a bishop who is a confirming bishop,
an eating bishop, a picture-taking bishop, a
touring and speaking and writing and drum-beat-
ing bishop. We will have everything excpet a
bishop in a position of power."

Father Gilbert Padilla, "Hispanic Ordinaries Scarcely Ordinary,"
PADRES 6 (Winter 1977): 16.

[30]It is extremely doubtful that COPS and UNO will materially
do more than act as a Chicano consumer pressure group. While
altering some of the more blatant circumstances of the barrio
(such as excessive insurance rates--issues that should not be
minimized), they are not major threats to the socio-economic
order. Aside from some material gains, their major effect will
be to teach some in the community organization techniques based
on the principles of Saul Alinsky. However, as Kenneth B. Clark
and Jeannette Hopkins in a study of anti-poverty programs note,
this does not mean that the organizations will result in major
changes.

"Saul Alinsky has organized the poor as a
counterforce to the anit-poverty programs in a
few cities. There is, however, no evidence that
the Alinsky approach, in spite of the extensive
publicity and success in a few skirmishes with
power groups, has contributed to any observable
changes of real significance in the basic condi-

tions of the poor in those communites in which he has worked." A Relevant War Against Poverty (New York: Harper and Row, 1968), pg. 253.

[31]Karl Marx, The Eighteenth Brumaire of Louis Bonaparte (New York: International Publishers, 1963), pg. 19.

[32]See for example, the sources cited in Footnote #1. All except Gomez call for more Chicano priests. Gomez, Somos Chicanos, notes that a complete break may be needed but he seems to prefer a Chicano National Catholic Church that would not be accountable to the U.S. hierarchy (pp. 168-170; 192-193).

[33]Phillip Berryman, The Religious Root of Rebellion: Christians in Central American Revolutions (Maryknoll, New York: Orbis Books, 1984). Also see Margaret Randall, Christians in the Nicaraguan Revolutions, translated by Mariana Valverde (Vancouver, B.C.: New Star Books, 1983.)

[34]Phillips Berryman, "Notes on Liberation Theology," CISPES ALERT 3:6 (Nov.-Dec., 1985) p. 5.

[35]See Chapter Two.

[36]Deborah Huntington, "Visions of the Kingom: The Latin American Church in Conflict," NACLA, Vol. XIX, Nov. 5 (Sept.-Oct. 1985) p. 45.

[37]In the forward of David E. Mutchler's The Church as a Political Factor in Latin America, With Particular Reference to Columbia and Chile (New York: Praeger Publishers, 1971), pg. vii.

Horowitz also notes that Mutchler demonstrates that the Church in Latin America as an institution "serves to make liberalism the style, while conservatism continues as the substance" especially if the Catholic base is perceived as being threatened by secularism or communism (pp. ix-x).

BIBLIOGRAPHY

Books and Monographs

Acosta, Oscar Zeta. The Revolt of the Cockroach People.
San Francisco: Straight Arrow Books, 1973.

Acuña, Rodolfo. Occupied America: The Chicano's Struggle Toward Liberation. New York: Canfield Press, 1972.

Allen, Robert. Black Awakening in Capitalist America. Garden
City, New York: Anchor Books, Doubleday and Company, Inc.,
1969.

Aptheker, Herbert, ed. Marxism and Christianity. New York:
Oxford University Press, 1970.

Bachrach, Peter, and Baratz, Morton S. Power and Poverty. New
York: Oxford University Press, 1970.

Bellah, Robert. Beyond Belief: Essays on Religion in a Post-
Traditional World. New York: Harper and Row, 1970.

Berryman, Phillip. The Religious Roots of Rebellion: Christians
in Central America Revolution. Maryknoll, New York: Orbis
Books, 1984.

Birnbaum, Norman, and Lenzer, Gertrud. Sociology and Religion.
Englewood Cliffs, New Jersey: Prentice-Hall, 1969.

Brackenridge, R. Douglas, and Garcia-Treto, Francisco O. Iglesia
Presbiteriana: A History of Presbyterians and Mexican Americans
in the Southwest. San Antonio: Trinity University Press,
1974.

Braden, Charles S. Religious Aspects of the Conquest of Mexico.
Durham, North Carolina: Duke University Press, 1930.

Cabrera, Arturo. Emerging Faces, the Mexican-American. San
Jose, California: William C. Brown Company, 1971.

Camara, Dom Helder. Revolution Through Peace. New York: Harper
and Row, 1971.

Chevalier, Francois. Land and Society in Colonial Mexico, The
Great Hacienda. Berkeley: University of California Press,
1963.

The Church in the Present-Day Transformation in the Light of
the Council - Medellin Conclusions. Washington, D.C.:
Division for Latin America - USCC, 1973.

Clark, Kenneth B., and Hopkins, Jeannett. A Relevant War
Against Poverty. New York: Harper and Row, 1968.

Clark, Margaret. Health in the Mexican-American Culture: A Community Study. Berkeley: University of
California Press, 1959, 1970.

Cortes, Carlos E., ed. Church Views of the Mexican American.
New York: Arno Press, 1974.

Cumberland, Charles C. Mexico: The Struggle for Modernity.
London: Oxford University Press, 1968.

Dehainaut, Raymond K. Faith and Ideology in Latin-American
Perspective. Sondeos Series, no. 85. Cuernavaca, Mexico:
CIDOC, 1972.

Demerath, N. J. III. Social Class in American Protestantism.
Chicago: Rand, McNally and Company, 1965.

Dolbeare, Kenneth M., and Dolbeare, Patricia.
American Ideologies: The Competing Political Beliefs of
the 1970's. 3rd ed. Chicago: Rand McNally College
Publishing Company, 1976.

Dunne, John Gregory. Delano. New York: Farrar, Straus, and
Giroux, 1967.

Elizondo, Rev. Virgilio P. Christianity and Culture.
Huntington, Indiana: Our Sunday Visitor, Inc., 1975.

Ellis, John Tracy. American Catholicism. 2nd ed. Chicago: The
University of Chicago Press, 1969.

Fernandez, Raul A. The United States-Mexico Border: A Politico-
Economic Profile. Notre Dame: Notre Dame Press, 1977.

Freire, Paulo. Pedagogy of the Oppressed. New York: Herder and
Herder, 1968, 1972.

Fromm, Erich. Marx's Concept of Man. New York: Frederich Ungar
Publishing Company, 1961, 1965.

Gamio, Manuel. The Life Story of the Mexican Immigrant. New
York: Dover Publications, 1971.

Gerrtz, Clifford. The Interpretation of Cultures. New York: Basic Books, Inc., 1973.

Gheerbrant, Alain. The Rebel Church in Latin America. Baltimore: Penguin, 1974.

Gibbons, William, S.J., ed. Seven Great Encyclicals. Glen Rock, New Jersey: Paulist Press, 1939, 1963.

Glazer, Nathan, and Moynihan, Daniel Patrick. Beyond the Melting Pot. Cambridge, Massachusetts: The M.I.T. Press, 1963.

Glock, Charles Y., and Hammond, Phillip E., eds. Beyond the Classics? Essays in the Scientific Study of Religion. New York: Harper and Row, 1973.

Godelier, Maurice. Perspectives in Marxist Anthropology. Translated by Robert Brain. Cambridge: Cambridge University Press, 1973, 1977.

Gomez, David F. Somos Chicanos: Strangers in Our Own Land. Boston: Beacon Press, 1973.

Gomez-Quinones, Juan. On Culture. Popular Series No. 1. Los Angeles: UCLA--Chicano Studies Center, 1977.

Goode, William J. Religion Among the Primitives. New York: Free Press, MacMillan Company, 1951, 1964.

Gott, Richard. Rural Guerrillas in Latin America. Middlesex, England: Penguin Books Ltd., 1970.

Grebler, Leo; Moore, Joan W.; and Guzman, Ralph C. The Mexican-American People. New York: The Free Press, 1970.

Greeley, Andrew M. The Catholic Experience. Garden City, New York: Doubleday and Company, 1967.

_____. Priests in the United States. Garden City, New York: Doubleday and Company, 1972.

_____., and Rossi, Peter H. The Education of Catholic Americans. Garden City, New York: Anchor Books, 1966, 1968.

Griffith, Beatrice. American Me. Boston: Houghton Mifflin Company, 1948.

Gutierrez, Gustavo. A Theology of Liberation. Maryknoll, New York: Orbis Books, 1973.

Hageman, Alice L., and Wheaton, Philip E., eds. Religion in Cuba Today: A New Church in a New Society. New York: Association Press, 1971.

Handein, Oscar. The Uprooted. Boston: Little, Brown, and Company, 1951.

Harris, Marvin. Cows, Pigs, Wars, and Witches: The Riddles of Culture. New York: Vintage Books, Random House, 1974.

Harvey, David. Social Justice and the City. Baltimore: John Hopkins, 1973.

Haseldon, Kyle. Death of a Myth. New York: Friendship Press, 1964.

Hedrick, B.C. Religious Syncretism in Spanish America. Miscellaneous Series. Greeley, Colorado: Museum of Anthropology, 1967.

Herberg, Will. Protestant, Catholic, Jew. Garden City, New York: Doubleday Anchor Book, 1955, 1960.

Hernandez, Deluvina. Mexican American Challenge to a Sacred Cow. Los Angeles: Chicano Studies Center, University of California, 1970. Herring, Herbert. A History of Latin America. 3rd ed. New York: Alfred A. Knopf, 1968.

Holland, Clifton L. The Religious Dimension in Hispanic Los Angeles, A Protestant Case Study. South Pasadena, California: William Carey Library, 1974.

Hurtado, Juan. An Attitudinal Study of Social Distance Between the Mexican American and the Church. San Antonio, Texas: Mexican American Cultural Center, 1975.

Johnson, John J. Political Change in Latin America: The Emergence of the Middle Sectors. Stanford: Stanford University Press, 1958.

Johnson, William Weber. Heroic Mexico. Garden City, New York: Doubleday and Company, Inc., 1968.

Junker, Buford H. Field Work: An Introduction to the Social Sciences. Chicago: The University of Chicago Press, 1960.

Katznelson, Ira. Black Men, White Cities. Chicago: University of Chicago Press, 1973, 1976.

Kee, Alistair, ed. A Reader in Political Theology.
Philadelphia: Westminister Press, 1974.

Kroeber, A.L., and Kluckhohn, Clyde. Culture. New York:
Vintage Books, 1952.

Kushner, Sam. Long Road to Delano. New York: International
Publishers, 1975.

LADOC. Paulo Freire. 'Keyhole' Series, No. 1. Washington,
D.C.: Division of Latin America - United States Catholic
Conference, n.d.

_____. The Theology of Liberation. 'Keyhole' Series, No.
2. Washington, D.C.: Division for Latin America - USCC,
n.d.

_____. Cuba. 'Keyhole' Series, No. 7. Washington, D.C.:
Division for Latin America - USCC, n.d.

_____. Helder Camara. 'Keyhole' Series, No. 12.
Washington, D.C.: Latin American Documentation - USCC, n.d.

_____. Latin Americans Discuss Marxism-Socialism.
'Keyhole' Series, No. 13. Washington, D.C.: Division for
Latin America - USCC, n.d.

Lampe, Philip E. Comparative Study of Assimilation of Mexican-
Americans: Parochial Schools Versus Public Schools. San
Frnacisco: R and E Research Associates, 1975.

Landis, Paul H. Social Control. Chicago: J.B. Lippincott Company, 1956.

Lanternari, Vittorio. The Religions of the Oppressed: A
Study of Modern Messianic Cults. New York: Alfred A.
Knopf, 1963.

Lenin, V.I. On Socialist-Ideology and Culture. Moscow:
Progress Publishers, 1975.

Lenski, Gerhard. The Religious Factor. Garden City, New York:
Doubleday, Anchor Books, 1961, 1963.

Leslie, Charles, ed. Anthropology of Folk Religion. New York:
Vintage Books, Random House, 1960.

Lessa, William A., and Vogt, Evon Z., eds. Reader in Comparative Religion: An Anthropological Approach. New York: Harper and Row, 1958, 1965.

Levy, Jacques E. Cesar Chavez: Autobiography of La Causa. New York: W.W. Norton and Company, 1975.

Lewis, Oscar. The Children of Sanchez. New York: Vintage Books, 1963.

Littwin, Lawrence. Latin America: Catholicism and Class Conflict. Encino, California: Dickenson Publishing Company, 1974.

London, Joan, and Anderson, Henry. So Shall Ye Reap. New York: Thomas Y. Crowell Company, 1970.

Lopez y Rivas, Gilberto. The Chicanos. New York: Monthy Review, 1973.

McLaughlin, Terence P., C.S.B., ed. The Church and the Reconstruction of theModern World: The Social Encyclicals of Pope Pius XI. Garden City, New York: Image Books, 1957.

McWilliams, Carey. North From Mexico: The Spanish Speaking People of the United States. New York: Greenwood Press, 1948, 1968.

_____. Southern California: An Island on the Land. Santa Barbara, California: Peregrine Smith, Inc., 1973.

Madsen, William. Mexican-Americans of South Texas. New York: Holt, Rinehart and Winston, 1964.

Marx, Karl. Contribution to the Critique of Hegel's Philosophy of Law. In Karl Marx, Frederick Engels, Collected Works, Vol. 3, pp. 3-130. New York: International Publishers, 1975.

_____. The 18th Brumaire of Louis Bonaparte. New York: International Publishers, 1963.

_____, and Engels, Frederick. On Religion. Moscow: Progress Publishers, 1957, 1975.

_____. The German Ideology. New York: International Publishers, 1947.

Matthiessen, Peter. Sal Si Puedes: Cesar Chavez and the New American Revolution. New York: Random House, 1969.

Mecham, Lloyd. Church and State in Latin America. Chapel Hill: The University of North Carolina Press, 1934.

Meier, Matt S., and Rivera, Feliciano. The Chicanos: A History of Mexican Americans. New York: Hill and Wang, 1972.

Moore, Joan. Mexican Americans. Englewood Cliffs, New Jersey: Prentice-Hall, 1970.

Morales, Armando. Ando Sangrando (I am bleeding): A Study of Mexican American-Police Conflict. La Puente, California: Perspectiva Publications, 1972.

Mutchler, David E. The Church as a Political Factor in Latin America. New York: Praeger Publishers, 1971.

Nelson, Eugene. Huelga. Delano, California: Farm Workers Press, 1966.

Padover, Saul K., ed. Karl Marx, On Religion. New York: McGraw-Hill Book Company, 1974.

Parkes, Henry Bamford. A History of Mexico. 3rd ed. Boston: Houghton Mifflin Company, 1969.

Paul VI, Pope. Populorum Progressio (On the Development of People). New York: Paulist Press, 1967.

Petras, James, and Zeitlin, Maurice, eds. Latin America: Reform or Revolution? New York: Fawcett Publications, 1968.

Petulla, Joseph. Christian Political Theology: A Marxian Guide. Maryknoll, New York: Orbis Books, 1972.

Phelan, John Leddy. The Hispanization of the Philippines. Madison: University of Wisconsin Press, 1959.

Pitt, Leonard. The Decline of the Californios. Berkeley: University of California Press, 1971.

Piven, Frances Fox, and Cloward, Richard A. Regulating the Poor: The Functions of Public Welfare. New York: Vintage Books, 1971.

Price, Glenn W. Origins of the War with Mexico, The Polk-Stockton Intrigue. Austin: The University of Texas Press, 1967.

Quigley, Robert E. American Catholic Opinions of Mexican Anti-clericalism 1910-1936. Sondeos, No. 27. Cuernavaca, Mexico: CIDOC, 1969.

Quirk, Robert E. The Mexican Revolution and the Catholic Church 1910-1929. Bloomington, Indiana: Indiana University Press, 1973.

Randall, Margaret. Christians in the Nicaraguan Revolution, translated by Mariana Valverde. Vancouver, B.C.: New Star Books, 1983.

Reed, John. Insurgent Mexico. New York: Simon and Schuster, 1969.

Ricard, Robert. The Spiritual Conquest of Mexico. Translated by Lesley Byrd Simpson. Berkeley: Univeristy of California Press, 1966.

Richey, Russell E., and Jones, Donald G. American Civil Religion. New York: Harper and Row, 1974.

Robertson, Roland. The Sociological Interpretations of Religion. New York: Schochen Books, 1970.

Romero, Juan. Reluctant Dawn, Historia del Padre A.J. Martinez, Cura de Taos. San Antonio, Texas: Mexican American Cultural Center, 1976.

Rosenbaum, Walter. Political Culture. New York: Praeger Publishers, 1975.

Ross, Stanley R., ed. Is the Mexican Revolution Dead? New York: Alfred A. Knopf, 1966.

Roucek, Joseph S. Social Control. New York: D. Van Nostrand Company, Inc., 1947.

Rubel, Arthur J. Across the Tracks: Mexican-Americans in a Texas City. Austin: The University of Texas Press, 1966.

Ruiz, Ramon Eduardo, ed. The Mexican War, Was It Manifest Destiny? New York: Holt, Rinehard and Winston, 1963.

Selsam, Howard, and Martel, Harry, eds. Reader in Marxist
Philosophy. New York: International Publishers, 1963.

Smith, Justin H. The War With Mexico. 2 vols. New York: The
Macmillan Company, 1919.

Steiner, Stan. La Raza: The Mexican Americans. New York:
Harper and Row, 1969.

Stoddard, Ellwyn R. Mexican Americans. New York: Random House,
1973.

Terrell, John Upton. Pueblos, Gods and Spaniards. New York:
Dial Press, 1973.

Torres, Father Camilo. Revolutionary Writings. Edited and with
an Introduction by Maurice Zeitlin. New York: Harper
Colophon Books, 1969.

Tucker, Robert C., ed. The Marx-Engels Reader. 2nd ed. New
York: W. W. Norton and Company, Inc., 1972, 1978.

Turner, Frederick C. Catholicism and Political Development in
Latin America. Chapel Hill: University of North Carolina
Press, 1971.

Vaillant, G.C. The Aztecs of Mexico. London: Penguin, 1950.

Valdez, Luis, and Steiner, Stan. Aztlan, An Anthology of Mexican
American Literature. New York: Vintage Books, 1972.

Vallier, Ivan. Catholicism, Social Control and Modernization in
Latin America. Englewood Cliffs, New Jersey: Prentice-
Hall, 1970.

Weber, Max. The Protestant Ethic and the Spirit of Capitalism.
New York: Charles Scribner's Sons, 1958.

_____. The Sociology of Religion. Boston: Beacon Press,
1963.

Wilkie, James W. Elitelore. Los Angeles: Latin American
Center, University of California, 1973.

Wolf, Eric. Sons of the Shaking Earth. Chicago: University of
Chicago Press, 1959.

Womack, John, Jr. Zapata and the Mexican Revolution. New York:
Vintage Books, 1968.

Yinger, J. Milton. _Religion, Society, and the Individual._ New York: The MacMillan Company, 1957.

Articles

Arroyo, Rev. Antonio M. Steven. "A Padre in Cuba." _PADRES_ (newsletter), Vol. VI, No. 3, Fall 1976.

Brandenburg, Frank R. "Causes of the Revolution." In _Revolution in Mexico: Years of Upheaval, 1910-1940_, pp. 16-23. Edited by James W. Wilkie and Albert L. Michaels. New York: Alfred A. Knopf, 1969.

Berryman, Phillip. "Notes on Liberation Theology." _CISPES ALBERT_, Vol. 3, No. 6 (Nov.-Dec. 1985).

Broom, Leonard, and Shevky, Eshref. "Mexicans in the United States: A Problem in Social Differentiation." _Sociology and Social Research_ 36 (January 1952): 150-158.

Camarillo, Alberto M. "Research Note on Chicano Community Leaders: The G.I. Generation." _Aztlan_ 2 (Fall 1971): 145-150.

Carrasco, Pedro. "Tarascan Folk Religion, Christian or Pagan?" In _The Social Anthropology of Latin America_, pp. 3-15. Edited by Walter Goldschmidt and Harry Hoijer. Los Angeles: Latin American Center, University of California, 1970.

Carrillo, Albert. "The Sociological Failure of the Catholic Church Toward the Chicano." _The Journal of Mexican American Studies_ 1 (Winter 1970): 75-83.

Chavez, Cesar. "The Mexican-American and the Church." In _Voices: Readings from El Grito_, pp. 215-218. Edited by Octavio Ignacio Romano-V. Berkeley: Quinto Sol Publications, 1973.

_____. "Peregrinacion, Penitencia, Revolucion." In _Aztlan: An Anthology of Mexican American Literature_, pp. 385-386. Edited by Luis Valdez and Stan Steiner. New York: Vintage Press, 1972.

Cleary, Edward. "The Church and Change in Latin America." _Pitt Magazine_, May 1975, pp. 9-12.

Cuba Review: Church, Theology, and Revolution. Vol. V, No. 3.

D'Antonio, William V., and Samora, Julian. "Occupational Strat-
ifications in Four Southwestern Communities." In Mexican-
Americans in the United States, pp. 363-375. Edited by John
H. Burma. Cambridge, Massachusetts: Harper and Row, 1970.

Diamond, Stanley. "The Marxist Tradition as a Dialectical
Anthropology." Dialectical Anthropology 1 (November 1975):
1-5.

Engelhardt, Zephyrin. "The Mission and Missionaries of
California." In A Documentary History of the Mexican Ameri-
cans, pp. 203-210. Edited by Wayne Moquin. New York:
Praeger Publishers, Inc., 1971.

Feuchtwang, Stephan. "Investigating Religion." In Marxist
Analysis and Social Anthropology, pp. 61-81. Edited by
Maurice Bloch. New York: John Wiley and Sons, 1975.

Fichter, Joseph H., S.J. "The Americanization of Catholicism."
In Anatomies of America: Sociological Perspecitves, pp.
285-295. Edited by Philip Ehrensaft and Amitai Etzioni.
Toronto: Collier-Macmillan, 1969.

Freeman, Donald. "Party, Vote, and the Mexican American in South
Tucson." In Chicano: The Evolution of a People, pp. 403-
412. Edited by Renato Rosaldo; Robert A. Calvert; and
Gustav L. Seligmann. Minneapolis: Winston Press, 1973.

Genovese, Eugene. "Class, Culture, and Historical Process."
Dialectical Anthropology 1 (November 1975): 71-79.

Geusau, Leo Alting von. "Revolution and Religion: The 'Radical'
Church in Brazil." Dialectical Anthropology 3 (February
1978): 21-42.

Godelier, Maurice. "Toward a Marxist Anthropology of Religion."
Dialectical Anthropology 1 (November 1975): 81-93.

Goldschmidt, Walter R. "Class Denominationalism in Rural
California Churches." American Journal of Sociology 49
(January 1944): 348-355.

Gomez-Quinones, Juan. "Toward a Perspective on Chicano History."
Aztlan 2 (Fall 1971): 1-49.

Gurley, John G. "The Materialist Conception of History." In
The Capitalist System, 2nd ed., pp. 42-50. Edited by
Richard C. Edwards; Michael Reich; and Thomas E. Weisskopf.
Englewood Cliffs, New Jersey: Prentice-Hall, 1972, 1978.

Harris, Marvin. "Race, Culture, and Manpower." In Peoples
and Cultures of Native South American, pp. 395-408. Edited
by Daniel R. Gross. Garden City, New York: Doubleday,
1973.

Huntington, Deborah. "Visions of the Kingdom: The Latin
American Church in Conflict." NACLA, Vol. XIX, No. 5.

Juarez, Rolando A. "What the Tape Recorder Has Created: A
Broadly-Based Exploration Into Contemporary Oral History
Practice." Aztlan 7 (Spring 1977): 99-118.

Kessell, John L. "Friars versus Bureaucrats: The Missions as a
Threatened Institution on the Arizona-Sonora Frontier, 1767-
1842." The Western Historical Quarterly 5 (April 1974):
151-162.

Knowlton, Clark S. "Patron-Peon Patterns Among the Spanish
Americans of New Mexico." Social Focus 41 (October 1962):
12-17.

Leonard, Irving A. "Visitas and Books." In The Conflict Between
Church and State in Latin America, pp. 65-77. Edited by
Frederick B. Pike. New York: Alfred A. Knopf, 1964.

Lucey, Robert E. "'Christianizing' Mexican Catholics." America,
16 August 1947, pp. 541-542.

_____. "Migratory Workers." The Commonweal, 15 January
1954, pp. 370-373.

La Luz: Hispanic Catholic Edition. Vol. 7, No. 10. October
1978.

McNamara, Patrick H. "Catholicism, Assimilation, and the Chicano
Movement: Los Angeles as a Case Study." In Chicanos an
Native Ameicans, The Territorial Minorities, pp. 124-130.
Edited by Rudolph O. de la Garza; Z. Anthony Kruszewski; and
Tomas A. Arciniega. Englewood Cliffs, New Jersey:
Prentice-Hall, 1973.

Martinez, Fr. Manuel, OFM. "The Perspective of the Hispanic
Community." In Entre Nosotros: Informes de Hermanas
y Padres (newsletter), Vol. I, No. 1, Fall 1978, pg. 10.

Munoz, Carlos. "Toward A Chicano perspective of Political
Analysis." Aztlan 1 (Fall 1970): 15-26.

Oxnam, G. Bromley, S.T.D. "The Mexican in Los Angeles from the Standpoint of the Religious Forces of the City." The Annals of the American Academy 93 (January 1921): 130-133.

Padilla, Fr. Gilbert. "Hispanic Ordinaries Scarcely Ordinary." PADRES (newsletter), Vol. VI, Winter 1977, pg. 16.

Perez H., Arnulfo. "God Does Not Exist." In Revolution in Mexico, pp. 195-198. Edited by James W. Wilkie, and Albert L. Michaels. New York: Alfred A. Knopf, 1969.

Quirk, Robert E. "Religion and the Mexican Social Revolution." In Religion, Revolution, and Reform, pp. 59-71. Edited by William V. D'Antonio, and Frederick B. Pike. New York: Praeger Publishers, 1964.

Ramirez, Ricardo, C.S.B. "La Familia, Channel of Faith and Culture." La Luz, October 1978, pp. 20-22.

Rocco, Raymond A. "The Chicano in the Social Sciences: Traditional Concepts, Myths, and Images." Aztlan 1 (Fall 1970): 75-98.

Romano-V., Octavio Ignacio. "Social Science, Objectivity, and the Chicanos;" and "The Anthropology and Sociology of the Mexican-Americans." In Voices: Readings from El Grito, pp. 30-42; and 43-56. Edited by Octavio Ignacio Romano-V. Berkeley: Quinto Sol Publications, 1973.

Shapiro, Harold A. "The Pecan Shellers of San Antonio, Texas." In Chicano: The Evolution of a People, pp. 193-202. Edited by Renato Rosaldo; Robert A. Calvert; and Gustav L. Seligmann. Minneapolis, Minnesota: Winston Press, 1973.

Spitzer, Allen. "Religious Structure in Mexico." Alpha Kappa Deltan 30 (1960): 54-58.

Ulibarri, Horacio. "Social and Attitudinal Characteristics of Spanish-Speaking Migrant and Ex-migrant Workers in the Southwest." In Mexican-Americans in the United States, pp. 29-39. Edited by John H. Burma. Cambridge: Schenkman Publishing Company, Inc., 1970.

"UNO." SOMOS, April/May 1978.

"Uprising in Texas." The Wall Street Journal, 13 July 1977, pg. 1.

Warner, W.L., and Srole, Leo. "Differential Assimilation of
American Ethnic Groups." In American Minorities. Edited by
Milton L. Barron. New York: Alfred A. Knopf, 1957.

Newspaper and Newsletters

Community Action on Latin America (CALA) - (newsletter)
Justicia O... (newspaper of La Raza Students' Association)

Denver Post

La Raza (Los Angeles Chicano magazine)

La Raza (Los Angeles Chicano newspaper)

Los Angeles Times

Machete (East Los Angeles College Chicano newspaper)

PADRES (newsletter)

El Popo (California State University at Northridge newspaper)

National Farm Worker Ministry (NFWM) Newsletter

The Tidings (Los Angeles diocesan newspaper)

Unpublished Material

Almaguer, Tomas. "Interpreting Chicano History: The 'World
System Approach to 19th Century California.'" Working
Papers Series #101. Berkeley: Institute for the Study of
Social Change, University of California, 1977.

Catolicos Por La Raza, Memorandum, 29 November 1969, with
attached documents from the Los Angeles County Assessor's
Office.

Flores, Henry. "Worker Citizen Participation in an Ethnic
Community: Some Interconnections." Paper presented at 1977
Annual meeting of the Western Political Science Association,
Phoenix, Arizona, March 31-April 2, 1977.

Hartmire, Wayne C., Jr. "The Church and the Emerging Farm
Worker's Movement." California Migrant Ministry, 22 July
1967. (Mimeographed.)

Hermanas-PADRES National Encuentro News Release, 15 August 1978, San Antonio, Texas.

McNamara, Patrick H. "Bishops, Priests and Prophecy." Ph.D. dissertation, University of California, Los Angeles, 1968.

"Mexican......and American." Transcript. Produced by NBC Religious Programs United in association with the Office for Film and Broadcasting, U.S. Catholic Conference. Airdate: February 15, 1976.

Ortegon, Samuel M. "Mexican Religious Population of Los Angeles." M.A. thesis, University of Southern California, 1932. Reprinted by R and E Associates, San Francisco, 1972.

PADRES National Congress, proceedings, San Antonio, Texas, February 2-5, 1975.

Penalosa, Fernando. "Class Consciousness and Social Mobility in a Mexican-American Community." Ph.D. dissertation, University of Southern California, 1963.

Personal Interviews

Chicano Leaders:

Interview, H.F., 30 August 1976.
Interview, N.L., 14 September 1976.
Interview, R.G., 16 September 1976.
Interview, S.R., 24 September 1976.
Interview, A.R., 3 December 1976.
Interview, C.R., 8 December 1976.
Interview, G.J., 10 and 15 December 1976.
Interview, G.N.A., 12 December 1976.
Interview, N.C., 21 December 1976.
Interview, S.C., 22 December 1976.
Interview, D.G., 31 December 1976.
Interview, B.P., 5 January 1977.

Chicano Population:

Interview, S.R., 15 February 1976.
Interview, S.L., 10 April 1976.
Interview, G.J., 20 April 1976.
Interview, M.A., 17 August 1976.
Interview, L.P., 1 September 1976.
Interview, R.B., 22 September 1976.
Interview, V.J., 6 December 1976.
Interview, G.J., 17 December 1976.
Interview, M.C., 28 December 1976.
Interview, P.M., 13 January 1977.
Interview, S.R.F., 2 February 1977.
Interview, D.M., 9 February 1977.
Interview, E.L.M., 14 February 1977.

Clergy:

Interview, L.R., 6 November 1976.
Interview, M.T., 9 November 1976.
Interview, O.L., 9 November 1976.
Interview, R.J., 10 December 1976.
Interview, D.E., 14 December 1976.
Interview, Rev. Chris Hartmire, 8 January 1977.
Interview, M.M., 10 January 1977.
Interview, Rev. Mark Day, 18 January 1977.
Interview, J.A., 20 January 1977.
Interview, S.E., 2 March 1977.

Ulibarri, Horacio, 115
United Farm Workers, 18-19,
    65, 104, 112-121, 123,
    135-140, 153, 159, 184
UNO, 158, 188

Valdez, Luis, 117
Valladoid, 37
Vatican II, 103, 143-144,
    150, 190
Vatican (Rome), 51, 55,
    154-155
Villa, 52
Virgin of Guadalupe (see
    Guadalupe)
Virgin of Los Remedios, 38
Vizzard, Fr. James, 119, 137
Voltaire, 36

Warner, W. L. 2, 21
War of the Reform, 51
Weber, Max, 5, 8, 23
Wilkie, James, 31
Willinger, Bishop A.J., 118,
    119
Wolf, Eric, 34

Yinger, J. Milton, 5

Zacatecas, 35
Zapata, 52, 117
Zumarraga, Juan de, 35, 36